THE ROUGH GUIDE

RUSSIAN
PHRASEBOOK

D0912408

Compiled by
LEXUS

ROUGH
GUIDES

www.roughguides.com

Credits

Russian Phrasebook

Compiled by Lexus with Irina and
Alistair Maclean
Lexus series editor: Sally Davies
Layout: Ajay Verma
Picture research: Rhiannon Furbear

Rough Guides Reference

Director: Andrew Lockett
Editors: Kate Berens, Ian Blenkinsop,
Tom Cabot, Tracy Hopkins,
Matthew Milton, Joe Staines

Publishing information

First edition published in 1997.
This updated edition published February 2012 by
Rough Guides Ltd, 80 Strand, London, WC2R 0RL
Email: mail@roughguides.com

Distributed by the Penguin Group:
Penguin Books Ltd, 80 Strand, London, WC2R 0RL
Penguin Group (USA), 375 Hudson Street, NY 10014, USA
Penguin Group (Australia), 250 Camberwell Road, Camberwell,
Victoria 3124, Australia
Penguin Group (New Zealand), Cnr Rosedale and Airborne Roads,
Albany, Auckland, New Zealand

Rough Guides is represented in Canada by Tourmaline Editions Inc.,
662 King Street West, Suite 304, Toronto, Ontario, M5V 1M7
Printed in Singapore by Toppan Security Printing Pte. Ltd.

A catalogue record for this book is available from the British Library.

978-1-84836-742-5

3 5 7 9 8 6 4 2 1

CONTENTS

How to use this book

The **Rough Guide Russian Phrasebook** is a highly practical introduction to the contemporary language. It gets straight to the point in every situation you might encounter: in bars and shops, on trains and buses, in hotels and banks, on holiday or on business. Laid out in clear A–Z style with easy-to-find, colour-coded sections, it uses key words to take you directly to the phrase you need – so if you want some help booking a room, just look up "room" in the dictionary section.

The phrasebook starts off with **Basics**, where we list some essential phrases, including words for numbers, dates and telling the time, and give guidance on pronunciation, along with a short section on the different regional accents you might come across. Then, to get you started in two-way communication, the **Scenarios** section offers dialogues in key situations such as renting a car, asking directions or booking a taxi, and includes words and phrases for when something goes wrong, from getting a flat tyre or asking to move apartments to more serious emergencies. You can listen to these and download them for free from www.roughguides.com/phrasebooks for use on your computer, MP3 player or smartphone.

Forming the main part of the guide is a double dictionary, first **English–Russian**, which gives you the essential words you'll need plus easy-to-use phonetic transliterations. Then, in the **Russian–English** dictionary, we've given not just the phrases you'll be likely to hear (starting with a selection of slang and colloquialisms) but also many of the signs, labels and instructions you'll come across in print or in public places. Scattered throughout the sections are travel tips

direct from the authors of the Rough Guides guidebook series.

Finally, there's an extensive **Menu reader**. Consisting of separate food and drink sections, each starting with a list of essential terms, it's indispensable whether you're eating out, stopping for a quick drink or looking around a local food market.

Счастливого пути!
sh-chasl**ee**vava poot**ee**!
Have a good trip!

BASICS

Pronunciation

Throughout this book Russian words have been transliterated into romanized form (see the Cyrillic Alphabet below) so that they can be read as though they were English, bearing in mind the notes on pronunciation given below:

a	as in **a**t	iy	i as in b**i**t followed
ay	as in m**ay**		by y as in **y**es
e	as in m**e**t	J	like the s in mea**s**ure
g	hard g as in **g**et	o	as in n**o**t
H	a guttural ch as in the	s	as in mi**ss**
	Scottish word lo**ch**	y	as in **y**es
i	as in b**i**t	ye	as in **ye**s
I	i sound as in **I** or **eye**		

Letters given in bold type indicate the part of the word to be stressed.

Abbreviations

adj	adjective	*pol*	polite
fam	familiar	*sing*	singular
pl	plural		

The Cyrillic alphabet

Set out below is the Cyrillic alphabet, the names of the letters and the system of transliteration used in this book:

А, а	ah	a as in at
Б, б	beh	b
В, в	veh	v
Г, г	geh	g as in get or v
Д, д	deh	d

Е, е	yeh	ye as in **ye**s
Ё, ё	yo	yo as in **yo**nder
Ж, ж	Jeh	J: pronounced like the s in mea**s**ure
З, з	zeh	z
И, и	ee	ee
Й, й	ee kratka-yeh	sometimes y as in bo**y**, but usually silent
К, к	ka	k
Л, л	el	l
М, м	em	m
Н, н	en	n
О, о	o	when stressed, o as in n**o**t; when unstressed, a as in **a**t
П, п	peh	p
Р, р	er	r
С, с	es	s
Т, т	teh	t
У, у	oo	oo as in b**oo**t
Ф, ф	ef	f
Х, х	Ha	H: a guttural ch as in Scottish lo**ch**
Ц, ц	tseh	ts as in ha**ts**
Ч, ч	cheh	ch as in **ch**urch
Ш, ш	sha	sh as in **sh**ip
Щ, щ	sh-cha	sh-ch
Ъ, ъ	tvyordi znak	hard sign: no sound, but indicates hardening of preceding consonant
Ы, ы	iy	i as in b**i**t followed by y as in **ye**s
Ь, ь	myaHkee znak	soft sign: no sound but softens the preceding letter

Э, э	eh	e as in end
Ю, ю	yoo	yoo
Я, я	ya	ya as in **yam**

б, в, г, д and з may be pronounced p, f, k, t and s respectively, usually when they occur at the end of a word or when preceding certain consonants. For example:

выход	вход
viyHat	fHot
exit	entrance

Combinations and diphthongs

АЙ, ай	ɪ: i sound as in **I** or **eye**; ee if unstressed
ЕЙ, ей	yay
ИЙ, ий	ee
ОЙ, ой	oy as in b**oy**; ɪ: i sound as in **I** or **eye** if unstressed
ЫЙ, ый	i as in b**i**t

Verbs

The basic form of the verb given in the English-Russian and Russian-English dictionaries in this book is the infinitive (e.g. to do, to go, to read etc). Most Russian verbs have two forms, known as the imperfective and perfective aspects. In the dictionaries, the two aspects of common verbs are given in this order: imperfective/ perfective. For example the verb 'to do' is given as:

делать d**ye**lat / сделать zd**ye**lat

The imperfective aspect is generally used to form what in English would be the present and imperfect (continuous) tenses and the future (with the future tense of быть **to be**). The perfective aspect is generally used to form what in English would be expressed by the perfect tense.

Questions

A statement can be turned into a question by using a questioning intonation:

we are returning to the hotel мы возвращаемся в гостиницу miy vazvrash-cha-yemsya vgast**ee**neetsoo

are we returning to the hotel? мы возвращаемся в гостиницу? miy vazvrash-cha-yemsya vgast**ee**neetsoo?

Basic phrases

yes да da

no нет nyet

OK хорошо Har**a**sho

hello здравствуйте zdr**a**svooytyeh

good morning доброе утро d**o**bra-yeh **oo**tra

good evening добрый вечер d**o**bri v**ye**chyer

good night (when leaving) до свидания da sveed**a**nya

good night (when going to bed) спокойной ночи spak**o**yn n**o**chee

goodbye до свидания da sveed**a**nya

hi! привет! preev**ye**t!

cheerio! пока! pak**a**!

see you! пока! pak**a**!

please пожалуйста paJ**a**lsta

yes please да, спасибо da, spas**ee**ba

thank you, thanks спасибо spas**ee**ba

no thank you нет, спасибо nyet, spas**ee**ba

thank you very much большое спасибо balsh**o**-yeh spas**ee**ba

don't mention it не за что n**ye**h-za-shta

how do you do? здравствуйте zdr**a**svooytyeh

how are you? как дела? kak dy**e**la?

fine, thanks хорошо, спасибо Har**a**sho, spas**ee**ba

nice to meet you
приятно познакомиться
pree-**ya**tna paznak**o**meetsa

excuse me (to get past, to say
sorry) извините eezveen**ee**tyeh

excuse me! (to get attention)
простите! prast**ee**tyeh!

excuse me (addressing someone
with question)
извините, пожалуйста…
eezveen**ee**tyeh, pa**J**alsta…

(I'm) sorry прошу прощения
prash**oo**-prash-ch**ye**nee-ya

sorry?/pardon me?
(didn't understand) простите?
prast**ee**tyeh?

what? что? shto?

what did you say? что вы
сказали? shto viy ska**za**lee?

I see (I understand)
понятно pan**ya**tna

I don't understand я не
понимаю ya nyeh pan**ee**ma-yoo

do you speak English?
вы говорите по-английски?
viy gavar**ee**tyeh pa-angl**ee**skee?

I don't speak Russian
я не говорю по-русски
ya nyeh gavar**yoo** pa-r**oo**skee

could you speak more slowly?
вы не могли бы говорить
помедленнее? viy nyeh magl**ee**bi
gavar**eet** pam**ye**dlyenyeh-yeh?

could you repeat that?
повторите, пожалуйста
paftar**ee**tyeh, pa**J**alsta

could you write it down?
запишите, пожалуйста
zapeesh**iy**tyeh, pa**J**alsta

I'd like… (said by man/woman)
я бы хотел/хотела…
ya biy нat**ye**l/нat**ye**la…

can I have…?
можно, пожалуйста…?
moJna, pa**J**alsta…?

do you have…? у вас есть…?
oo vas yest…?

how much is it? сколько это
стоит? sk**o**lka eta st**o**-eet?

cheers! (toast) ваше здоровье!
v**a**sheh zdar**o**vyeh!

it is… это… **e**ta…

where is the…? где…?
gdyeh…?

is it far from here? это далеко
отсюда? **e**ta dalyek**o** atsy**oo**da?

what's the time?
который час? kat**o**ri chas?

Dates

To express the date, use the ordinals given on p.15 with the months overleaf.

the second of November
второе ноября ftaro-yeh
na-yabrya

the thirty-first of January
тридцать первое января treetsat
pyerva-yeh yanvarya

Days

Sunday воскресенье
vaskryesyenyeh

Monday понедельник
panyedyelneek

Tuesday вторник ftorneek

Wednesday среда sryeda

Thursday четверг chyetvyerk

Friday пятница pyatneetsa

Saturday суббота soobota

Months

January январь yanvar

February февраль fyevral

March март mart

April апрель apryel

May май mI

June июнь ee-yoon

July июль ee-yool

August август avgoost

September сентябрь syentyabr

October октябрь aktyabr

November ноябрь na-yabr

December декабрь dyekabr

Time

what time is it? который час?
katori chas?

(it's) one o'clock час chas

(it's) two o'clock два часа dva
chasa

(it's) three o'clock три часа
tree chasa

(it's) four o'clock четыре часа
chyetiyryeh chasa

(it's) five o'clock* пять часов
pyat chasof

* For numbers of five and above, use часов.

For time past the hour, refer to the next hour. половина второго 'half past one' literally means 'half of the second'.

five past one пять минут
  второго pyat meen**oo**t ftar**o**va

ten past two десять минут
  третьего d**ye**syat meen**oo**t
  tr**ye**tyeva

quarter past one четверть
  второго ch**ye**tvyert ftar**o**va

quarter past two четверть
  третьего ch**ye**tvyert tr**ye**tyeva

half past one половина
  второго palav**ee**na ftar**o**va

half past two половина
  третьего palav**ee**na tr**ye**tyeva

twenty to ten без двадцати
  десять byez dvatsat**ee** d**ye**sat

quarter to two без четверти
  два byez ch**ye**tvyertee dva

quarter to ten без четверти
  десять byez ch**ye**tvyertee d**ye**sat

at one o'clock в час fchas

at two/three/four o'clock
  в два/три/четыре часа v dva/
  tree/chyet**iy**ryeh chas**a**

at five o'clock в пять часов
  fpyat chas**o**f

at half past four в половине
  пятого fpalav**ee**nyeh p**ya**tava

14.00 hours четырнадцать
  ноль-ноль chyet**iy**rnatsat nol-nol

17.30 семнадцать тридцать
  syemnatsat tr**ee**tsat

noon полдень p**o**ldyen

midnight полночь p**o**lnach

am утра **oo**tra

pm (in the afternoon) дня dnya
  (in the evening) вечера v**ye**chyera

hour час chas

minute минута meen**oo**ta

second секунда syek**oo**nda

quarter of an hour четверть
  часа ch**ye**tvyert chas**a**

half an hour полчаса polchas**a**

three quarters of an hour
  сорок пять минут s**o**rak pyat
  meen**oo**t

Numbers

0 ноль nol

1 один ad**ee**n

2 два dva

3 три tree

4 четыре chyet**iy**ryeh

5 пять pyat

6 шесть shest

7 семь syem

8 восемь v**o**syem

9 девять d**ye**vyat

10 десять d**ye**syat

11 одиннадцать ad**ee**natsat

12 двенадцать dvyen**a**tsat

13 тринадцать treen**a**tsat

14 четырнадцать chyetiyrnatsat

15 пятнадцать pyatnatsat

16 шестнадцать shesnatsat

17 семнадцать syemnatsat

18 восемнадцать vasyemnatsat

19 девятнадцать dyevyatnatsat

20 двадцать dvatsat

21 двадцать один dvatsat adeen

22 двадцать два dvatsat dva

30 тридцать treetsat

40 сорок sorak

50 пятьдесят pyadyesyat

60 шестьдесят shesdyesyat

70 семьдесят syemdyesyat

80 восемьдесят vosyemdyesyat

90 девяносто dyevyanosta

100 сто sto

101 сто один sto adeen

102 сто два sto dva

200 двести dvyestee

300 триста treesta

400 четыреста chyetiyryesta

500 пятьсот pyatsot

600 шестьсот shes-sot

700 семьсот syemsot

800 восемьсот vasyemsot

900 девятьсот dyevyatsot

1,000 тысяча tiysyacha

2,000 две тысячи dvyeh tiysyachi

3,000 три тысячи tree tiysyachi

4,000 четыре тысячи chyetiyryeh tiysyachi

5,000 пять тысяч pyat tiysyach

10,000 десять тысяч dyesyat tiysyach

20,000 двадцать тысяч dvatsat tiysyach

100,000 сто тысяч sto tiysyach

1,000,000 миллион meelee-on

Ordinals

1st первый pyervi

2nd второй ftaroy

3rd третий tryetee

4th четвёртый chyetvyorti

5th пятый pyati

6th шестой shestoy

7th седьмой syedmoy

8th восьмой vasmoy

9th девятый dyevyati

10th десятый dyesyati

11th одиннадцатый adeenatsati

12th двенадцатый dvyenatsati

13th тринадцатый treenatsati

14th четырнадцатый

chyet**iy**rnatsati

15th пятнадцатый pyat**n**atsati

16th шестнадцатый shesnatsati

17th семнадцатый syem**n**atsati

18th восемнадцатый
vasyemnatsati

19th девятнадцатый
dyevyat**n**atsati

20th двадцатый dvatsati

21st двадцать первый
dvatsat p**ye**rvi

22nd двадцать второй
dvatsat ftar**oy**

23rd двадцать третий
dvatsat tr**ye**tee

24th двадцать четвёртый
dvatsat chyetv**yo**rti

25th двадцать пятый
dvatsat p**ya**ti

26th двадцать шестой
dvatsat shest**oy**

27th двадцать седьмой
dvatsat syedm**oy**

28th двадцать восьмой
dvatsat vasm**oy**

29th двадцать девятый
dvatsat dyev**ya**ti

30th тридцатый treetsati

31st тридцать первый
treetsat p**ye**rvi

Regional accents

In most former Soviet republics (such as the Ukraine or Belarus or Georgia) Russian was spoken and studied at school as the first language, so people of a certain age group – those aged 30 and above – will speak Russian fluently (although some pretend not to). If you are travelling to these countries this phrasebook will serve you well, in spite of the accent differences.

Accents in Russia itself do differ, but not as dramatically as in the UK or US. And even across the Urals – in Siberia and out to Vladivostok – there are no major accent differences. (Some remote places do have dialects bordering on a separate language and in rare cases even a Russian native speaker may not understand what is being said there.) What Russian regional accents you may hear are, broadly, northern, southern and central Russian or the Moscow accent. What Russian regional accents you may hear are, broadly, northern, southern and central Russian or the Moscow accent. The northern is the only accent to pronounce an unstressed o as o, the others pronouncing this as a.

What is most significant is not so much the difference in actual sounds as that speech be 'educated'. A person will be seen as uneducated if he/she puts the stress in the wrong places (Mikhail Gorbachev was famous for this). For example, pozvoneesh (позвонишь) is incorrect and should be pozvoneesh or, in the south, pazvoneesh.

Standard Russian, as taught to foreigners, is most like the accent which you will hear in Moscow and central Russia. Here are some examples of the few differing pronunciations which you may hear in Russia:

	unstressed 'o' becomes 'a' except in the north	'sh' becomes 'ch'	'v' becomes 'g'
	ПОНЯТНО	ЧТО	НИЧЕГО
	I see	what	nothing
Moscow and central Russia	panyatna	shto	neechevo
The north	ponyatno	shto	neechevo
Old St Petersburg	panyatna	chto	neechego
The south	panyatna	shto	neechevo

SCENARIOS

Download these scenarios as MP3s from
www.roughguides.com/phrasebooks

1. Accommodation

▶ What's an inexpensive hotel you can recommend?
Вы можете порекомендовать недорогую гостиницу?
viy mo_j_etyeh paryekamyendava_t_ nyedarago**o**-yoo gast**ee**neetsoo?

▶▶ I'm sorry, they all seem to be fully booked.
К сожалению, похоже, ни в одной нет мест.
k sa_j_aly**e**nee-yoo, pa_Ho_jeh, neevadno**y** nyet myest

▶ Can you give me the name of a good middle-range hotel?
Есть ли хорошая гостиница средней категории?
y**e**stlee _Ha_rosha-ya gast**ee**neetsa sry**e**dnyay katyego**ree**-ee?

▶▶ Let me have a look; do you want to be in the centre?
Давайте посмотрим, вы хотите быть в центре?
dav**i**tyeh pasmo**t**reem, viy _Ha_t**ee**etyeh biyt fts**e**ntryeh?

▶ If possible.
Если возможно.
y**e**slee vazmo_J_na

▶▶ Do you mind being a little way out of town?
Вас устроит, если это будет за городом?
vas oostro-eet, y**e**slee **e**ta bo**o**dyet za**g**aradam?

▶ Not too far out.
Если не слишком далеко.
y**e**slee nyeh sl**ee**shkam dalyek**o**

▶ Where is it on the map?
Где это на карте?
gdyeh **e**ta na k**a**rtyeh?

▶ Can you write the name and address down?
Напишите, пожалуйста, название и адрес?
napeesh**iy**tyeh, pa_J_alsta, nazv**a**nee-yeh ee **a**dryes

▶ I'm looking for a room in a private house.
Я хочу снять комнату в частном доме.
ya _Ha_ch**oo** snyat k**o**mnatoo fch**a**stnam d**o**myeh

2. Banks

bank account	банковский счет	bankofskee sh-chot
cheque	чек	chyek
to deposit	класть/положить на счет	klast/palaJiyt na sh-chot
rouble	рубль	roobl
pin number	пин-код	peen kod
pound	фунт	foont
to withdraw	снимать/снять со счета	sneemat/snyat sa sh-chota

▶ Can you change this into roubles?
Вы не могли бы обменять это на рубли?
viy nyeh magleebi abmyenyat eta na rooblee?

▶▶ How would you like the money?
Какие купюры вы хотите?
kakee-yeh koopyooriy viy Hateetyeh?

▶ Small notes.
Мелкие купюры.
myelkee-yeh koopyooriy

▶ Big notes.
Крупные купюры.
kroopniy-yeh koopyooriy

▶ Do you have information in English about opening an account?
Есть ли у вас информация на английском языке об открытии счета?
yestlee oo vas eenfarmatsi-ya na angleeskam yazikyeh ab atkriytee-ee sh-chota?

▶▶ Yes, what sort of account do you want?
Да, какой счет вы хотите открыть?
da, kakoy sh-chot viy Hateetyeh atkriyt?

▶ I'd like a current account.
Текущий счет.
tyekoosh-chee sh-chot

▶▶ Your passport, please.
Ваш паспорт, пожалуйста.
vash paspart, paJalsta

▶ Can I use this card to draw some cash?
Я могу снять деньги по этой карточке?
ya magoo snyat dyengee pa-etl kartochkyeh?

▶▶ You have to go to the cashier's desk.
Вам нужно подойти к кассе.
vam noozhna padltee k-kas-syeh

▶ I want to transfer this to my account at Citybank.
Я хотела бы перевести это на мой счет в ситибанке.
ya Hatyela biy pyeryevyestee eta na moy sh-chot v seeteebankyeh

▶▶ OK, but we'll have to charge you for the phonecall.
Хорошо, но вам придется оплатить телефонный звонок.
Harasho, no vam preedyotsa aplateet tyelyefon-ni zvanok

3. Booking a room

shower	душ	doosh
telephone in the room	телефон в номере	tyelyefon vnomyeryeh
payphone in the lobby	таксофон в фойе	taksafon f-fa-**yeh**

▶ Do you have any rooms?
У вас есть свободные номера?
oo vas yest svabodni-yeh namyera?

▶▶ For how many people?
На сколько человек?
na skolka chyelavyek?

▶ For one/for two.
На одного/на двоих.
na adnavo/na dva-eeн

▶▶ Yes, we have rooms free.
Да, у нас есть свободные номера.
da, oo nas yest svabodni-yeh namyera

▶▶ For how many nights?
На сколько ночей?
na skolka nachyay?

▶ Just for one night.
Только на одну ночь.
tolka na adnoo noch

▶ How much is it?
Сколько это стоит?
skolka eta sto-eet?

>> 3060 roubles with bathroom and 2380 roubles without bathroom.
3060 Рублей с ванной и 2380 без ванной.
tree tïysyachee shesdyesyat rooblyay svan-nl ee dvyeh tïysyachee treesta vosyemdyesyat byez van-ni

▶ Does that include breakfast?
Это включает завтрак?
eta fklyoocha-yet zaftrak?

▶ Can I see a room with bathroom?
Можно посмотреть номер с ванной?
moлna pasmatryet nomyer svan-nl?

▶ OK, I'll take it.
Хорошо, это подойдет.
Harasho, eta padldyot

▶ When do I have to check out?
Во сколько нужно освободить номер?
va skolka nooлna asvabadeet nomyer?

▶ Is there anywhere I can leave luggage?
Где можно оставить багаж?
gdyeh moлna astaveet bagaл?

4. Car hire

automatic	автоматическая передача	aftamateechyeska-ya pyeryedacha
full tank	полный бак	polni bak
manual	ручная передача	roochna-ya pyeryedacha
rented car	прокатная машина	prakatna-ya mashiyna

▶ I'd like to rent a car.
Я хотела бы взять на прокат машину.
ya Hatyela biy vzyat na prakat mashiynoo

> ▶▶ For how long?
> **На какой срок?**
> na kakoy srok?

▶ Two days.
На два дня.
na dva dnya

▶ I'll take the…
Я возьму…
ya vazmoo…

▶ Is that with unlimited mileage?
Это с неограниченным километражем?
eta snyeh-agraneechyen-niym keelamyetrajem?

> ▶▶ It is.
> **Да.**
> da

> ▶▶ Can I see your driving licence, please?
> **Ваши водительские права, пожалуйста?**
> vashiy vadeetyelskee-yeh prava, paжalsta?

> ▶▶ And your passport.
> **И ваш паспорт.**
> ee vash paspart

▶ Is insurance included?
Входит ли сюда страховка?
fHodeetlee syooda straHofka?

> ▶▶ Yes, but you have to pay the first 3400 roubles.
> **Да, но вам придется заплатить первые 3400 рублей.**
> da, no vam preedyotsa zaplateet pyervi-yeh tree tiysyachee chyetiyryesta rooblyay

> ▶▶ Can you leave a deposit of 3400 roubles?
> Вы сможете оставить задаток в размере 3400 рублей?
> viy smojetyeh astaveet zadatak vrazmyeryeh tryoh tiysyach
> chyetiyryohsot rooblyay?

▶ And if this office is closed, where do I leave the keys?
Если офис закрыт, где нужно оставить ключи?
yeslee ofees zakriyt, gdyeh noojna astaveet klyoochee?

> ▶▶ You drop them in that box.
> Бросьте их в тот ящик.
> brostyeh eeн ftot yash-cheek

5. Car problems

brakes	тормоза	tarmaza
to break down	ломаться/сломаться	lamatsa/slamatsa
clutch	сцепление	stseplyenee-yeh
diesel	дизель	deezyel
flat battery	разряженный аккумулятор	razryaJen-ni akoomoolyatar
flat tyre	спущенная шина	spoosh-chyen-na-ya shiyna
petrol	бензин	byenzeen

▶ Excuse me, where is the nearest petrol station?
Извините, пожалуйста, где ближайшая заправочная станция?
eezveeneetyeh, paJalsta, gdyeh bleeлsha-ya zapravachna-ya stantsi-ya?

> ▶▶ In the next town, about 5km away.
> В следующем городе, примерно в пяти километрах.
> fslyedoosh-chyem goradyeh, preemyerna fpyatee keelamyetraн

▶ The car has broken down.
Машина сломалась.
mashiyna slamalas

> ▶▶ Can you tell me what happened?
> Вы можете сказать, что случилось?
> viy moJetyeh skazat, shto sloocheelas?

▶ I've got a flat tyre.
У меня спустила шина.
oo menya spoosteela shiyna

▶ I think the battery is flat.
Кажется, разряжен аккумулятор.
ka**J**etsa, razrya**J**en akoomoolyatar

>> Can you tell me exactly where you are?
Вы можете точно сказать, где вы находитесь?
viy mo**J**etyeh tochna skaz**at**, gdyeh viy na**H**odeetyes?

▶ I'm about 2km outside of Vyazma on the M1.
Я примерно в двух километрах от Вязьмы на дороге М1.
ya preem**y**erna vdvoo**H** keelamy**e**tra**H** at vy**a**zmi na dar**o**gyeh em-ad**ee**n

>> What type of car? What colour?
Какого типа машина? Какого цвета?
kak**o**va t**ee**pa mash**i**yna? kak**o**va tsv**y**eta?

▶ Can you send a tow truck?
Вы можете прислать эвакуатор?
viy mo**J**etyeh preesl**at** evakoo-**a**tar?

6. Children

baby	ребенок	ryeb**yo**nak
boy	мальчик	m**a**lcheek
child	ребенок	ryeb**yo**nak
children	дети	d**ye**tee
cot	детская кроватка	d**ye**tska-ya krav**a**tka
formula	детская смесь	d**ye**tska-ya smy**es**
girl	девочка	d**ye**vachka
highchair	высокий детский стул	vis**o**kee d**ye**tskee stool
nappies (diapers)	подгузники	padg**oo**zneekee

▶ We need a babysitter for tomorrow evening.
Нам нужна няня завтра вечером.
nam noo**J**na ny**a**nya z**a**ftra v**ye**chyeram

>> For what time?
На какое время?
na kak**o**-yeh vr**ye**mya?

▶ From 7.30 to 11.00.
С семи тридцати до одиннадцати.
s-sy**e**mee treetsat**ee** da ad**ee**natsatee

▶▶ How many children? How old are they?
Сколько детей? Какого они возраста?
skolka dyet**yay**? kak**o**va an**ee** v**o**zrast?

▶ Two children, aged four and eighteen months.
Двое детей, в возрасте четырех и восемнадцати месяцев.
dv**o**-yeh dyet**yay**, v-v**o**zrastyeh chyetir**yo**н ee vasyemn**a**tsatee m**ye**syatsef

---

▶ Where can I change the baby?
Где я могу перепеленать ребенка?
gdyeh ya mag**oo** pyeryepyelyen**a**t ryeb**yo**nka?

Could you please warm this bottle for me?
Вы не могли бы подогреть эту бутылочку?
viy nyeh magleebi padagryet etoo bootiylachkoo?

Can you give us a child's portion?
Вы можете подать нам детскую порцию?
viy moJetyeh padat nam dyetskoo-yoo portsi-yoo?

We need two child seats.
Нам нужны два детских кресла.
nam nooJniy dva dyetskeeн kryesla

Is there a discount for children?
Есть ли скидка для детей?
yestlee skeetka dlya dyetyay?

7. Communications: Internet

@, at	"собачка"	sabachka
computer	компьютер	kampyooter
email	электронная почта	elyektron-na-ya pochta
Internet	Интернет	eenternet
keyboard	клавиатура	klavee-atoora
mouse	мышь	miysh

▶ Is there somewhere I can check my emails?
Где я могу проверить мою электронную почту?
gdyeh ya magoo pravyereet ma-yoo elyektron-noo-yoo pochtoo?

▶ Do you have Wi-Fi?
У вас есть wi-fi?
oo vas yest vı-fı?

▶ Is there an Internet café around here?
Есть ли поблизости интернет-кафе?
yestlee pableezastee eenternet-kafeh?

▶▶ Yes, there's one in the shopping centre.
Да, есть одно в торговом центре.
da, yest adno ftargovam tsentryeh

▶▶ Do you want fifteen minutes, thirty minutes or one hour?
Вам пятнадцать минут, тридцать минут или один час?
vam pyatnatsat meenoot, treetsat meenoot eelee adeen chas?

▶ Thirty minutes please. Can you help me log on?
Тридцать минут, пожалуйста. Вы можете мне помочь войти в систему?
treetsat meenoot, paJalsta, viy moJetyeh mnyeh pamoch vitee fseestyemoo?

▶▶ OK, here's your password.
Хорошо, вот ваш пароль.
Harasho, vot vash par**ol**

▶ Can you change this to an English keyboard?
Вы можете переключить клавиатуру на английский язык?
viy mo**J**etyeh pyeryeklyooch**ee**t klavee-at**oo**roo na angl**ee**skee yaz**iy**k?

▶ I'll take another quarter of an hour.
Мне еще четверть часа, пожалуйста.
mnyeh yesh-ch**o** ch**ye**tvyert ch**a**sa, pa**J**alsta

▶ Is there a printer I can use?
Я могу воспользоваться принтером?
ya mag**oo** vasp**o**lzavatsa pr**ee**nteram?

8. Communications: phones

mobile phone	мобильный телефон	mab**ee**lni tyely**e**fon
(cell phone)	(сотовый телефон)	(s**o**tavi tyely**e**fon)
payphone	таксофон	taksaf**o**n
phone call	телефонный звонок	tyelyef**o**n-ni zvan**o**k
phone card	телефонная карта	tyelyef**o**n-na-ya k**a**rta
phone charger	зарядное то для телефона	zary**a**dna yehoostr**o**ystva dlya tyelyef**o**na
SIM card	SIM-карта	seem-k**a**rta

▶ Can I call abroad from here?
Я могу позвонить отсюда за границу?
ya mag**oo** pazvan**ee**t ats**yoo**da za gran**ee**tsoo?

▶ How do I get an outside line?
Как мне выйти на внешнюю линию?
kak mnyeh v**iy**tee na vn**ye**shnyoo-yoo l**ee**nee-yoo?

▶ What's the code to call the UK/ US from here?
Какой код набирать, чтобы позвонить отсюда в Великобританию/в США?
kak**oy** kod nabeer**a**t, sht**o**bi pazvan**ee**t ats**yoo**da v-vyeleekabreet**a**nee-yoo/ fseh-sheh-**a**?

zero	ноль	nol
one	один	ad**ee**n
two	два	dva
three	три	tree
four	четыре	chyet**iy**ryeh
five	пять	pyat
six	шесть	shest
seven	семь	syem
eight	восемь	v**o**syem
nine	девять	d**ye**vyat

► Hello, can I speak to Galina?
Алло, можно Галину, пожалуйста?
allo, mojna galeenoo, paJalsta?

►► Yes, that's me speaking.
Да, я слушаю.
da, ya sloosha-yoo

► Do you have a charger for this?
У вас есть зарядное устройство для этого телефона?
oo vas yest zaryadna-yeh oostroystva dlya etava tyelyefona?

► Can I buy a SIM card for this phone?
Я могу купить sim-карту для этого телефона?
ya magoo koopeet seem-kartoo dlya etava tyelyefona?

9. Directions

► Hi, I'm looking for Kozitsky Lane.
Добрый день, я ищу козицкий переулок.
dobri dyen, ya eesh-choo kazeetskee pyeryeh-oolak

► Hi, Kozitsky Lane, do you know where it is?
Добрый день, вы не знаете, где находится козицкий переулок?
dobri dyen, viy nyeh zna-yetyeh, gdyeh kazeetskee pyeryeh-oolak?

▶▶ Sorry, never heard of it.
Извините, никогда о таком не слышала.
eezveen**ee**tyeh, neekagd**a** atak**o**m nyeh sl**iy**shala

▶ Hi, can you tell me where Kozitsky Lane is?
Добрый день, не подскажете, где козицкий переулок?
d**o**bri dyen, nyeh patsk**a**Jetyeh, gdyeh kazeetskee pyeryeh-**oo**lak?

▶▶ I'm a stranger here too.
Я тоже приезжая.
ya t**o**Jeh pree-**ye**zJa-ya

▶ Where?   ▶ Which direction?
Где?   В каком направлении?
gdyeh?   fkak**o**m napravl**ye**nee-ee?

▶▶ Around the corner.   ▶▶ Left at the second traffic lights.
За углом.   Налево после второго светофора.
za oogl**o**m   nal**ye**va p**o**slyeh ftar**o**va svyetaf**o**ra

▶▶ Then it's the first street on the right.
Затем первая улица справа.
zat**ye**m p**ye**rva-ya **oo**leetsa spr**a**va

вон там	von tam	over there
дальше	dalsheh	further
мимо...	meema...	past the...
назад	nazat	back
напротив	naproteef	opposite
недалеко (от)	nyedalyeko (ot)	near
перед	pyeryet	in front of
поворот	pavarot	turn off
прямо	pryama	straight ahead
слева	slyeva	on the left
следующий	slyedoosh-chee	next
справа	sprava	on the right
сразу за	srazoo za	just after
улица	ooleetsa	street

10. Emergencies

▶ Help!
Помогите!

accident	несчастный случай	nyesh-chasni sloochee
(in a car)	авария	avaree-ya
ambulance	скорая помощь	skora-ya pomash-ch
consul	консул	konsool
embassy	посольство	pasolstva
fire brigade	пожарная команда	paJarna-ya kamanda
police	милиция	meeleetsi-ya

pamageetyeh!

▶ Can you help me?
Вы можете мне помочь?
viy moJetyeh mnyeh pamoch?

▶ Please come with me! It's really very urgent!
Пожалуйста, пойдемте со мной – это очень срочно!
paJalsta, pIdyomtyeh samnoy – eta ochyen srochna!

▶ I've lost my keys.
Я потеряла ключи.
ya patyeryala klyoochee

▶ My car is not working.
Моя машина сломалась.
ma-ya mashiyna slamalas

▶ My purse has been stolen.
У меня украли кошелек.
oo myenya ookralee kashelyok

▶ I've been mugged.
Меня обокрали.
myenya abakralee

▶▶ What's your name?
Как ваше имя?
kak vasheh eemya?

▶▶ I need to see your passport.
Ваш паспорт, пожалуйста.
vash paspart, paJalsta

▶ I'm sorry, all my papers have been stolen.
Извините, у меня украли все документы.
eezveeneetyeh, oo myenya ookralee fsyeh dakoomyentiy

11. Friends

▶ Hi, how're you doing?
Привет, как дела?
preevy**et**, kak dyel**a**?

▶▶ OK, and you?
Хорошо, а у тебя?
Harash**o**, a-ootyeb**ya**?

▶ Yeah, fine.
Хорошо.
Harash**o**

▶ Not bad.
Неплохо.
nyepl**o**Ha

▶ D'you know Andrei?
Ты знаком с андреем?
tiy znak**o**m sandr**yeh**-yem?

▶ And this is Olga.
А это – ольга.
a-**e**ta – **o**lga

▶▶ Yeah, we know each other.
Да, мы знакомы.
da, miy znak**o**miy

▶ Where do you know each other from?
Где вы познакомились?
gdyeh viy paznak**o**meelees?

▶▶ We met at Sasha's place.
Мы познакомились у саши.
miy paznak**o**meelees oos**a**shiy

▶ That was some party, eh?
Неплохая была вечеринка, а?
nyeplaHa-ya biyla vyechyer**ee**nka, ah?

▶▶ The best.
Отличная.
atl**ee**chna-ya

▶ Are you guys coming for a beer?
А вы пойдете с нами выпить пива?
viy pld**yo**tyeh sn**a**mee v**iy**peet p**ee**va?

▶▶ Cool, let's go.
Отлично, пойдем.
atl**ee**chna, pld**yo**m

▶▶ No, I'm meeting Yulia.
Нет, я встречаюсь с юлей.
nyet, ya fstryecha-yoos s **yoo**lyay

▶ See you at Sasha's place tonight.
Увидимся у саши сегодня вечером.
oo**vee**deemsya oo **sa**shiy syev**o**dnya **vye**chyeram

▶▶ See you!
Пока!
pak**a**!

12. Health

▶ I'm not feeling very well.
Мне нехорошо.
mnyeh nyeh нarash**o**

▶ Can you get a doctor?
Вы не могли бы вызвать врача?
viy nyeh magl**ee**biy v**iy**zvat vracha?

▶ Where does it hurt?
Где у вас болит?
gdyeh oo vas bal**eet**?

▶▶ It hurts here.
Здесь.
zdyes

▶ Is the pain constant?
Боль постоянная?
bol pasta-**ya**n-na-ya?

▶▶ It's not a constant pain.
Нет, не постоянная.
nyet, nyeh pasta-**ya**n-na-ya

▶ Can I make an appointment?
Могу ли я записаться к врачу?
mag**oo**lee ya zapees**a**tsa kvrach**oo**?

▶ Can you give me something for…?
Вы можете дать мне что-нибудь от…?
viy m**o**Jethyeh dat mnyeh sht**o**neeboot at…?

▶ Yes, I have insurance.
Да, у меня есть страховка.
da, oo myen**ya** yest straH**o**fka

antibiotics	антибиотики	anteebee-**o**teekee
antiseptic ointment	антисептическая мазь	anteesyept**ee**chyeska-ya mas
cystitis	цистит	tsist**eet**
dentist	зубной врач	zoobn**oy** vrach
diarrhoea	диарея	dee-ar**yeh**-ya
doctor	врач	vrach
hospital	больница	baln**ee**tsa
ill	болен	b**o**lyen
medicine	лекарство	lyek**a**rstva
painkillers	болеутоляющие средства	b**o**lyeh-ootal**ya**-yoosh-chee-yeh sr**ye**tstva
pharmacy	аптека	apt**ye**ka
to prescribe	прописывать/ прописать	prap**ee**siyvat/ prapees**a**t
thrush	молочница	mal**o**chneetsa

13. Hotels

maid	горничная	gorneechna-ya
manager	администратор	admeeneestratar
room service	обслуживание в номере	apslooJivanee-yeh vnomyeryeh

▶ Hello, we've booked a double room in the name of Cameron.
Здравствуйте, у нас забронирован двухместный номер на имя Кэмерон.
zdrastvooytyeh, oo nas zabraneeravan dvooнmyesni nomyer na eemya Cameron

▶▶ That was for four nights, wasn't it?
На четыре ночи, правильно?
na chyetiyryeh nochee, praveelna?

▶ Yes, we're leaving on Saturday.
Да, мы уезжаем в субботу.
da, miy oo-yeJ-Ja-yem fsoobotoo

▶▶ Can I see your passport please?
Ваш паспорт, пожалуйста.
vash paspart, paЈalsta

▶▶ There you are, room 321 on the third floor.
Вот, пожалуйста, номер триста двадцать один на третьем этаже.
vot, paЈalsta, nomyer treesta dvatsat adeen na tryetyem etaЈeh

▶ I can't get this keycard to work.
У меня не работает эта ключ-карта.
oo menya nyeh rabota-yet eta klyooch-karta

▶▶ Sorry, I need to reactivate it.
Извините, мне нужно ее реактивировать.
eezveeneetyeh, mnyeh nooЈna yeh-yo rye-akteeveeravat

▶ What time is breakfast?
В какое время завтрак?
fkako-yeh vryemya zaftrak?

▶ There aren't any towels in my room.
В моем номере нет полотенец.
vma-yom nomyeryeh nyet palatyenyets

▶ My flight isn't until this evening, can I keep the room a bit longer?
Я улетаю только вечером, я могу оставить за собой номер еще ненадолго?
ya oolyeta-yoo tolka vyechyeram, ya magoo astaveet za saboy nomyer yesh-cho nyenadolga?

► Can I settle up? Is this card OK?
Можно расплатиться? Эта карта подходит?
moJna rasplateetsa? eta karta padHodeet?

14. Language difficulties

a few words	несколько слов	nyeskalka slof
interpreter	переводчик	pyeryevotcheek
to translate	переводить/	pyeryevadeet/
	перевести	pyeryevestee

►► Your credit card has been refused.
Ваша кредитная карта не проходит.
vasha kryedeetna-ya karta nyeh praHodeet

► What? I don't understand. Do you speak English?
Что? Я не понимаю. Вы говорите по-английски?
shto? ya nyeh paneema-yoo, viy gavareetyeh pa-angleeskee?

►► This isn't valid.
Это не действительно.
eta nyeh dyaystveetyelna

► Could you say that again?
Повторите, пожалуйста?
paftareetyeh, paJalsta

► Slowly.
Медленно.
myedlyen-na

► I understand very little Russian.
Я понимаю чуть-чуть по-русски.
ya paneema-yoo choot-choot paroos-skee

► I speak Russian very badly.
Я очень плохо говорю по-русски.
ya ochyen ploHa gavaryoo paroos-skee

►► You can't use this card to pay.
Вы не можете платить этой карточкой.
viy nyeh moJetyeh plateet etl kartachkl

▶▶ Do you understand?
Вы понимаете?
viy paneema-yetyeh

▶ Sorry, no.
Извините, нет.
eezveeneetyeh, nyet

▶ Is there someone who speaks English?
Кто-нибудь здесь говорит по-английски?
ktoneeboot zdyes gavareet pa-angleeskee?

▶ Oh, now I understand.
А, теперь я понимаю.
ah, tyepyer ya paneema-yoo

▶ Is that OK now?
Теперь все в порядке?
tyepyer fsyo fparyatkyeh

15. Meeting people

▶ Hello.
Добрый день.
dobri dyen

▶▶ Hello, my name's Tanya.
Добрый день, меня зовут таня.
dobri dyen, menya zavoot tanya

▶ Graham, from England, Thirsk.
Меня зовут грээм, из англии, из города тирск.
menya zavoot Graham, eez anglee-ee, eez gorada Thirsk

▶▶ Don't know that, where is it?
Не слышала о таком, где это?
nyeh sliyshala atakom, gdyeheta?

▶ Not far from York, in the North; and you?
Не далеко от йорка, на севере, а вы?
nyeh dalyeko at yorka, na syevyeryeh, aviy?

▶▶ I'm from Moscow; here by yourself?
Я из москвы; вы здесь один?
ya eez maskviy; viy zdyes adeen?

▶ No, I'm with my wife and two kids.
Нет, я с женой и двумя детьми.
nyet, ya sJenoy ee dvoomya dyetmee

▶ What do you do?
Кем вы работаете?
kyem viy rab**o**ta-yetyeh?

▶▶ I'm in computers.
Я занимаюсь компьютерами.
ya zaneem**a**-yoos kamp**yoo**teramee

▶ Me too.
Я тоже.
ya t**o**Jeh

▶ Here's my wife now.
А вот и моя жена.
av**o**t ee ma-**ya** Jen**a**

▶▶ Nice to meet you.
Приятно познакомиться.
pree-**ya**tna paznak**o**meetsa

16. Nightlife

heavy metal	тяжелый металл	tyaJ**o**li my**e**tal
folk	фольк	folk
jazz	джаз	dJaz
hip-hop	хип-хоп	Heep-H**o**p
electro	электро	el**ye**ktra
rock	рок	rok

▶ What's a good club for…?
Какой здесь есть хороший клуб с музыкой в стиле…?
kak**oy** zdyes yest Har**o**shi kloop sm**oo**ziki fst**ee**lyeh…?

▶▶ There's going to be a great gig at the Zvyezda Club tomorrow night.
Отличная программа будет в клубе "Звезда" завтра вечером.
atl**ee**chna-ya pragr**a**m-ma b**oo**dyet fkl**oo**byeh zvyezd**a** z**a**ftra v**ye**chyeram

▶ Where can I hear some local music?
Где я могу послушать местную музыку?
gdyeh ya mag**oo** pasl**oo**shat m**ye**snoo-yoo m**oo**zikoo?

▶ **What's a good place for dancing?**
Куда здесь можно пойти потанцевать?
kooda zdyes mo**zh**na pi**tee** patantsev**a**t?

▶ **Can you write down the names of the best bars around here?**
Вы можете написать названия лучших местных баров?
viy mo**zh**etyeh napees**a**t nazv**a**nee-ya l**oo**chshi**h** m**ye**sni**h** b**a**raf?

▶▶ **That depends what you're looking for.**
Это зависит от того, что вы ищете.
eta zav**ee**seet at tav**o**, shto viy **ee**sh-chyetyeh

▶ **The place where the locals go.**
Место, куда ходят местные жители.
m**ye**sta, kood**a** **н**odyat m**ye**sni-yeh **zh**iytyelee

▶ **A place for a quiet drink.**
Место, где можно спокойно выпить.
m**ye**sta, gdyeh mo**zh**na spak**oy**na v**iy**peet

▶▶ **The casino across the river is very good.**
Казино на противоположном берегу реки очень хорошее.
kazeen**o** na prateevapal**o**znam byeryeg**oo** ryek**ee** **o**chyen **н**ar**o**sheh-yeh

▶ I suppose they have a dress code.
Я полагаю, у них дресс-код.
ya palaga-yoo, oo neeн dryes-kod

▶▶ You can wear what you like.
Вы можете надеть что хотите.
viy moJetyeh nadyet shto Hateetyeh

▶ What time does it close?
В какое время они закрываются?
fkako-yeh vryemya anee zakriva-yootsa?

17. Post offices

авиапочта	avee-a pochta	airmail
открытка	atkriytka	post card
почта	pochta	post office
марка	marka	stamp

▶ What time does the post office close?
Во сколько закрывается почта?
vaskolka zakriyva-yetsa pochta?

▶▶ Eight o'clock weekdays.
В восемь часов по будням.
v-vosyem chasof pa boodnyam

▶ Is the post office open on Saturdays?
Открыта ли почта по субботам?
atkriytalee pochta pa soobotam?

▶▶ Until two o'clock.
До двух часов.
da dvooн chasof

▶ I'd like to send this registered to England.
Я хотела бы послать это заказным в англию.
ya Hatyela biy paslat eta zakazniym vanglee-yoo

▶▶ Certainly, that will cost 340 roubles.
Да, конечно, это будет стоить 340 рублей.
da, kanyeshna, eta boodyet sto-eet treesta sorak rooblyay

▶ And also two stamps for England, please.
А также две марки для англии, пожалуйста.
ah takJeh dvyeh markee dlya anglee-ee, paJalsta

▶ Do you have some airmail stickers?
Есть ли у вас наклейки авиапочты?
yestlee oo vas naklyaykee avee-a pochtiy?

▶ Do you have any mail for me?
Есть ли у вас почта для меня?
yestlee oo vas pochta dlya myenya?

МЕЖДУНАРОДНЫЙ	myeJdoonarodni	international
ПИСЬМА	peesma	letters
ВНУТРЕННИЙ	vnootryen-nee	domestic
ПОСЫЛКИ	pasiylkee	parcels
ДО ВОСТРЕБОВАНИЯ	da vastryebiyvanee-ya	poste restante

18. Restaurants

bill	счет	sh-chot
menu	меню	myenyoo
table	стол	stol

▶ Can we have a non-smoking table?
Есть ли у вас столик для некурящих?
yestlee oo vas stoleek dlya nyekooryash-cheeн?

▶ There are two of us.
Нас двое.
nas dvo-yeh

▶ There are four of us.
Нас четверо.
nas chyetvyera

▶ What's this?
Что это?
shto-eta?

▶▶ It's a type of fish.
Это такая рыба.
eta taka-ya riyba

▶▶ It's a local speciality.
Это местное фирменное блюдо.
eta myestna-yeh feermyen-na-yeh blyooda

▶▶ Come inside and I'll show you.
Входите, я вам покажу.
fнadeetyeh, ya vam pakaJoo

▶ We would like two of these, one of these and one of those.
Нам, пожалуйста, две порции этого, одну – этого и одну – этого.
nam, paJalsta, dvyeh portsiy-ee etava, adnoo etava ee adnoo etava

▶▶ And to drink?
А выпить?
aviypeet?

▶ Red wine.   ▶ White wine.
Красное вино.   Белое вино.
krasna-yeh veeno   byela-yeh veeno

▶ A beer and two orange juices.
Одно пиво и два апельсиновых сока.
adno peeva ee dva apyelseenaviyн soka

▶ Some more bread please.
Еще хлеба, пожалуйста.
yesh-cho Hlyeba, paJalsta

▶▶ How was your meal?
Вам понравилось?
vam panraveelas?

▶ Excellent, very nice!
Да, замечательно, очень вкусно!
da, zamyechatyelna, ochyen fkoosna

▶▶ Anything else?
Еще что-нибудь?
yesh-cho shtoneeboot?

▶ Just the bill thanks.
нет, спасибо, только счет.
nyet, spaseeba, tolka sh-chot

19. Self-catering accommodation

air-conditioning	кондиционер	kandeetsi-anyer
apartment	квартира	kvarteera
cooker	плита	pleeta
fridge	холодильник	Haladeelneek
heating	отопление	ataplyenee-yeh
hot water	горячая вода	garyacha-ya vada
lightbulb	лампочка	lampachka
toilet	туалет	too-alyet

▶ The toilet's broken, can you get someone to fix it?
Туалет сломан, вы можете вызвать кого-нибудь, чтобы его починить?
too-alyet sloman, viy moJetyeh viyzvat kavo-neeboot, shtobi yevo pacheeneet?

▶ There's no hot water.
Нет горячей воды.
nyet garyachay vadiy

▶ Can you show me how the air-conditioning works?
Вы можете показать мне, как работает кондиционер?
viy moJetyeh pakazat mnyeh, kak rabota-yet kandeetsi-anyer?

▶▶ OK, what apartment are you in?
Хорошо, в какой вы квартире?
Harash**o**, fkak**oy** viy kvart**ee**ryeh?

▶ We're in number five.
Мы в номере пять.
miy vn**o**meryeh pyat

▶ Can you move us to a quieter apartment?
Вы можете переселить нас в квартиру потише?
viy m**o**jetyeh pyeryesyel**ee**t nas fkvart**ee**roo pat**ee**sheh?

▶ Is there a supermarket nearby?
Есть ли поблизости супермаркет?
yestlee pabl**ee**zastee soopyerm**a**rkyet?

▶▶ Have you enjoyed your stay?
Вы довольны своим пребыванием?
viy dav**o**lni sva-**ee**m pryebiv**a**nee-yem?

▶ Brilliant holiday, thanks!
Отличный отдых, спасибо!
atl**ee**chni **o**d-dih, spas**ee**ba!

20. Shopping

▶▶ Can I help you?
Я могу вам помочь?
ya mag**oo** vam pam**o**ch?

▶ Can I just have a look around?
Я могу просто посмотреть?
ya mag**oo** pr**o**sta pasmatr**ye**t?

▶ Yes, I'm looking for…
Да, я ищу…
da, ya eesh-ch**oo**…

▶ How much is this?
Сколько это стоит?
sk**o**lka **e**ta st**o**-eet?

▶▶ Seven hundred and sixty-eight roubles.
Семьсот шестьдесят восемь рублей.
syems**o**t shesdyes**ya**t v**o**syem roobl**ya**y

▶ OK, I think I'll have to leave it; it's a little too expensive for me.
Пожалуй, это слишком дорого для меня.
pa**J**al**oo**y, **e**ta sl**ee**shkam d**o**raga dlya myen**ya**

▶▶ How about this?
А вот это?
ah vot **e**ta?

▶ Can I pay by credit card?
Я могу заплатить кредитной картой?
ya mag**oo** zaplat**ee**t kryed**ee**tnl k**a**rtl?

▶ It's too big.
Это велико.
eta vyeleek**o**

▶ It's too small.
Это мало.
eta mal**o**

▶ It's for my son – he's about this high.
Это для моего сына – он примерно такого роста.
eta dlya ma-yev**o** s**iy**na – on preem**ye**rna tak**o**va r**o**sta

▶▶ Will there be anything else?
Что-нибудь еще?
sht**o**-neeboot yesh-ch**o**?

▶ That's all thanks.
Нет, спасибо, это все.
nyet, spas**ee**ba, **e**ta fsyo

МОСКВА
кафе & lounge

▶ Make it seven hundred roubles and I'll take it.
Я возьму, если отдадите за семьсот рублей.
ya vazm**oo**, **ye**slee atdad**ee**tyeh za syems**o**t roobl**yay**

▶ Fine, I'll take it.
Хорошо, я возьму это.
Harash**o**, ya vazm**oo e**ta

ЗАКРЫТО	zakr**iy**ta	closed
КАССА	k**a**s-sa	cash desk
ОБМЕНИВАТЬ/	abm**y**en**ee**vat/abmyen**ya**t	to exchange
ОБМЕНЯТЬ		
ОТКРЫТО	atkr**iy**ta	open
РАСПРОДАЖА	raspr**a**daJa	sale

21. Shopping for clothes

to alter	изменять/изменить	eezmyen**ya**t/eezmyen**ee**t
bigger	побольше	pab**o**lsheh
just right	как раз	k**a**k ras
smaller	поменьше	pam**ye**nsheh
to try on	мерить/померить	m**ye**reet/pam**ye**reet

▶▶ Can I help you?
Я могу вам помочь?
ya mag**oo** vam pam**o**ch?

▶ No thanks, I'm just looking.
Нет, спасибо, я просто смотрю.
nyet, spas**ee**ba, ya pr**o**sta smatr**yoo**

▶▶ Do you want to try that on?
Вы хотите это померить?
viy нat**ee**tyeh **e**ta pam**ye**reet?

▶ Yes, and I'll try this one too.
Да, и это я тоже померяю.
da, ee **e**ta ya t**o**Jeh pam**ye**rya-yoo

▶ Do you have it in a bigger size?
У вас есть размер побольше?
oo vas yest razm**ye**r pab**o**lsheh?

▶ Do you have it in a different colour?
У вас есть другой цвет?
oo vas yest droog**oy** tsvyet?

▶▶ That looks good on you.
Вам идет.
vam eed**yo**t

▶ Can you shorten this?
Вы можете это укоротить?
viy mo**je**tyeh **e**ta ookarat**eet**?

▶▶ Sure, it'll be ready on Friday, after 12.00.
Конечно, будет готово в пятницу, после двенадцати.
kan**ye**shna, **boo**dyet gat**o**va fp**ya**tneetsoo, p**o**slyeh dvyen**a**tsatee

22. Sightseeing

art gallery	картинная галерея	kart**een**-na-ya galer**yeh**-ya
bus tour	автобусная экскурсия	afto**boo**sna-ya eksk**oor**see-ya
city centre	центр города	tsentr g**o**rada
closed	закрыто	zakr**i**ta
guide	гид	geed
museum	музей	mooz**yay**
open	открыто	atkr**i**ta

▶ I'm interested in seeing the old town.
Хотела бы посмотреть на старый город.
нat**ye**la biy pasmatr**ye**t na st**a**ri g**o**rat

▶ Are there guided tours?
Есть ли экскурсии с гидом?
yestlee eksk**oo**rsee-ee sg**ee**dam?

▶▶ I'm sorry, it's fully booked.
К сожалению, мест нет.
k saJal**ye**nee-yoo, myest nyet

▶ How much would you charge to drive us around for four hours?
Сколько вы возьмете за четырехчасовую поездку по городу?
sk**o**lka viy vazm**yo**tyeh za chyetiyr**yo**н-chasav**oo**-yoo pa-**ye**stkoo pa g**o**radoo?

▶ Can we book tickets for the concert here?
Здесь можно заказать билеты на концерт?
zdyes m**o**Jna zakaz**at** beel**ye**tiy na kants**ert**?

▶▶ Yes, in what name?
Да, на чьё имя?
da, na chyo **ee**mya?

▶▶ Which credit card?
Какой кредитной картой вы будете платить?
kak**oy** kryed**ee**tnl k**a**rtl viy b**oo**dyetyeh plat**ee**t?

▶ Where do we get the tickets?
Где можно получить билеты?
gdyeh m**o**Jna palooch**ee**t beel**ye**tiy?

▶▶ Just pick them up at the entrance.
Заберите их при входе.
zabyer**ee**tyeh eeн pree fн**o**dyeh

▶ Is it open on Sundays?
Открыт ли он по воскресеньям?
atr**iy**tlee on pa vaskryes**ye**nyam?

▶ How much is it to get in?
Сколько стоит входной билет?
sk**o**lka st**o**-eet fн**a**dn**o**y beel**ye**t?

▶ Are there reductions for groups of 6?
Есть ли скидки для групп из 6 человек?
yestlee sk**ee**tkee dlya groop eez shest**ee** chyelav**ye**k?

▶ That was really impressive!
Это было очень впечатляюще!
eta biyla ochyen fpyechatlya-yoosh-chyeh!

23. Taxis

▶ Can you get us a taxi?
А вы можете вызвать нам такси?
a viy moJetyeh viyzvat nam taksee?

▶▶ For now? Where are you going?
На сейчас? Куда вам ехать?
na seechas? kooda vam yeнat?

▶ To the town centre.
В центр города.
ftsentr gorada

▶ I'd like to book a taxi to the airport for tomorrow.
Я хотела бы заказать такси в аэропорт на завтра.
ya Hatyela biy zakazat taksee va-eraport na zaftra.

▶▶ Sure, at what time? How many people?
Конечно, в какое время? Сколько человек?
kanyeshna, fkako-yeh vryemya? skolka chyelavyek?

▶ How much is it to the Bolshoi Theatre?
Сколько стоит проезд до большого театра?
skolka sto-eet pra-yest da balshova tyeh-atra?

▶ Right here is fine, thanks.
Я выйду здесь, спасибо.
ya viydoo zdyes, spaseeba

▶ Can you wait here and take us back?
Вы можете подождать здесь и отвезти нас обратно?
viy moJetyeh padaJdat zdyes ee atvyestee nas abratna?

▶▶ How long are you going to be?
Сколько времени вам потребуется?
skolka vryemyenee vam patryeboo-yetsa?

24. Trains

to change	делать/сделать	dyelat/zdyelat
trains	пересадку	pyeryesatkoo
platform	платформа	platforma
return	обратный билет	abratni beelyet
single	билет в один конец	beelyet vadeen kanyets
station	вокзал	vakzal
(underground, bus)	станция	stantsiy-ya
stop	остановка	astanofka
ticket	билет	beelyet

▶ How much is…?
Сколько стоит …?
skolka sto-eet…?

▶ A single, second class to…
Купейный билет в один конец до …
koopayni beelyet vadeen kanyets da…

▶ Two returns, second class to…
Два обратных купейных билета до…
dva abratniyн koopayniyн beelyeta da…

▶ For today.
На сегодня.
na syevodnya

▶ For tomorrow.
На завтра.
na zaftra

▶ For next Tuesday.
На следующий вторник.
na slyedoosh-chee ftorneek

▶▶ There's a supplement for the Intercity.
За поезд дальнего следования нужно доплатить.
za po-yest dalnyeva slyedavanee-ya nooJna daplateet

▶▶ Do you want to make a seat reservation?
Вы хотите забронировать место?
viy Hateetyeh zabraneeravat myesta?

▶▶ You have to change at Moscow.
Вам нужно сделать пересадку в москве.
vam nooJna zdyelat pyeryesatkoo vmaskvyeh

▶ Is this seat free?
Это место свободно?
eta myesta svabodna?

▶ Excuse me, which station are we at?
Извините, пожалуйста, что это за станция?
eezveeneetyeh, paJalsta, shto eta zastantsiy-ya?

▶ Is this where I change for Rostov?
Это здесь нужно сделать пересадку на ростов?
eta zdyes nooJna zdyelat pyeryesatkoo na rastof?

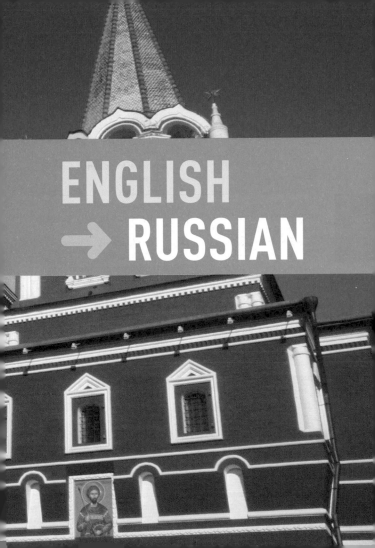

ENGLISH

→ RUSSIAN

A

a, an Russian has no word for 'a' or 'an'

about: about 20 около двадцати okala dvatsatee

it's about 5 o'clock около пяти часов okala pyatee chasof

a film about Russia фильм о России feelm a rassee-ee

above над nad

abroad за границей za graneetsay

absolutely! конечно! kanyeshna!

absorbent cotton вата vata

accelerator акселератор aksyelyeratar

accept принимать/ принять preeneemat/ preenyat

accident несчастный случай nyesh-chasni sloochee

there's been an accident произошёл несчастный случай pra-eezashol nyesh-chasni sloochee

accommodation жильё Jilyo

ache боль bol

my back aches у меня болит спина oo menya baleet speena

across: across the road через дорогу chyeryes darogoo

adaptor адаптер adapter

address адрес adryes

what's your address? какой ваш адрес? kakoy vash adryes?

address book алфавитная записная книжка alfaveetna-ya zapeesna-ya kneeshka

admission charge: how much is the admission charge? сколько стоит билет? skolka sto-eet beelyet?

adult взрослый человек vzrosli chyelavyek

advance: in advance заранее zaranyeh-yeh

aeroplane самолёт samalyot

after после poslyeh

after you после вас poslyeh vas

after lunch после обеда poslyeh abyeda

afternoon: in the afternoon днём dnyom

this afternoon сегодня днём syevodnya dnyom

aftershave лосьон после бритья lasyon poslyeh breetya

aftersun cream крем после загара kryem poslyeh zagara

afterwards потом patom

again снова snova

against против proteef

age возраст vozrast

ago: a week ago неделю назад nyedyelyoo nazat

an hour ago час назад chas nazat

agree: I agree (said by man/ woman) я согласен/ согласна ya saglasyen/ saglasna

Aids СПИД speed

air воздух vo**z**dooн

  by air самолётом
  samal**yo**tam

  **air-conditioning: with
  air-conditioning** с
  кондиционером skandeetsi-
  an**ye**ram

airline авиалиния **a**vee-a-
l**ee**nee-ya

airmail: by airmail авиапочтой
avee-a-p**o**chtı

airmail envelope
международный конверт
mye**J**doonar**o**dni kanv**ye**rt

airport аэропорт a-erap**o**rt

  to the airport, please в
  аэропорт, пожалуйста
  va-erap**o**rt, pa**J**alsta

airport bus автобус-экспресс
в аэропорт aft**o**boos-**e**kspr**e**s
va-erap**o**rt

aisle seat место у прохода
m**ye**sto oo pra**H**oda

alcohol спиртное speertn**o**-yeh

alcoholic: is it alcoholic? это
спиртное? **e**ta speertn**o**-yeh?

all (things) всё fsyo

  (people) все fsyeh

  all the children все дети fsyeh
  d**ye**tee

  all of it всё fsyo

  all of them все fsyeh

  all day весь день vyes dyen

  that's all, thanks это всё,
  спасибо **e**ta fsyo, spas**ee**ba

allergic: I'm allergic to... у
меня аллергия на... oo men**ya**

alyerg**ee**-ya na...

**allowed: is smoking allowed
here?** можно ли здесь
курить? m**o**Jnalee zdyes
koor**ee**t?

all right хорошо нarash**o**

  I'm all right со мной всё
  в порядке samn**oy** fsyo
  fpar**ya**tkyeh

  are you all right? с вами
  всё в порядке? sv**a**mee fsyo
  fpar**ya**tkyeh?

almond миндаль meend**a**l

almost почти pacht**ee**

alone (male/female) один/одна
ad**ee**n/adn**a**

already уже ooJ**e**h

also тоже t**o**Jeh

although хотя нat**ya**

altogether всего fsyev**o**

always всегда fsyegd**a**

am: at seven am в семь часов
утра fsyem chas**of** oot**ra**

amazing (*surprising*)
удивительный oodee**vee**tyelni

(*very good*) потрясающий
patrya**sa**-yoosh-chee

ambulance скорая помощь
sk**o**ra-ya p**o**mash-ch

call an ambulance!
вызовите скорую помощь!
v**iy**zaveetyeh sk**oo**roo-yoo p**o**mash-ch!

America Америка am**y**er**ee**ka

American (*adj*) американский
amyer**ee**k**a**nskee

I'm American (*male/female*) я
американец/американка ya
amyer**ee**k**a**nyets/amyer**ee**k**a**nka

among среди sryed**ee**

amount количество
kal**ee**echyestva

(*money*) сумма s**oo**m-ma

amp: 13-amp fuse
предохранитель на
тринадцать ампер
predaнran**ee**tyel na tr**ee**natsat
amp**y**er

and и ee

angry сердитый syerd**ee**ti

animal животное Ji**vo**tna-yeh

ankle лодыжка lad**iy**shka

anniversary (*wedding*) юбилей
yoobeel**yay**

**annoy: this man's annoying
me** этот человек мне
досаждает **e**tat chyelav**y**ek
mn**yeh** das**a**Jda-yet

annoying: it's annoying это
раздражает **e**ta razdra**J**a-yet

another другой droog**oy**

can we have another room?
можно другой номер? m**o**Jna
droog**oy** n**o**myer?

another beer, please
ещё одно пиво,
пожалуйста yesh-ch**o** adn**o**
p**ee**va, pa**J**alsta

antibiotics антибиотики
anteebee-**o**teekee

antifreeze антифриз anteefr**ee**s

antihistamine антигистамин
anteegeestam**ee**n

antique антиквариат
anteekvaree-**a**t

antique shop
антикварный магазин
anteekv**a**rni magaz**ee**n

antiseptic антисептическое средство anteesepteechyeska-yeh sryetstva

any: have you got any bread/ tomatoes? у вас есть хлеб/ помидоры? oo vas yest Hlyep/ pameedori?

do you have any …? у вас есть …? oo vas yest …?

sorry, I don't have any извините, у меня нет eezveeneetyeh, oo menya nyet

anybody кто-нибудь kto-neeboot

does anybody speak English? кто-нибудь говорит по-английски? kto-neeboot gavareet pa-angleeskee?

there wasn't anybody there там никого не было tam neekavo nyebila

anything что-нибудь shto-neeboot

DIALOGUE

anything else? что-нибудь ещё? shto-neeboot yesh-cho?

nothing else, thanks больше ничего, спасибо bolsheh neechyevo, spaseeba

would you like anything to drink? вы хотите что-нибудь выпить? viy Hateetyeh shto-neeboot viypeet?

I don't want anything, thanks спасибо, я ничего не хочу spaseeba, ya neechyevo nyeh Hachoo

apart from кроме kromyeh

apartment квартира kvarteera

apartment block многоквартирный дом mnogakvarteerni dom

aperitif аперитив apyereeteef

apology извинение eezveenyenee-yeh

appendicitis аппендицит apyendeetsiyt

appetizer закуска zakooska

apple яблоко yablaka

appointment приём preeyom

DIALOGUE

good morning, how can I help you? доброе утро, чем я могу вам помочь? dobra-yeh ootra, chyem ya magoo vam pamoch?

I'd like to make an appointment (said by man/ woman) я бы хотел/ хотела записаться на приём yabi Hatyel/Hatyela zapeesatsa na preeyom

what time would you like? какое время для вас удобно? kako-yeh vryemya dlya vas oodobna?

three o'clock в три часа ftree chasa

I'm afraid that's not possible, is four o'clock all right? боюсь, что в три часа не получится, в четыре вас устроит? bayoos, shto ftree chasa nyeh

yes, that will be fine да, это меня устроит da, eta myenya oostro-eet

the name was ...? ваше имя ...? vasheh eemya ...?

---

apricot абрикос abreekos

April апрель apryel

area район rI-on

area code междугородный код myeJdoogarodni kod

arm рука rooka

arrange: will you arrange it for us? вы организуете это для нас? viy arganeezoo-yetyeh eta dlya nas?

arrival прибытие preebyItee-yeh

arrive приезжать/приехать pree-yeJJat/pree-yeHat

when do we arrive? когда мы приезжаем? kagda miy pree-yeJ-Ja-yem?

has my fax arrived yet? ещё не пришёл факс для меня? yesh-cho nyeh preeshol faks dlya menya?

we arrived today мы приехали сегодня miy pree-yeHalee syevodnya

art искусство eeskoostva

art gallery картинная галерея karteen-na-ya galyeryeh-ya

artist художник HoodoJneek

as: as big as такой же большой как ... takoyJeh

balshoy kak ...

as soon as possible как можно быстрее kak moJna bistryeh-yeh

ashtray пепельница pyepyelneetsa

ask спрашивать/спросить sprashivat/spraseet

I didn't ask for this (said by man/woman) это не то, что я заказал/заказала eta nyeh to, shto ya zakazal/zakazala

could you ask him to ...? попросите его, пожалуйста ... papraseetyeh yevo, paJalsta ...

asleep: she's asleep она спит ana speet

aspirin аспирин aspeereen

asthma астма astma

astonishing поразительный parazeetyelni

at: at the hotel в гостинице vgasteeneetseh

at the station на станции na stantsi-ee

at six o'clock в шесть часов fshest chasof

at Sasha's у Саши oo sashi

athletics атлетика atlyeteeka

ATM банкомат bankamat

at sign собачка sabachka

attractive привлекательный preevlyekatyelni

aubergine баклажан baklaJan

August август avgoost

aunt тётя tyotya

Australia Австралия afstralee-ya

Australian (*adj*) австралийский afstral**ee**skee

I'm Australian (*male/female*) я австралиец/австралийка ya afstral**ee**-yets/afstral**ee**ka

Austria Австрия **a**fstree-ya

automatic (*adj*) автоматический aftamat**ee**chyeskee

(*noun:* car) с автоматической коробкой передач saftamat**ee**chyeski kar**o**pki pyeryed**a**ch

autumn осень **o**syen

in the autumn осенью **o**senyoo

avenue аллея al**yeh**-ya

average (not good) посредственный pasr**ye**tstvyen-ni

on average в среднем fsr**ye**dnyem

awake: is he awake? он проснулся? on prasn**oo**lsya?

away: go away! уходите! ooHad**ee**tyeh!

is it far away? это далеко? **e**ta dalyek**o**?

awful ужасный ooJ**a**sni

B

baby ребёнок ryeb**yo**nak

baby food детское питание d**ye**tska-yeh peet**a**nee-yeh

baby's bottle бутылочка для кормления ребёнка boot**iy**lachka dlya karml**ye**nee-ya ryeb**yo**nka

baby-sitter няня n**ya**nya

back (of body) спина sp**ee**na

(back part) задняя часть z**a**dnya-ya chast

at the back сзади z-z**a**dee

I'd like my money back (said by man/woman) я хотел/хотела бы получить обратно деньги ya Hat**yel**/Hat**ye**la biy palooch**ee**t abr**a**tna d**ye**ngee

to come back возвращаться/вернуться vazvrash-ch**a**tsa/vyern**oo**tsa

to go back (by transport) уезжать/уехать oo-yeJ-J**a**t/oo-**ye**Hat

(on foot) возвращатьсвернуться vazvrash-ch**a**tsa/vyern**oo**tsa

backache боль в спине bol fspeen**yeh**

bacon бекон byek**o**n

bad плохой plaH**oy**

not bad неплохо nyeplo**ha**

a bad headache сильная головная боль s**ee**lna-ya galavn**a**-ya bol

badly плохо plo**ha**

bag сумка s**oo**mka

(handbag) дамская сумка d**a**mska-ya s**oo**mka

(suitcase) чемодан chyemod**a**n

baggage багаж bag**a**sh

baggage checkroom камера хранения k**a**myera Hran**ye**nee-ya

baggage claim выдача багажа v**iy**dacha bag**a**Ja

bakery булочная b**oo**lachna-ya

balcony балкон balk**o**n

   a room with a balcony
   номер с балконом n**o**myer
   zbalk**o**nam

bald лысый l**iy**si

ball мяч myach

ballet балет bal**ye**t

ballpoint pen шариковая
   ручка shareekava-ya r**oo**chka

banana банан banan

band (orchestra) оркестр ark**ye**str

bandage бинт beent

Bandaid пластырь pl**a**stir

bank (money) банк bank

bank account банковский счёт
   b**a**nkofskee sh-chot

banknote банкнота bankn**o**ta

bar бар bar

   a bar of chocolate плитка
   шоколада pl**ee**tka shakal**a**da

barber's парикмахерская
   pareenma**ye**rska-ya

bargaining

how much is this? сколько
   это стоит? sk**o**lka **e**ta st**o**-
   eet?

100,000 roubles сто тысяч
   рублей sto t**iy**syach roobl**ya**y

that's too expensive это
   слишком дорого **e**ta
   sl**ee**shkam d**o**raga

how about 70,000? как
   насчёт семидесяти тысяч?
   kak nash-ch**o**t syem**ee**edyestee
   t**iy**syach?

I'll let you have it for
   90,000 отдам за
   девяносто тысяч ad-d**a**m
   za dyevyan**o**sta t**iy**syach

can you reduce it a bit
   more?/OK, it's a deal
   сбросьте ещё немного/
   ладно, идёт sbr**o**styeh yesh-
   cho nyemn**o**ga/l**a**dna, eed**yo**t

basket корзина karz**ee**na

bath ванна v**a**n-na

   can I have a bath? можно
   ли принять ванну? m**o**Jnalee
   preen**ya**t v**a**n-noo?

bathhouse баня b**a**nya

bathroom ванная v**a**n-na-ya

   with a private bathroom с
   ванной sv**a**n-ni

bath towel банное полотенце
   b**a**n-na-yeh palat**ye**ntseh

bathtub ванна v**a**n-na

battery (for radio) батарейка
   batar**ya**yka

   (for car) аккумулятор
   akoomool**ya**tar

bay бухта b**oo**нta

be быть biyt

beach пляж plyash

   on the beach на пляже na
   pl**ya**Jeh

beach mat пляжная подстилка
   pl**ya**Jna-ya patst**ee**lka

beach umbrella пляжный зонт
   pl**ya**Jni zont

beans фасоль (*sing*) fas**o**l

   French beans фасоль fas**o**l

broad beans бобы bab**iy**

beard борода barad**a**

beautiful красивый kras**ee**vi

because потому что patam**oo**shta

  because of из-за **ee**z-za

bed кровать krav**a**t

  I'm going to bed now я ложусь спать ya laj**oo**s spat

bed and breakfast проживание и завтрак praJiv**a**nee-yeh ee **za**ftrak

bedroom спальня sp**a**lnya

beef говядина gav**ya**deena

beer пиво p**ee**va

  two beers, please два пива, пожалуйста dva p**ee**va, paJ**a**lsta

before перед p**ye**ryet

begin начинаться/начаться nacheen**a**tsa/nach**a**tsa

  when does it begin? когда начало? kagd**a** nach**a**la?

beginner (*male/female*) начинающий/начинающая nacheen**a**-yoosh-chee/ nacheen**a**-yoosh-cha-ya

beginning: at the beginning в начале vnach**a**lyeh

behind за z**a**

  behind me за мной za mn**oy**

Belgium Бельгия b**ye**lgee-ya

believe верить/поверить v**ye**reet/pav**ye**reet

below под pod

belt ремень ryem**ye**n

bend (in road) поворот pavar**o**t

berth (on ship) койка k**oy**ka

beside: beside the ... рядом с ... r**ya**dam s ...

best лучший l**oo**chshi

better лучше l**oo**chsheh

  are you feeling better? вам лучше? vam l**oo**chsheh?

between между m**ye**Jdoo

beyond за za

bicycle велосипед vyelaseep**ye**t

big большой balsh**oy**

  too big слишком большой sl**ee**shkam balsh**oy**

  it's not big enough недостаточно большой nyedast**a**tachna balsh**oy**

bike велосипед vyelaseep**ye**t

  (*motorbike*) мотоцикл matats**iy**kl

bill счёт sh-chot

  (*US: banknote*) банкнота bankn**o**ta

  could I have the bill, please? счёт, пожалуйста sh-chot, paJ**a**lsta

bin мусорное ведро m**oo**sarna-yeh vyedr**o**

bird птица pt**ee**tsa

birthday день рождения dyen raJd**ye**nee-ya

  happy birthday! с днём рождения! sdnyom raJd**ye**nee-ya!

biscuit печенье pyech**ye**nyeh

bit: a little bit немножко nyeh-mn**o**shka

  a big bit большой кусок balsh**oy** koos**o**k

a bit of ... кусочек ...
koos**o**chyek...

a bit expensive дороговато
daraga**va**ta

bite (by insect) укус
(насекомого) ook**oo**s
(nasy**e**komava)

(by dog) укус (собаки) ook**oo**s
(sab**a**kee)

bitter (taste) горький
g**o**rkee

black чёрный ch**o**rni

black market чёрный рынок
ch**o**rni r**i**ynak

Black Sea Чёрное море ch**o**rna-
yeh m**o**ryeh

blanket одеяло adyeh-y**a**la

bleach (for toilet) хлорка Hl**o**rka

bless you! будьте здоровы!
b**oo**t-tyeh zdar**o**vi!

blind слепой slyep**oy**

blinds шторы sht**o**ri

blocked (road) перегороженный
pyeryegar**o**Jen-ni

(sink) засоренный zas**o**ryen-ni

blond (*adj*) белокурый byelak**oo**ri

blood кровь krof

high blood pressure
высокое давление vis**o**ka-yeh
davl**ye**nee-yeh

blouse блузка bl**oo**ska

blow-dry укладка феном
ookl**a**tka f**ye**nam

I'd like a cut and blow-dry
пожалуйста, постригите и
сделайте укладку феном
paJ**a**lsta, pastreeg**ee**tyeh ee
sd**ye**lityeh ookl**a**tkoo f**ye**nam

blue синий s**ee**nee

blue eyes голубые глаза
galoob**iy**-yeh gl**a**za

blusher румяна pl room**ya**na

boarding pass посадочный
талон pas**a**dachni tal**o**n

boat лодка l**o**tka

(for passengers) корабль
kar**a**bl

when is the next boat to...?
когда следующий рейс в...?
kagd**a** sl**ye**doo-sh-chee ryays v...?

body тело t**ye**la

**boil: do we have to boil the
water?** нужно ли кипятить
воду? n**oo**Jnalee keepyat**ee**t
v**o**doo?

boiled egg варёное яйцо
var**yo**na-yeh yits**o**

boiled water кипячёная вода
keepyach**o**na-ya vad**a**

boiler кипятильник
keepyat**ee**lneek

bone кость kost

bonnet (of car) капот kap**o**t

book (*noun*) книга kn**ee**ga

(*verb*) заказывать/заказать
zak**a**zivat/zakaz**a**t

can I book a seat? могу ли
я заказать билет mag**oo**lee ya
zakaz**a**t beel**ye**t?

DIALOGUE

**I'd like to book a table for
two** (said by man/woman) я
хотел/хотела бы заказать
столик на двоих ya Hat**ye**l/
Hat**ye**la biy zakaz**a**t st**o**leek na
dva-**ee**H

what time would you like it booked for? на какое время? na kako-yeh vryemya?

half past seven на половину восьмого na palaveenoo vasmova

that's fine хорошо Harasho

and your name? ваше имя? vasheh eemya?

bookshop, bookstore книжный магазин kneeJni magazeen

boot (footwear) ботинок bateenak (of car) багажник bagaJneek

border (of country) граница graneetsa

bored: I'm bored мне скучно mnyeh skooshna

boring скучный skooshni

born: I was born in Manchester (said by man/woman) я родился/родилась в Манчестере ya radeelsa/radeelas vmanchyesteryeh

I was born in 1960 (said by man/woman) я родился/родилась в тысяча девятьсот шестидесятом году ya radeelsa/radeelas ftiysyacha dyevyatsot shesteedyesyatam gadoo

borrow занимать/занять zaneemat/zanyat

may I borrow ...? вы не одолжите ...? viy nyeh adalJiyteh ...?

both оба oba

bother: sorry to bother you извините за беспокойство eezveeneetyeh za byespakoystva

bottle бутылка bootiylka

a bottle of vodka бутылка водки bootiylka votkee

bottle-opener открывалка atkrivalka

bottom (of person) зад zat

at the bottom of ... (street etc) в конце ... (улицы) fkantseh (ooleetsi)

(hill) у подножия ... oo padnoJi-ya...

bouncer вышибала vishibala

bowl тарелка taryelka

box коробка karopka

box office театральная касса tyeh atralna-ya kas-sa

boy мальчик malcheek

boyfriend друг drook

bra бюстгальтер byoostgalter

bracelet браслет braslyet

brake тормоз tormas

brandy коньяк kanyak

bread хлеб Hlyep

white bread белый хлеб byeli Hlyep

brown bread чёрный хлеб chorni Hlyep

rye bread ржаной хлеб rJanoy Hlyep

wholemeal bread хлеб из непросеянной муки Hlyep eez nyeprasyeh-yani mookee

break (verb) ломать/сломать lamat/slamat

I've broken the ... (said by man/woman) я сломал/ сломала ... ya slamal/slamala

I think I've broken my wrist (said by man/woman) кажется, я сломал/сломала запястье kaJetsa, ya slamal/slamala zapyastyeh

break down ломаться/ сломаться lamatsa/slamatsa

I've broken down у меня сломалась машина oo menya slamalas mashyna

breakdown поломка palomka

breakdown service экстренная техпомощь ekstryen-na-ya tyeHpomosh-ch

breakfast завтрак zaftrak

break-in: I've had a break-in мою комнату обокрали ma-yoo komnatoo abakralee

breast грудь grood

breathe дышать dishat

breeze ветерок vyetyerok

bribe взятка vzyatka

bridge (over river) мост mosst

brief краткий kratkee

briefcase портфель partfyel

bright (light etc) яркий yarkee

bright red ярко-красный yarka-krasni

brilliant (idea, person) блестящий blyestyash-chee

bring приносить/принести preenaseet/preenyestee

I'll bring it back later я верну это позже ya vyernoo eta poJ-Jeh

Britain Великобритания vyeleeka-breetanee-ya

British британский breetanskee

brochure брошюра brashoora

broken сломанный sloman-ni

bronchitis бронхит branheet

brooch брошь brosh

broom метла myetla

brother брат brat

brother-in-law (husband's brother) деверь dyevyer
(wife's brother) шурин shooreen

brown коричневый kareechnyevi

    brown hair каштановые волосы kashtanavi-yeh volasi

    brown eyes карие глаза karee-yeh glaza

bruise синяк seenyak

brush щётка sh-chotka
(artist's) кисть keest

bucket ведро vyedro

buffet (on train etc) буфет boofyet
(in restaurant) шведский стол shvetskee stol

buggy (for child) детская коляска dyetska-ya kalyaska

building здание zdanee-yeh

bulb (light bulb) лампочка lampachka

Bulgaria Болгария balgaree-ya

bumper бампер bampyer

bunk койка koyka

bureau de change обмен валюты abmyen valyooti

burglary ограбление agrablyenee-yeh

burn (noun) ожог aJok
(verb) гореть/сгореть garyet/sgaryet

    this is burnt это горелое eta garyela-yeh

burst: a burst pipe лопнувшая труба lopnoofsha-ya trooba

bus автобус aftoboos

    what number bus is it to …? какой автобус идёт до…? kakoy aftoboos eedyot da…?

    when is the next bus to …? когда следующий автобус до …? kagda slyedoosh-chee aftoboos da …?

    what time is the last bus? когда приходит последний автобус? kagda preeHodeet paslyednee aftoboos?

DIALOGUE

does this bus go to …? идёт ли этот автобус до …? eedyotlee etat aftoboos da …?

no, you need a number … нет, вам нужен номер … nyet, vam nooJen nomyer …

---

business бизнес beeznes

bus station автобусная станция aftoboosna-ya stantsi-ya

bus stop остановка автобуса astanofka aftoboosa

bust бюст byoost

busy (restaurant etc) оживлённый aJivlyon-ni

    I'm busy tomorrow (said by man/woman) я буду занят/занята завтра ya boodoo zanyat/zanyata zaftra

but но no

butcher's мясной магазин myasnoy magazeen

butter масло masla

button пуговица p**oo**gaveetsa

buy покупать/купить pakoopat/
koopeet

> **where can I buy ...?** где
> можно купить ...? gdyeh
> moJna koopeet ...?

by: by train/by car/by plane
на поезде/на машине/на
самолёте na p**o**-yezdyeh/na
mash**i**ynyeh/na samal**yo**tyeh

> **the book is written by ...**
> книга написана ... kn**ee**ga
> nap**ee**sana ...

> **by the window** около окна
> **o**kala akn**a**

> **by the sea** у моря oo m**o**rya

> **by Thursday** к четвергу
> kchyetvyerg**oo**

bye! пока! pak**a**

C

cabaret кабаре kabar**eh**

cabbage капуста kap**oo**sta

cabin (on ship) каюта ka-**yoo**ta

cable car фуникулёр
fooneekool**yor**

café кафе kaf**eh**

cagoule куртка от дождя
k**oo**rtka ad-daJd**ya**

cake торт tort

> **a piece of cake** кусок торта
> koos**o**k t**o**rta

cake shop кондитерская
kand**ee**tyerska-ya

call (verb) звать/позвать zvat/
pazv**a**t

(verb: to phone) звонить/
позвонить zvan**ee**t/
pazvan**ee**t

> **what's it called?** как это
> называется? kak **e**ta naziva-
> y**e**tsa?

> **he/she is called ...** его/её
> зовут ... yev**o**/ye-**yo** zav**oo**t ...

> **please call the doctor**
> вызовите, пожалуйста, врача
> v**i**yzaveetyeh, paJ**a**lsta, vrach**a**

> **please give me a call
> at 7.30 am tomorrow**
> позвоните мне, пожалуйста,
> завтра в семь тридцать утра
> pazvan**ee**tyeh mnyeh, paJ**a**lsta,
> z**a**ftra fsyem tr**ee**tsat ootr**a**

> **please ask him to call me**
> пожалуйста, попросите
> его мне позвонить paJ**a**lsta,
> papras**ee**tyeh yev**o** mnyeh
> pazvan**ee**t

call back: I'll call back later
я вернусь позже ya vyern**oo**s
p**o**J-Jeh

> (phone back) я перезвоню
> попозже ya pyeryezvan**yoo**
> pap**o**J-Jeh

**call round: I'll call round
tomorrow** я зайду завтра ya
zid**oo** z**a**ftra

camcorder видеокамера
veedyeh-ok**a**myera

camera фотоаппарат fota-apar**a**t

camera shop магазин кино- и
фотоаппаратуры magaz**ee**n
keena-ee-f**o**ta-aparat**oo**ri

camp (verb) жить в палатках Jiyt
fpal**a**tkah

can we camp here? можно ли здесь разбить лагерь? moJnalee zdyes razbeet lagyer?

camping gas газовый баллончик gazavi baloncheek

campsite кемпинг kyempeeng

can банка banka

a can of beer банка пива banka peeva

can: can you ...? вы можете ...? viy moJetyeh ...?

can you show me ...? вы можете показать мне ...? viy moJetyeh pakazat mnyeh ...?

can I have ...? можно мне, пожалуйста ... moJna mnyeh, paJalsta ...

I can't ... я не могу ... ya nyeh magoo ...

Canada Канада kanada

Canadian канадский kanatskee

I'm Canadian (male/female) я канадец/канадка ya kanadyets/ kanatka

canal канал kanal

cancel отменять/отменить atmyenyat/atmyeneet

candies конфеты kanfyeti

candle свеча svyecha

can-opener открывалка atkrivalka

cap (hat) шапка shapka

(of bottle) крышка kriyshka

car машина mashiyna

by car на машине na mashiynyeh

carafe графин grafeen

a carafe of white wine,

please графин белого вина, пожалуйста grafeen byelava veena, paJalsta

card (birthday etc) открытка atkriytka

here's my (business) card моя карточка, пожалуйста ma-ya kartachka, paJalsta

cardigan кофта kofta

cardphone телефон, принимающий карточки tyelyefon, preeneema-yoosh-chee kartachkee

cards карты karti

careful осторожный astaroJni

be careful! осторожно! astaroJna!

caretaker (male/female) сторож storash

car ferry автопаром aftaparom

car park стоянка sta-yanka

carpet ковёр kavyor

car rental прокат автомобилей prakat aftamabeelyay

carriage (of train) вагон vagon

carrier bag сумка soomka

carrot морковь markof

carry нести nyestee

carry-cot переносная кроватка pyeryenasna-ya kravatka

carton пакет pakyet

case (suitcase) чемодан chyemadan

cash наличные деньги naleechni-yeh dyengee

will you cash this for me? (travellers' cheque) обменяйте, пожалуйста, на наличные abmyen**yay**tyeh, pa**j**alsta, na na**lee**chni-yeh

cash desk касса kas-sa

cash dispenser банкомат bankama**t**

cassette кассета kas-s**ye**ta

cassette recorder кассетный магнитофон kas-s**ye**tni magneeta**fo**n

castle замок **za**mak

casualty department палата скорой помощи pa**l**ata sk**o**ri po**m**ash-chee

cat кошка k**o**shka

catch (*verb*: ball) ловить/ поймать la**vee**t/pi**ma**t

where do we catch the bus to…? откуда идёт автобус до …? at**koo**da eed**yot** af**to**boos da…?

cathedral собор sa**bo**r

Catholic (*adj*) католический kata**lee**chyeskee

cauliflower цветная капуста tsvyet**na**-ya kap**oo**sta

cave пещера pyesh-ch**ye**ra

caviar икра eek**ra**

Travel tip Caviar should be bought in a delicatessen or supermarket rather than a market, where the stuff on sale is almost certainly of illicit origin and may be unsafe to eat. You can take as much red caviar as you wish out of the country, but no more than 250 grams of black.

---

red caviar красная икра kr**a**sna-ya eek**ra**

black caviar чёрная икра ch**o**rna-ya eek**ra**

ceiling потолок pata**lo**k

celery сельдерей syeldyer**yay**

cemetery кладбище kl**a**dbeesh-chyeh

centigrade по Цельсию pa ts**e**lsee-yoo

centimetre сантиметр santeem**ye**tr

central центральный tsen**tra**lni

central heating центральное отопление tsen**tra**lna-yeh atapl**ye**nee-yeh

centre центр tsentr

how do we get to the city centre? как попасть в центр города? kak pap**a**st ftsentr g**o**rada?

cereal сухой завтрак soo**ho**y z**a**ftrak

certainly да, конечно da, kan**ye**shna

certainly not ни в коем случае nee fk**o**-yem sl**oo**cha-yeh

chair стул stool

champagne шампанское sham**pa**nska-yeh

change (*noun*: money) мелочь m**ye**lach

(*verb*: money) обменивать/ обменять abm**ye**neevat/ abmyen**ya**t

can I change this for…? можно обменять это на…?

моłна abmyenyat eta na…?

I don't have any change у
меня нет мелочи oo menya
nyet myelachee

**can you give me change for
a 10,000 rouble note?** вы не
могли бы разменять десять
тысяч? viy nyeh magleebi
razmyenyat dyesyat tiysyach?

**do we have to change
(trains)?** нужно ли
нам сделать пересадку?
noożnalee nam zdyelat
pyeryesatkoo?

**yes, change at St
Petersburg/no, it's a
direct train** да, сделайте
пересадку в Санкт-
Петербурге/нет, это
прямой поезд da, zdyelityeh
pyeryesatkoo fsankt-
peetyerboorgyeh/nyet, eta
pryamoy po-yest

changed: to get changed
переодеваться/переодеться
pyeryeh-adyevatsa/pyeryeh-
adyetsa

charge (*noun*) цена tsena
(*verb*) назначать/назначить
цену naznachat/naznacheet
tsenoo

cheap дешёвый dyeshovi
**do you have anything
cheaper?** у вас нет ничего
подешевле? oo vas nyet
neechyevo padyeshevlyeh?

check (US: bill) счёт sh-chyot

(US: cheque) чек chyek
check (*verb*) проверять/
проверить pravyeryat/
pravyereet

**could you check the…,
please?** проверьте…,
пожалуйста pravyertyeh…,
paжalsta

check in регистрироваться/
зарегистрироваться
ryegeestreeravatsa/
zaryegeestreeravatsa

**where do we have to
check in?** где проходит
регистрация? gdyeh praнodeet
ryegeestratsi-ya?

check-in регистрация
ryegeestratsi-ya

cheek щека sh-chyeka

cheerio! пока! paka!

cheers! (toast) ваше здоровье!
vasheh zdarovyeh!

cheese сыр siyr

chemist's аптека aptyeka

cheque чек chyek

do you take cheques?
вы принимаете чеки? viy
preeneema-yetyeh chyekee?

cheque book чековая книжка
chyekava-ya kneeshka

cheque card чековая карточка
chyekava-ya kartachka

cherry вишня veeshnya

chess шахматы shaнmati

chest грудь grood

chewing gum жвачка жvachka

chicken цыплёнок tsiplyonak

chickenpox ветрянка vyetryanka

hot chocolate горячий шоколад gar**ya**chee shakal**at**

choose выбирать/выбрать vibeer**at**/v**iy**brat

Christian name имя **ee**mya

Christmas Рождество ra**J**dyestv**o**

  Christmas Eve канун рождества kan**oon** ra**J**dyestv**a**

  merry Christmas! счастливого Рождества! sh-chasl**ee**vava ra**J**dyestv**a**!

church церковь ts**e**rkaf

cider сидр **s**eedr

cigar сигара seeg**a**ra

cigarette сигарета seegar**ye**ta

  (Russian non-filter) папироса papeer**o**sa

cigarette lighter зажигалка za**J**ig**a**lka

cinema кино keen**o**

circle круг krook

  (in theatre) ярус **ya**roos

CIS СНГ es-en-geh

city город g**o**rat

city centre центр города tsentr g**o**rada

clean (*adj*) чистый ch**ee**sti

  can you clean these for me? вы можете почистить это viy m**o**Jetyeh pach**ee**steet **e**ta?

cleaning solution (for contact lenses) раствор для линз rastv**o**r dlya leenz

cleansing lotion очищающий лосьон ach**ee**sh-cha-y**oo**sh-chee las**yo**n

clear (obvious) ясный **ya**sni

---

child ребёнок ryeb**yo**nak

  children дети d**ye**tee

child minder няня n**ya**nya

children's pool бассейн для детей bas**ay**n dlya dyet**yay**

children's portion детская порция d**ye**tska-ya p**o**rtsi-ya

chin подбородок padbar**o**dak

China Китай Keet**I**

Chinese (*adj*) китайский keet**I**skee

chips картофель фри kart**o**fyel free

  (US: crisps) чипсы ch**ee**psi

chocolate шоколад shakal**at**

  milk chocolate молочный шоколад mal**o**chni shakal**at**

  plain chocolate шоколад shakal**at**

ИП Полторжков ИНН 781406092313 (812)3164676

21.02.2014 12.54

Товарный чек № 92337

1. (2201189000296) Яйца
   Деревянные вл. кр 23 х 1.00 х
   1036.00   1036.00

2. (5780042000273) 6местные
   матрешки 6м НХП КС 63/88 27
   х 1.00 х 1215.00   1215.00

ВСЕГО РУБ   2250.00

                                                     0.00

ИТОГО РУБ   2250.00

                                          Кредит   2250.00

(21.02.2014 11.13)

Отдел: 1 Кассир: Администра

clever умный **oo**mni

cliff скала sk**a**la

climbing альпинизм alpeen**ee**zm

clinic клиника kl**ee**neeka

cloakroom (for coats) гардероб gardyer**o**p

clock часы chas**iy**

close (*verb*) закрывать/закрыть zakriv**a**t/zakr**iy**t

DIALOGUE

what time do you close? когда вы закрываетесь? kagd**a** viy zakriv**a**-yetyes?

we close at 8pm on weekdays and 6pm on Saturdays мы закрываемся в восемь в будние дни и в шесть по субботам miy zakriv**a**-yemsya vv**o**syem vb**oo**dnee-yeh dnee ee fshest pa soob**o**tam

do you close for lunch? у вас есть обеденный перерыв? oo vas yest abyedyen-ni pyeryer**iy**f?

yes, between 1 and 2pm да, с часу до двух da, schas**oo** da dv**oo**H

closed закрыто zakr**iy**ta

cloth (fabric) ткань tkan
(for cleaning etc) тряпка tr**ya**pka

clothes одежда ad**ye**Jda

cloud облако **o**blaka

cloudy облачный **o**blachni

clutch сцепление stsepl**ye**nee-yeh

coach междугородный автобус myeJdoo-gar**o**dni aft**o**boos
(on train) вагон vag**o**n

coach trip автобусная экскурсия aft**o**boosna-ya eksk**oo**rsee-ya

coast берег b**ye**ryek

on the coast на побережье na pabyer**ye**Jeh

coat пальто palt**o**
(jacket) куртка k**oo**rtka

coathanger вешалка v**ye**shalka

cockroach таракан tarak**a**n

cocoa какао kaka-**o**

code (for phoning) код kod

what's the (dialling) code for Moscow? какой код для Москвы? kak**oy** kod dlya maskv**iy**?

coffee кофе k**o**fyeh

two coffees, please две чашки кофе, пожалуйста dvyeh ch**a**shkee k**o**fyeh, paJ**a**lsta

coin монета man**ye**ta

Coke Кока-кола k**o**ka-k**o**la

cold холодный Hal**o**dni
(*noun*) простуда prast**oo**da

I'm cold мне холодно mnyeh H**o**ladna

I have a cold у меня простуда oo men**ya** prast**oo**da

collapse: he's collapsed он потерял сознание on patyer**ya**l saznanee-yeh

collar воротник varatn**ee**k

collect: I've come to collect... (said by man/woman) я пришёл/ пришла за... ya preesh**o**l/

preeshla za...

collect call звонок с оплатой вызываемым абонентом zvanok saplati visiva-yemim abanyentam

college колледж kaledJ

colour цвет tsvyet

do you have this in other colours? у вас есть это другого цвета? oo vas yest eta droogova tsvyeta?

colour film цветная плёнка tsvyetna-ya plyonka

comb расчёска rash-choska

come приходить/прийти preeHadeet/preetee

come back возвращаться/ вернуться vazvrash-chatsa/ vyernootsa

I'll come back tomorrow я вернусь завтра ya vyernoos zaftra

come in входить/войти fHadeet/ vitee

comfortable удобный oodobni

communism коммунизм kamooneezm

communist (adj) коммунистический kamooneesteechyeskee

Communist party

коммунистическая партия kamooneesteechyeska-ya partee-ya

compact disc компакт-диск kampakt-deesk

company (business) компания kampanee-ya

compartment (on train) купе koopeh

complain жаловаться/ пожаловаться Jalavatsa/ paJalavatsa

complaint жалоба Jalaba

I have a complaint у меня есть жалоба oo myenya yest Jalaba

completely совершенно savyershen-na

computer компьютер kampyooter

concert концерт kantsert

concierge (in hotel) дежурная dyeJoorna-ya

conditioner (for hair) ополаскиватель apalaskeevatyel

condom презерватив pryezyervateef

conference конференция kanfyeryentsi-ya

confirm подтверждать/ подтвердить patvyerJdat/ patverdeet

congratulations! поздравляю! pazdravlya-yoo!

connecting flight стыковочный рейс stikovachni ryays

connection (transport) пересадка pyeryesatka

conscious в сознании fsaznanee-ee

constipation запор zapor

consulate консульство konsoolstva

contact (verb) связаться с svyazatsa s

contact lenses контактные линзы kantaktni-yeh leenzi

contraceptive противозачаточное средство proteevazachatachna-yeh sryetstva

convenient удобный oodobni

that's not convenient это не удобно eta nyeh oodobna

cook (verb) готовить/ приготовить gatoveet/ preegatoveet

the meat is not cooked мясо не прожарено myasa nyeh praJaryena

cooker плита pleeta

cookie печенье pyechyenyeh

cooking utensils кухонная посуда kooHan-na-ya pasooda

cool прохладный praHladni

cork пробка propka

corkscrew штопор shtopar

corner: on the corner на углу na oogloo

in the corner в углу voogloo

cornflakes кукурузные хлопья kookooroozni-yeh Hlopya

correct (right) правильный praveelni

corridor коридор kareedor

cosmetics косметика kasmyeteeka

cost (noun) стоимость sto-eemast

how much does it cost? сколько это стоит? skolka eta sto-eet?

cot детская кроватка dyetska-ya kravatka

cottage (in the country) дача dacha

cotton хлопок Hlopak

cotton wool вата vata

couch (sofa) диван deevan

couchette спальное место spalna-yeh myesta

cough (noun) кашель kashel

cough medicine средство от кашля sryedstva at kashlya

could: could you...? вы не могли бы ..? viy nyeh magleebi...?

could I have...? можно мне...? moJna mnyeh...?

country страна strana

(countryside) деревня dyeryevnya

in the country за городом zagaradam

countryside деревня dyeryevnya

couple (two people) пара para

a couple of hours пару часов paroo chasof

courgette кабачок kabachok

courier курьер kooryer

course (main course etc) блюдо blyooda

of course конечно kanyeshna

of course not конечно, нет kanyeshna, nyet

cousin (male/female) кузен/кузина koozen/koozeena

cow корова karova

cracker крекер krekyer

craft shop художественный салон Hoodojestvyen-ni salon

crash (*noun*) авария avaree-ya

I've had a crash (said by man/woman) я попал/попала в аварию ya papal/papala vavaree-yoo

crazy сумасшедший soomashetshi

cream (in coffee etc) сливки pl sleefkee

(in cake, lotion) крем kryem

(colour) кремовый kryemavi

soured cream сметана smyetana

creche ясли pl yaslee

credit card кредитная карточка kryedeetna-ya kartachka

do you take credit cards? вы принимаете кредитные карточки? viy preeneema-yetyeh kryedeetni-yeh kartachkee?

can I pay by credit card? могу ли я заплатить кредитной карточкой? magoolee ya zaplateet kryedeetni kartachki?

which card do you want to use? какой карточкой вы хотите заплатить? kakoy kartachki viy Hateetyeh zaplateet?

Mastercard/Visa

yes, sir да, пожалуйста da, paJalsta

what's the number? какой номер? kakoy nomyer?

and the expiry date? когда истекает срок действия? kagda eesteyka-yet srok dyeystvee-ya?

credit crunch кредитный кризис kryedeetni kreezees

Crimea Крым kriym

crisps хрустящий картофель Hroostyash-chee kartofyel

crockery посуда pasooda

crossing (by sea, across river) переправа pyeryeprava

crossroads перекрёсток pyeryekryostak

crowd толпа talpa

crowded переполненный pyeryepolnyen-ni

crown (on tooth) коронка karonka

cruise круиз kroo-ees

crutches костыли kastilee

cry (*verb*) плакать/заплакать plakat/zaplakat

cucumber огурец agooryets

pickled cucumber солёный огурец salyoni agooryets

cup чашка chashka

a cup of tea, please чашку чая, пожалуйста chashkoo cha-ya, paJalsta

cupboard шкаф shkaf

cure (*verb*) лечить/вылечить lyech**ee**t/v**i**ylyech**ee**t

curly кудрявый kood**rya**vi

current (electrical) ток tok

curtains занавески zanav**ye**skee

cushion подушка pad**oo**shka

custom обычай ab**i**ychee

Customs таможня tam**o**Jnya

Customs form таможенная декларация tam**o**Jen-na-ya dyeklar**a**tsi-ya

cut (*noun*) порез par**ye**s
(*verb*) резать/разрезать r**ye**zat/ razr**ye**zat

I've cut myself (said by man/woman) я порезался/ порезалась ya par**ye**zalsa/ par**ye**zalas

cutlery столовые приборы st**a**lovi-yeh preeb**o**rı

cycling велоспорт vyelasp**o**rt

cyclist (*male/female*) велосипедист/велосипедистка vyelaseepyed**ee**st/ vyelaseepyed**ee**stka

Czech Republic Чешская республика ch**ye**shska-ya ryesp**oo**bleeka

D

dad папа p**a**pa

daily ежедневно yeJedn**ye**vna
(*adj*) ежедневный yeJedn**ye**vni

damage (*verb*) повреждать/

повредить pavryeJd**a**t/ pavryed**ee**t

it's damaged это повреждено **e**ta pavryeJd**ye**no

I'm sorry, I've damaged this (said by man/woman) извините, я повредил/повредила это eezveen**ee**tyeh, ya pavryed**ee**l/ pavryed**ee**la **e**ta

damn! чёрт! chort!

damp сырой sir**o**y

dance (*noun*) танец t**a**nyets
(*verb*) танцевать tantsev**a**t

would you like to dance? можно пригласить вас на танец? m**o**Jna preeglas**ee**t vas na t**a**nyets?

dangerous опасный ap**a**sni

Danish (*adj*) датский d**a**tskee

dark (*adj*: colour) тёмный t**yo**mni

dark green тёмно-зелёный t**yo**mna-zyel**yo**ni

it's getting dark темнеет tyemn**ye**-yet

date: what's the date today? какое сегодня число? kak**o**-yeh syev**o**dnya cheesl**o**?

let's make a date for next Monday договоримся на следующий понедельник dagavar**ee**msya na sl**ye**doosh-chee panyed**ye**lneek

dates (fruit) финики f**ee**neekee

daughter дочь doch

daughter-in-law невестка nyev**ye**stka

dawn рассвет ras-sv**ye**t

at dawn на рассвете na ras-sv**ye**tyeh

day день dyen

the day before накануне nakan**oo**nyeh

the day after tomorrow послезавтра p**o**slyeh-z**a**ftra

the day before yesterday позавчера pazafch**ye**ra

next day на следующий день na sl**ye**doosh-chee dyen

every day каждый день k**a**Jdi dyen

all day весь день vyes dyen

in two days' time через два дня ch**ye**ryes dva dnya

have a nice day всего хорошего! fsyev**o** Har**o**sheva!

day trip однодневная экскурсия adnadn**ye**vna-ya eksk**oo**rsee-ya

dead мёртвый m**yo**rtvi

deaf глухой gloo**Ho**y

deal (business) сделка zd**ye**lka

it's a deal (said by man/woman) согласен/согласна sagl**a**syen/ sagl**a**sna

death смерть smyert

decaffeinated coffee кофе без кофеина k**o**fyeh byes kafyeh-**ee**na

December декабрь dyek**a**br

decide решать/решить ryesh**a**t/ ryesh**iy**t

we haven't decided yet мы ещё не решили miy yesh-ch**o** nyeh ryesh**iy**lee

decision решение ryesh**e**nee-yeh

deck (on ship) палуба p**a**looba

deckchair шезлонг shezl**o**ng

deep глубокий gloob**o**kee

definitely: we'll definitely come мы обязательно придём miy abyaz**a**tyelna preed**yo**m

it's definitely not possible это совершенно невозможно **e**ta savyersh**e**n-na nyevazm**o**Jna

degree (qualification) диплом deepl**o**m

delay (*noun*) задержка zad**ye**rshka

delay: the flight was delayed рейс задержался ryays zadyerJ**a**lsa

deliberately умышленно oom**iy**shlen-na

delicatessen кулинария kooleenar**ee**-ya

delicious вкусный fk**oo**sni

deliver доставлять/ доставить dastavl**ya**t/ dast**a**veet

delivery (of mail) доставка dast**a**fka

democratic демократический dyemakrat**ee**chyeskee

Denmark Дания d**a**nee-ya

dental floss нитка для чистки зубов n**ee**tka dlya ch**ee**stkee zoob**o**f

dentist зубной врач zoobn**o**y vrach

---

it's this one here вот этот vot **e**tat

this one? этот? **e**tat?

no that one нет, вот этот nyet, vot **e**tat

here здесь zdyes

yes да da

dentures зубной протез zoobn**oy** prat**e**s

deodorant дезодорант dyezadar**a**nt

department отдел ad-d**ye**l

department store универмаг ooneevy**e**rmak

departure (train) отправление atpravly**e**nee-yeh

(plane) вылет v**i**ylyet

departure lounge зал ожидания zal a**J**ed**a**nee-ya

depend: it depends как сказать kak skaz**a**t

it depends on… это зависит от… **e**ta zav**ee**seet at…

deposit (as security) задаток zad**a**tak

(as part payment) взнос vznos

dessert десерт dyes**ye**rt

destination: what's your destination? куда вы едете? ko**o**da viy y**e**deetyeh?

develop проявлять/проявить pra-yavly**a**t/pra-yav**ee**t

diabetic (*noun*) диабетик dee-ab**ye**teek

dial (*verb*) набирать/набрать номер nabeer**a**t/nabr**a**t n**o**myer

dialling code код kod

diamond бриллиант breelee-**a**nt

diaper пелёнка pyely**o**nka

diarrhoea понос pan**o**s

do you have something for

diarrhoea? у вас есть что-нибудь от поноса? oo vas yest shto-neeboot at pan**o**sa?

diary (for personal experiences) дневник dnyevn**ee**k

(business) записная книжка zapeesn**a**-ya kn**ee**shka

dictionary словарь slav**a**r

didn't

see **not**

die умирать/умереть oomeer**a**t/ oomyery**e**t

diesel дизельное топливо d**ee**zyelna-yeh t**o**pleeva

diet диета dee-y**e**ta

I'm on a diet я на диете ya na dee-y**e**tyeh

I have to follow a special diet (said by man/woman) я должен/должна соблюдать особую диету ya d**o**lJen/ dalJn**a** sablyood**a**t as**o**boo-yoo dee-y**e**too

difference разница r**a**zneetsa

what's the difference? в чём разница? fchom r**a**zneetsa?

different разный r**a**zni

they are different они разные an**ee** r**a**zni-yeh

a different table другой столик droog**oy** st**o**leek

difficult трудный tr**oo**dni

difficulty трудность tr**oo**dnast

dining room столовая stal**o**va-ya

dinner (evening meal) ужин **oo**Jin

to have dinner ужинать/поужинать **oo**Jinat/pa**oo**Jinat

direct (*adj*) прямой pryam**oy**

is there a direct train? есть
ли прямой поезд? **yest**lee
pryam**oy** po-**yest**?

direction направление
napravl**ye**nee-yeh

which direction is it? в
каком это направлении?
fkak**om** eta napravl**ye**nee-ee?

is it in this direction? это в
этом направлении? eta v**e**tam
napravl**ye**nee-ee?

directory enquiries
справочная spr**a**vachna-ya

dirt грязь gryas

dirty грязный gr**ya**zni

disabled инвалид eenval**ee**t

**is there access for the
disabled?** есть ли доступ для
инвалидов? **yest**lee d**o**stoop dlya
eenval**ee**daf?

disappear исчезать/исчезнуть
eeschyez**at**/eeschy**e**znoot

my watch has disappeared
мои часы пропали ma-**ee** cha-
s**iy** prap**a**lee

**disappointed: I am
disappointed** (said by man/
woman) я разочарован/
разочарована ya razachar**o**van/
razachar**o**vana

disappointing неважный
nyev**a**jni

disaster катастрофа
katastr**o**fa

disco дискотека deeskat**ye**ka

discount скидка sk**ee**tka

is there a discount? нет ли
скидки? n**ye**tlee sk**ee**tkee?

disease болезнь bal**ye**zn

disgusting отвратительный
atvrat**ee**tyelni

dish блюдо bl**yoo**da

dishcloth кухонное полотенце
k**oo**Han-na-yeh palat**ye**ntseh

disinfectant
дезинфицирующее средство
dyezeen-feets**iy**roo-yoosh-chyeh-
yeh sr**ye**tstva

disk (for computer) диск deesk

disposable diapers/nappies
одноразовые пелёнки
adnar**a**zavi-yeh pyel**yo**nkee

distance расстояние rasta-
yanee-yeh

in the distance на
расстоянии na rasta-**ya**nee-ee

district район ri-**on**

disturb беспокоить byespak**o**-eet

diversion (detour) объезд ab**yest**

divorced: I'm divorced (said
by man/woman) я разведён/
разведена ya razvyed**yon**/
razvyedyen**a**

dizzy: I feel dizzy у меня
кружится голова oo myen**ya**
kr**oo**Jitsa galav**a**

do делать/сделать d**ye**lat/sd**ye**lat

what shall we do? что нам
делать? shto nam d**ye**lat?

how do you do it? как это
делается? kak eta d**ye**la-yetsa?

will you do it for me?
пожалуйста, сделайте это для
меня paJ**a**lsta, zd**ye**lityeh eta dlya
men**ya**

how do you do? здравствуйте! zdra**stvooy**tyeh!

nice to meet you приятно познакомиться pree-**ya**tna pazna**ko**meetsa

what do you do? (work) кем вы работаете? kyem viy ra**bo**ta-yetyeh?

I'm a teacher, and you? (said by man/woman) я учитель/учительница, а вы? ya ooch**ee**tyel/ ooch**ee**tyelneetsa, a**viy**?

I'm a student (said by man/woman) я студент/ студентка ya stood**yent**/ stood**yent**ka

what are you doing this evening? что вы делаете сегодня вечером? shto viy d**ye**la-yetyeh syev**o**dnya v**ye**chyeram?

we're going out for a drink, do you want to join us? мы идём куда-нибудь выпить, не хотите пойти с нами? miy eed**yom** koo**da**-neeboot v**iy**peet, nyeh Ha**tee**tyeh p**ee**tee sn**a**mee?

do you want cream? вы хотите сливки? viy Ha**tee**tyeh sl**ee**fkee?

I do, but she doesn't я да, а она нет ya da, a a**na** nyet

doctor врач vrach
(title) доктор d**o**ktar

we need a doctor нам нужен врач nam n**oo**Jen vrach

please call a doctor вызовите, пожалуйста, врача v**iy**zaveetee, pa**J**alsta, vrach**a**

where does it hurt? где у вас болит? gdyeh oo vas bal**eet**?

right here здесь zdyes

does that hurt now? а теперь больно? atyep**yer** b**o**lna?

yes да da

take this to the chemist получите это в аптеке paloocheetyeh **e**ta vapt**ye**kyeh

document документ dak**oom**yent

dog собака sab**a**ka

doll кукла k**oo**kla

domestic flight внутренний рейс vn**oo**tryen-nee ryays

don't! (to adult/child) перестаньте/ перестань! pyeryest**a**ntyeh/ pyeryest**a**n!

don't do that! (to adult/child) не делайте/делай этого! nyeh d**ye**lityeh/d**ye**li **e**tava!

door дверь dvyer

doorman швейцар shv**ye**ytsar

double двойной dvin**oy**

double bed двуспальная кровать dv**oo**spalna-ya krav**a**t

double room двухместный номер dv**oo**Hm**ye**sni n**o**myer

doughnut пончик p**o**ncheek

down вниз vnees

put it down over there
положите там palaJiytyeh tam

it's down there on the right
это там, справа eta tam, sprava

it's further down the road
это дальше по дороге eta
dalsheh pa darogyeh

download (*verb*) загружать/
загрузить zagrooJat/zagroozeet

downmarket (restaurant etc)
дешёвый dyeshovi

downstairs внизу vneezoo

dozen дюжина dyooJina

half a dozen полдюжины
poldyooJini

draught beer бочковое пиво
bachkova-yeh peeva

draughty: it's draughty дует
doo-yet

drawer ящик yash-cheek

drawing рисунок reesoonak

dreadful ужасный ooJasni

dream сон son

(aspiration) мечта myechta

dress (*noun*) платье platyeh

dressed: to get dressed
одеваться/одеться adyevatsa/
adyetsa

dressing (for cut) перевязка
pyeryevyaska

(for salad) приправа preeprava

dressing gown халат Halat

drink (*noun*) напиток napeetak
(verb) пить/выпить peet/viypeet

a cold drink
прохладительный напиток
praHladeetyelni napeetak

can I get you a drink?
не хотите ли что-нибудь
выпить? nyeh Hateetyehlee shto-
neeboot viypeet?

**what would you like (to
drink)?** что бы вы хотели
(выпить)? shtobi viy Hatyelee
(viypeet)?

no thanks, I don't drink
спасибо, я не пью spaseeba, ya
nyeh pyoo

**I'll just have a drink
of water** стакан воды,
пожалуйста stakan vadiy,
paJalsta

drinking water питьевая вода
peetyeva-ya vada

is this drinking water? это
питьевая вода? eta peetyeva-ya
vada?

drive водить машину vadeet
mashiynoo

we drove here мы приехали
сюда на машине miy pree-
yeHalee syooda na mashiynyeh

I'll drive you home я отвезу
вас домой ya atvyezoo vas
damoy

driver водитель vadeetyel

driving licence водительские
права vadeetyelskee-yeh prava

drop: just a drop, please (of
drink) чуть-чуть, пожалуйста
choot-choot, paJalsta

drug (medical) лекарство
lyekarstva

drugs (narcotics) наркотики
narkoteekee

drunk (*adj*) пьяный pyani

dry (adj) сухой sooHoy

dry-cleaner's химчистка Heemcheestka

duck утка ootka

due: he was due to arrive yesterday он должен был приехать вчера on dolJen biyl pree-yeHat fchyera

when is the train due? когда приходит поезд? kagda preeHodeet po-yest?

dull (pain) тупой toopoy

(weather) пасмурный pasmoorni

dummy (baby's) пустышка poostiyshka

during в течение ftyechyenee-yeh

dust пыль piyl

dustbin мусорный ящик moosarni yash-cheek

dusty пыльный piylni

duty-free беспошлинный byesposhleen-ni

duty-free shop магазин беспошлинной торговли magazeen byesposhleen-ni targovlee

duvet одеяло adye-yala

DVD DVD deeveedee

E

each (every) каждый kaJdi

how much are they each? сколько стоит каждый? skolka sto-eet kaJdi?

ear ухо ooHa

earache: I have earache у меня болит ухо oo menya baleet ooHa

early рано rana

early in the morning рано утром rana ootram

I called by earlier (said by man/woman) я заходил/ заходила раньше ya zaHadeel/zaHadeela ransheh

earrings серьги syergee

east восток vastok

in the east на востоке na vastokyeh

Easter Пасха pasHa

eastern восточный vastochni

Eastern Europe Восточная Европа vastochna-ya yevropa

easy лёгкий lyoHkee

eat есть/поесть yest/pa-yest

we've already eaten, thanks мы уже поели, спасибо miy ooJeh pa-yelee, spaseeba

eau de toilette туалетная вода too-alyetna-ya vada

economy class экономический класс ekanameechyeskee klass

Edinburgh Эдинбург edeenboork

egg яйцо yitso

eggplant баклажан baklaJan

either: either... or... или... или... eelee... eelee...

either of them любой из них lyooboy eez neeH

elastic (*noun*) резинка
ryezee**nka**

elastic band резинка
ryezee**nka**

elbow локоть lokat

electric электрический
elyektree**chyeskee**

electrical appliances
электрические приборы
elyektree**chyeskee**-yeh pree**bori**

electric fire электрокамин
elyektraka**meen**

electrician электрик
el**yektreek**

electricity электричество
elyektree**chyestva**

elevator лифт leeft

else: something else что-
то другое shto-ta droogo-yeh

somewhere else где-
нибудь в другом месте
gd**yeh**-neeboot vdroog**om**
m**ye**styeh

DIALOGUE

**would you like anything
else?** вы хотите ещё что-
нибудь? viy Ha**tee**tyeh yesh-
ch**o** shto-neeboot?

no, nothing else, thanks
нет, спасибо, больше
ничего nyet, spas**ee**ba,
b**ol**sheh neechy**evo**

e-mail (*noun*) электронная
почта elyektr**on**-na-ya p**o**chta

(*verb*: person) писать/написать
по электронной почте pee**sat**/
na**pee**sat pa elyektr**on**-ni p**o**chtyeh

(*file*) отправлять/отправить
по электронной почте
atprav**lyat**/at**pra**veet

embassy посольство pas**ol**stva

emergency критическая
ситуация kree**tee**chyeska-ya
seetoo-**a**tsi-ya

this is an emergency!
требуется неотложная
помощь! tr**ye**boo-yetsa nyeh-
atl**o**Jna-ya p**o**mash-ch!

emergency exit запасной
выход zapasn**oy** v**iy**Hat

empty пустой poost**oy**

end (*noun*) конец kan**ye**ts

at the end of the street в
конце улицы fkants**eh oo**leetsi

when does it end? когда
это заканчивается? kagd**a e**ta
zak**an**cheeva-yetsa?

engaged (toilet/telephone) занято
z**a**nyata

(to be married: *male/female*)
помолвлен/помолвлена
pam**ol**vlyen/pam**ol**vlyena

engine (car) двигатель dv**ee**gatyel

England Англия **a**nglee-ya

English (*adj*) английский
angl**ee**skee

(language) английский язык
angl**ee**skee yaz**iy**k

I'm English (*male/female*) я
англичанин/англичанка ya
anglee**cha**neen/anglee**chan**ka

do you speak English? вы
говорите по-английски? vi
gava**reet**-yeh pa-angl**ee**skee?

enjoy: to enjoy oneself
хорошо проводить/

провести время Harasho
pravadeet/pravyestee vryemya

how did you like the film?
вам понравился фильм?
vam panraveelsya feelm?

**I enjoyed it very much,
did you enjoy it?** мне
очень понравился, а вам?
mnyeh **o**chyen panraveelsa,
a vam?

enjoyable приятный pree-**ya**tni

enlargement (of photo)
увеличение
oovyeleechy**e**nee-yeh

enormous огромный agr**o**mni

enough достаточно dast**a**tachna

that's enough достаточно
dast**a**tachna

that's not enough этого
недостаточно **e**tava
nyedast**a**tachna

it's not big enough это не
достаточно большое **e**ta nyeh
dast**a**tachna balsh**o**-yeh

entrance вход fHot

(to house) подъезд pady**e**st

envelope конверт kanv**y**ert

epileptic эпилептик
epeel**ye**pteek

equipment оборудование
abar**oo**davanee-yeh

(for climbing etc) снаряжение
snarya**J**enee-yeh

(for photography)
фотоаппаратура f**o**ta-ap-
parat**oo**ra

error ошибка ash**i**ypka

escalator эскалатор eskal**a**tar

especially особенно
as**o**byen-na

essential основной asnavn**oy**

it is essential that...
необходимо, чтобы... nyeh-
apHad**ee**ma, shtob**i**...

ethnic (restaurant, dress etc)
национальный natsi-an**a**lni

EU Европейский Союз
yevrap**yay**skee sa-**yoo**s

Europe Европа yevr**o**pa

European (adj) европейский
yevrap**yay**skee

even даже d**a**Jeh

even if... даже если d**a**Jeh
yeslee

evening вечер v**ye**chyer

this evening сегодня
вечером syev**o**dnya v**ye**chyeram

in the evening вечером
v**ye**chyeram

evening meal ужин **oo**Jin

eventually в конце концов
fkants**eh** kants**of**

ever когда-нибудь kagda-neeb**oo**t

**have you ever been
to Novgorod?** вы
когда-нибудь были в
Новгороде? viy kagda-
neeb**oo**t b**i**ylee vn**o**vgarad**y**eh?

**yes, I was there two years
ago** (said by man/woman) да,
я там был/была два года
назад da, ya tam biyl/bil**a** dva
g**o**da naz**a**t

every каждый ka**J**di

every day каждый день ka**J**di dyen

everyone все fsyeh

everything всё fsyo

everywhere везде vyezd**yeh**

exactly! совершенно верно savyer**sh**en-na **vyer**na

exam экзамен ek**za**myen

example пример pree**myer**

for example например napree**myer**

excellent отличный at**lee**chni

excellent! отлично! at**lee**chna!

except кроме **kro**myeh

excess baggage излишек багажа eez**lee**shek baga**J**a

exchange rate обменный курс ab**myen**-ni koors

exciting увлекательный oovlyeka**tyel**ni

excuse me (to get past, to say sorry) извините! eezveen**ee**tyeh!

(to get attention) простите! prast**ee**tyeh!

(addressing someone with question) извините, пожалуйста… eezveen**ee**tyeh, pa**J**alsta…

exhausted: I'm exhausted (said by man/woman) я очень устал/ устала ya **o**chyen oos**tal**/oos**ta**la

exhaust pipe выхлопная труба vi**H**lapna-ya troo**ba**

exhibition выставка **viy**stafka

exit выход **viy**Hat

where's the nearest exit? где ближайший выход? gdyeh blee**J**Ishi **viy**Hat?

expect ожидать a**J**i**dat**

expensive дорогой darag**oy**

experienced опытный **o**pitni

explain объяснять/ объяснить abyas**nyat**/ abyas**neet**

can you explain that? вы можете это объяснить? viy **mo**Jetyeh eta abyas**neet**?

express (mail) срочное письмо **sro**chna-yeh pees**mo**

(train, bus) экспресс eks**pres**

extension (telephone) добавочный (номер) da**ba**vachni (**no**myer)

extension 221, please добавочный двести двадцать один, пожалуйста da**ba**vachni **dvyes**tee **dva**tsat a**deen**, pa**J**alsta

extension lead удлинитель oodleen**ee**tyel

extra: can we have an extra one? можно ещё один? **mo**Jna yesh-**cho** a**deen**?

do you charge extra for that? вы берёте дополнительную плату за это? viy byer**yo**tyeh dapaln**ee**tyelnoo-yoo **pla**too za **e**ta?

extraordinary удивительный oodeev**ee**tyelni

extremely крайне kr**I**nyeh

eye глаз glas

will you keep an eye on my suitcase for me?

присмотрите, пожалуйста, за моим чемоданом preesmatr**ee**tyeh, pa**J**alsta, za ma-**ee**m chyemad**a**nam

eyebrow pencil карандаш для бровей karand**a**sh dlya brav**yay**

eye drops глазные капли glazn**iy**-yeh k**a**plee

eyeglasses очки achk**ee**

eyeliner карандаш для глаз karand**a**sh dlya glas

eye shadow тени для век pl t**ye**nee dlya vyek

F

face лицо leets**o**

factory фабрика f**a**breeka

faint (*verb*) падать/упасть в обморок p**a**dat/**uu**p**a**st v**o**bmarak

 she's fainted она упала в обморок an**a** oop**a**la v**o**bmarak

 I feel faint мне дурно mnyeh d**oo**rna

fair (*funfair*) парк аттракционов park at-tr**a**ktsi-onaf

 (*trade*) выставка v**iy**stafka

 (*adj: just*) справедливый spravyedl**ee**evi

fairly довольно dav**o**lna

fake подделка pad-d**ye**lka

fall (*verb*) падать/упасть p**a**dat/ oop**a**st

 she's had a fall она упала an**a** oop**a**la

fall (US: *autumn*) осень **o**syen

 in the fall осенью **o**syenyoo

false ложный l**o**Jni

family семья syem**ya**

famous знаменитый znamyen**ee**ti

fan (*electrical*) вентилятор vyenteel**ya**tar

 (sport: *male/female*) любитель/ любительница lyoob**ee**tyel/ lyoob**ee**tyelneetsa

fantastic замечательный zamyech**a**tyelni

far далеко dalyek**o**

DIALOGUE

is it far from here? это далеко отсюда? **e**ta dalyek**o** ats**yoo**da?

no, not very far нет, не очень далеко nyet, nyeh **o**chyen dalyek**o**

well how far? как далеко? kak dalyek**o**?

it's about 20 kilometres примерно двадцать километров preem**ye**rna dv**a**tsat keelam**ye**traf

fare стоимость проезда st**o**-eemast pra-**ye**zda

farm ферма f**ye**rma

fashionable модный m**o**dni

fast быстрый b**iy**stri

fat (*person*) толстый t**o**lsti

 (*on meat*) жир Jir

father отец at**ye**ts

father-in-law (*wife's father*) тесть tyest

 (*husband's father*) свёкор sv**yo**kar

faucet кран kran

fault (mechanical) неисправность
nyeh-eespra**v**nast

sorry, it was my fault
извините, это моя вина
eezvee**nee**tyeh, eta ma-**ya** veena

it's not my fault это не моя
вина **e** ta nyeh ma-**ya** veena

faulty: this is faulty это не
работает **e**ta nyeh ra**bo**ta-yet

favourite любимый lyoo**bee**mi

fax (noun) факс faks

(verb) посылать/послать по
факсу pasi**lat**/pa**slat** pa **fa**ksoo

I want to send a fax Я хочу
послать факс ya Ha**choo** pa**slat**
faks

fax (machine) факс faks

February февраль fyev**ral**

feel чувствовать/
почувствовать choo**stva**vat/
pa**choo**stvavat

I feel hot мне жарко mnyeh
Jarka

I feel unwell мне нехорошо
mnyeh nyeh-Hara**sho**

I feel like going for a walk
мне хочется прогуляться
mnyeh **Ho**chetsa pragoo**lyat**sa

how are you feeling? как вы
себя чувствуете? kak viy syeb**ya**
choo**stvoo**-yetyeh?

I'm feeling better мне лучше
mnyeh **loo**chsheh

felt-tip (pen) фломастер
fla**ma**styer

fence забор za**bor**

fender (of car) бампер **ba**mpyer

ferry паром pa**rom**

festival фестиваль fyestee**val**

Travel tip Spring and autumn
are when Russian festi-
vals tend to take place. In
Moscow, the Golden Mask
competition to choose the
best of the previous year's
drama, dance, opera and
puppetry in Russia sees
dozens of shows over two
weeks in February/March
culminating in a gala awards
ceremony.

---

fetch: I'll fetch him я схожу за
ним ya sHa**Joo** za neem

**will you come and fetch me
later?** вы зайдёте за мной
попозже? viy zid**yo**tyeh za mnoy
papo**J**-Jeh?

feverish: I'm feverish меня
лихорадит myen**ya** leeHa**ra**deet

few: a few несколько **nye**skalka

a few days несколько дней
nyeskalka dnyay

fiancé жених Jen**ee**H

fiancée невеста nyev**ye**sta

field поле **po**lyeh

fight (noun) драка **dra**ka

figs инжир een**Jiyr**

file фйла fil

fill in заполнять/заполнить
zapal**nyat**/za**pol**neet

do I have to fill this in? мне
нужно это заполнить? mnyeh
nooJna **e**ta za**pol**neet?

fill up наполнять/наполнить
napal**nyat**/na**pol**neet

fill it up, please полный бак, пожалуйста polni bak, paJalsta

filling (in cake, sandwich) начинка nacheenka

(in tooth) пломба plomba

film (movie) фильм feelm

(for camera) плёнка plyonka

filthy грязный gryazni

find (*verb*) находить/найти naHadeet/nitee

I can't find it я не могу это найти ya nyeh magoo eta nitee

I've found it (said by man/woman) я нашёл/нашла это ya nashol/nashla eta

find out узнавать/узнать ooznavat/ooznat

could you find out for me? вы не могли бы узнать для меня viy nyeh magleebi ooznat dlya myenya?

fine (weather) хороший Haroshi

(punishment) штраф shtraf

DIALOGUE

how are you? как у вас дела? kak oo vas dyela?

I'm fine thanks хорошо, спасибо Harasho, spaseeba

is that OK? так хорошо? tak Harasho?

that's fine thanks хорошо, спасибо Harasho, spaseeba

finger палец palyets

finish (*verb*) заканчивать/ закончить zakancheevat/ zakoncheet

I haven't finished yet (said by man/woman) я ещё не закончил/закончила ya yeshcho nyeh zakoncheel/ zakoncheela

when does it finish? когда это заканчивается? kagda eta zakancheeva-yetsa?

Finland Финляндия feenlyandee-ya

fire (in hearth) огонь agon

(campfire) костёр kastyor

(blaze) пожар paJar

fire! пожар! paJar!

can we light a fire here? здесь можно разложить костёр? zdyes moJna razlaJiyt kastyor?

my room is on fire! в моём номере пожар! vma-yom nomyereh paJar!

fire alarm пожарная тревога paJarna-ya tryevoga

fire brigade пожарная команда paJarna-ya kamanda

fire escape пожарная лестница paJarna-ya lyesneetsa

fire extinguisher огнетушитель agnyetooshiytyel

first первый pyervi

I was first (said by man) я был первым ya biyl pyervim

(said by woman) я была первой ya biyla pyervi

at first сначала snachala

the first time первый раз pyervi ras

first turn on the left первый

поворот налево pyervi pavarot
nalyeva

first aid первая помощь pyerva-
ya pomash-ch

first-aid kit походная аптечка
paHodna-ya aptyechka

first class (travel etc) первым
классом pyervim klasam

first floor второй этаж ftaroy
etash

(US) первый этаж pyervi etash

first name имя eemya

fish (noun) рыба riyba

fit (attack) приступ preestoop

fit: it doesn't fit me это мне не
по размеру eta mnyeh nyeh pa
razmyeroo

fitting room примерочная
pryemyerachna-ya

fix (verb: arrange) чинить/
починить cheeneet/
pacheeneet

can you fix this? (repair) вы
можете это починить? viy
moJetyeh eta pacheeneet?

fizzy газированный gazeerovan-ni

flag флаг flag

flash (for camera) вспышка
fspiyshka

flat (noun: apartment) квартира
kvarteera

(adj) плоский ploskee

I've got a flat tyre у меня
спустила шина oo menya
spoosteela shiyna

flavour вкус fkoos

flea блоха blaHa

flight рейс ryays

flight number номер рейса
nomyer ryaysa

flood наводнение
navadnyenee-yeh

floor (of room) пол pol

(storey) этаж etash

on the floor на полу na paloo

florist цветочный магазин
tsvyetochni magazeen

flour мука mooka

flower цветок tsvyetok

flu грипп greep

**fluent: he speaks fluent
Russian** он бегло говорит
по-русски on byegla gavareet
pa-rooskee

fly (noun) муха mooHa

(verb) лететь/полететь lyetyet/
palyetyet

can we fly there? туда
можно полететь? tooda moJna
palyetyet?

fog туман tooman

foggy туманный tooman-ni

folk dancing народные танцы
pl narodni-yeh tantsi

folk music народная музыка
narodna-ya moozika

follow следовать/
последовать slyedavat/
paslyedavat

follow me следуйте за мной
slyedooytyeh za mnoy

food еда yeda

food poisoning пищевое
отравление peesh-chyevo-yeh
atravlyenee-yeh

food shop/store гастроном

gastran**o**m

foot (of person) ступня stoopn**ya**

  on foot пешком pyeshk**o**m

football (game) футбол footb**o**l

  (ball) футбольный мяч footb**o**lni myach

football match футбольный матч footb**o**lni match

for: do you have something for a headache/diarrhoea? у вас есть что-то от головной боли/поноса? oo vas yest sht**o**-ta at galavn**o**y b**o**lee/pan**o**sa?

who's the chicken Kiev for? для кого котлеты по-Киевски? dlya kav**o** katl**ye**ti pa-k**ee**-yefskee?

that's for me это для меня **e**ta dlya men**ya**

and this one? а это? a **e**ta?

that's for her это для неё **e**ta dlya nyeh-**yo**

where do I get the bus for Belorussky station? откуда идёт автобус до Белорусского вокзала? atk**oo**da eed**yo**t aft**o**boos da byelar**oo**skava vakz**a**la?

the bus for the railway station leaves from Tverskaya street автобус до вокзала идёт с Тверской улицы aft**o**boos da vakz**a**la eed**yo**t stvyersk**o**y **oo**leetsi

how long have you been here? вы давно приехали? viy davn**o** pree-**ye**Halee?

I've been here for two days, how about you? я здесь уже два дня, а вы? ya zdyes oo**Je**h dva dnya, a viy?

I've been here for a week я здесь уже неделю ya zdyes oo**Je**h nyed**ye**lyoo

forehead лоб lop

foreign иностранный eenastr**a**n-ni

foreigner (*male/female*) иностранец/иностранка eenastr**a**nyets/eenastr**a**nka

forest лес lyes

> Travel tip Forested areas outside the cities are potentially infested with encephalitis-bearing ticks (*kleshy*) during May and June. Russians take care to cover their heads, shoulders and arms at this time of year when walking in forests, and you should do the same.

forget забывать/забыть zabiv**a**t/ zab**iy**t

  I forget, I've forgotten (said by man/woman) я забыл/забыла ya zab**iy**l/zab**iy**la

fork (for eating) вилка v**ee**lka

form (document) бланк blank

formal (dress) вечерний vyechyernee

fortnight две недели dvyeh nyedyelee

fortunately к счастью ksh-chastyoo

forward: could you forward my mail? вы не могли бы переслать мне мою почту viy nyeh magleebi pyeryeslat mnyeh ma-**yoo** pochtoo

forwarding address адрес для пересылки adryes dlya pyeryesiylkee

foundation (make-up) тональный крем tanalni kryem

fountain фонтан fantan

foyer (hotel, theatre) фойе fay-**yeh**

fracture перелом pyeryelom

France Франция frantsi-ya

free (no charge) бесплатный byesplatni

   is it free (of charge)**?** это бесплатно? eta byesplatna?

freeway автострада aftastrada

freezer морозилка marazeelka

French (adj, language) французский frantsooskee

French fries картофель фри kartofyel free

frequent частый chasti

   how frequent is the bus to Suzdal? как часто ходят автобусы в Суздаль? kak chasta Hodyat aftoboosi fsoozdal?

fresh (weather, breeze)

прохладный praHladni

   (fruit etc) свежий svyeЈi

fresh orange juice свежий апельсиновый сок svyeЈi apyelseenavi sok

Friday пятница pyatneetsa

fridge холодильник Haladeelneek

fried жареный Јaryeni

fried egg яичница ya-eeshneetsa

friend (male/female) друг/подруга drook/padrooga

friendly дружеский drooЈeskee

from: when does the next train from Yaroslavl arrive? когда приходит следующий поезд из Ярославля? kagda preeHodeet slyedoosh-chee po-yest eez yaraslavlya?

   from Monday to Friday с понедельника до пятницы spanyedyelneeka da pyatneetsi

   from Moscow to Tver от Москвы до Твери at maskviy da tvyeree

---

   where are you from? вы откуда? viy atkooda?

   I'm from England я из англии ya eez anglee-ee

---

front передняя часть pyeryednya-ya chast

   in front впереди fpyeryedee

   in front of the hotel перед гостиницей pyeryed gasteeneetsay

at the front спереди
spy**e**ryedee

frost мороз mar**o**s

frozen замёрзший zam**yo**rshi

frozen food замороженные
продукты zamar**o**Jeni-yeh
prad**oo**kti

fruit фрукты fr**oo**kti

fruit juice фруктовый сок
fr**oo**ktovi sok

frying pan сковородка
skavar**o**tka

FSS ФСБ (Федеральная
Служба Безопасности)
ef-es-b**eh** (fyedyer**a**lna-ya sl**oo**Jba
byezap**a**snastee)

full полный p**o**lni

  this fish is full of bones в
  этой рыбе одни кости v**e**ti
  r**i**ybyeh adn**ee** k**o**stee

  I'm full (said by man/woman) я

наелся/наелась ya na-y**e**lsya/
na-y**e**las

full board полный пансион
p**o**lni pansee-**o**n

fun: it was fun было весело
b**i**yla vy**e**syela

funeral похороны pl poн**a**rani

funny (strange) странный
stran-ni

  (amusing) забавный zab**a**vni

fur мех myeн

  fur hat меховая шапка
  myeнav**a**-ya sh**a**pka

furniture мебель my**e**byel

further дальше d**a**lsheh

  it's further down the road
  это дальше по улице **e**ta
  d**a**lsheh pa **oo**leetseh

DIALOGUE

  how much further is it to
  Klin? далеко ли ещё до
  Клина? dalyek**o**lee yesh-ch**o**
  da kl**ee**na?

  about 5 kilometres около
  пяти километров **o**kala
  pyat**ee** keelamy**e**traf

fuse предохранитель
pryedaнran**ee**tyel

  the lights have fused свет
  перегорел svyet
  pyeryegar**ye**l

fuse wire проволока для
предохранителя pr**o**valaka dlya
pryedaнran**ee**tyelya

future будущее
b**oo**doosh-chyeh-yeh

  in future в будущем
  vb**oo**doosh-chyem

G

game (cards etc) игра eegra

  (match) матч match

  (meat) дичь deech

garage (for fuel) заправочная станция byenzakalonka

  (for repairs) станция техобслуживания stantsi-ya tyenapslooJivanee-ya

  (for parking) гараж garash

garden сад sat

garlic чеснок chyesnok

gas газ gas

  (US: petrol) бензин byenzeen

gas cylinder (camping gas) газовый баллон gazavi balon

gas-permeable lenses газопроницаемые линзы gazapraneetsa-yemi-yeh leenzi

gas station бензоколонка byenzakalonka

gate ворота varota

  (at airport) выход viyнat

gay гомосексуалист gomaseksoo-aleest

Travel tip Although homosexuality is no longer illegal in Russia, society remains extremely homophobic. Most Russian gays and lesbians adopt a low profile and seldom come out to family and friends. Moscow's gay clubs are reliable havens, while St Petersburg has a flourishing gay scene.

---

gay bar бар для гомосексуалистов bar dlya gomaseksoo-aleestaf

gear передача pyeryedacha

gearbox коробка передач karopka pyeryedach

general (adj) общий opsh-chee

general delivery до востребования da vastryebavanee-ya

gents' toilet мужской туалет mooshskoy too-alyet

genuine (antique etc) подлинный podleen-ni

German (adj) немецкий nyemyetskee

Germany Германия gyermanee-ya

get (fetch) приносить/принести preenaseet/preenyestee

  could you get me another one, please? принесите, пожалуйста, ещё один preenyeseetyeh, paJalsta, yesh-cho adeen

  how do I get to...? как попасть в...? kak papast v...?

  do you know where I can get them? вы не знаете, где я могу их достать viy nyeh zna-yetyeh, gdyeh ya magoo еeн dastat?

  can I get you a drink? что вы будете пить? shto viy boodyetyeh peet?

  no, I'll get this one, what would you like? нет,

позвольте мне, что бы
вы хотели? nyet, pazvoltyeh
mnyeh, shto biy viy Hatyelee?

a glass of red wine бокал
красного вина bakal
krasnava veena

get back (return) возвращаться/
вернуться vazvrash-chatsa/
vyernootsa

get in (arrive) приезжать/
приехать pree-yeJat/pree-
yeHat

get off выходить/выйти
viHadeet/viytee

  where do I get off? где
  мне выходить? gdyeh mnyeh
  viHadeet?

get on (to train etc) садиться/
сесть sadeetsa/syest

get out (of car etc) выходить/
выйти viHadeet/viytee

get up (in the morning) вставать/
встать fstavat/
fstat

gift подарок padarak

gift shop магазин сувениров
magazeen soovyeneeraf

gin джин djin

  a gin and tonic, please
  джин с тоником, пожалуйста
  djin stoneekam, paJalsta

girl (child) девочка dyevachka

  (young woman) девушка
  dyevooshka

girlfriend подруга padrooga

give давать/дать davat/dat

  can you give me some

change? вы не разменяете?
viy nyeh razmyenya-yetyeh?

I gave it to him (said by man/
woman) я отдал/отдала ему
это ya ad-dal/ad-dala yemoo eta

will you give this to…?
передайте это,
пожалуйста,… pyeryedItyeh
eta, paJalsta,…

**how much do you want
  for this?** сколько вы
  хотите за это? skolka viy
  Hateetyeh za eta?

40,000 roubles сорок
  тысяч рублей sorak tiysyach
  rooblyay

I'll give you 30,000 я дам
  вам тридцать тысяч ya
  dam vam treetsat tiysyach

give back возвращать/вернуть
vazvrash-chat/vyernoot

glad: I'm glad (said by
man/woman) я рад/рада
ya rat/rada

glass (material) стекло styeklo

  (for drinking) стакан stakan

  a glass of wine бокал вина
  bakal veena

glasses очки achkee

gloves перчатки pyerchatkee

glue (*noun*) клей klyay

go (on foot) идти/пойти eet-tee/
pItee

  (by transport) ехать/поехать
  yeHat/pa-yeHat

  we'd like to go to the

Kremlin мы хотели бы сходить в Кремль miy нatyeleebi shadeet fkryeml

where are you going? куда вы идёте? kooda viy eedyotyeh?

where does this bus go? куда идёт этот автобус? kooda eedyot etat aftoboos?

let's go! пойдемте! pidyomtyeh!

she's gone (left) она ушла ana ooshla

where has he gone? куда он ушёл? kooda on ooshol?

I went there last week (said by man/woman) я там был/была на прошлой неделе ya tam biyl/bila na proshlı nyedyelyeh

hamburger to go гамбургер на вынос gamboorgyer na viynas

go away уходить/уйти ooнadeet/ooytee

go away! уходите! ooнadeetyeh!

go back (return) возвращаться/вернуться vazvrash-chatsa/vyernootsa

go down (the stairs etc) спускаться/спуститься spooskatsa/spoosteetsa

go in входить/войти fнadeet/vitee

go out: do you want to go out tonight? вы не хотите куда-нибудь пойти сегодня вечером? viy nyeh нateetyeh kooda-neebood pitee syevodnya vyechyeram?

go through проходить/пройти

praнadeet/pritee

go up (the stairs etc) подниматься/подняться padneematsa/padnyatsa

goat коза kaza

God бог boн

goggles защитные очки zash-cheetni-yeh achkee

gold золото zolata

good хороший нaroshi

good! хорошо! нarasho!

it's no good это не годится eta nyeh gadeetsa

goodbye до свидания da sveedanya

good evening добрый вечер dobri vyechyer

Good Friday Страстная Пятница strasna-ya pyatneetsa

good morning доброе утро dobra-yeh ootra

good night (leaving) до свидания da sveedanya

(when going to bed) спокойной ночи spakoynı nochee

goose гусь goos

got: we've got to leave нам нужно идти nam nooжna eet-tee

have you got any...? у вас есть... oo vas yest...

government правительство praveetyelstva

gradually постепенно pastyepyen-na

gram(me) грамм gram

grammar грамматика gram-mateeka

granddaughter внучка
vn**oo**chka

grandfather дедушка
d**ye**dooshka

grandmother бабушка
b**a**booshka

grandson внук vn**oo**k

grapefruit грейпфрут
gry**a**ypfr**oo**t

grapefruit juice
грейпфрутовый сок
gry**a**ypfr**oo**tavi sok

grapes виноград veen**a**gr**a**t

grass трава trav**a**

grateful благодарный blagad**a**rni

gravy соус s**o**-oos

great (*excellent*) замечательный
zamyech**a**tyelni

   that's great! здорово!
zd**o**rava!

   a great success большой

успех balsh**oy** oosp**ye**н

Great Britain Великобритания
vyeleekabreet**a**nee-ya

Greece Греция gry**e**tsi-ya

greedy жадный J**a**dni

green зелёный zyel**yo**ni

greengrocer's овощной
магазин av**a**sh-chn**oy** magaz**ee**n

grey серый s**ye**ri

grilled жареный на рашпере
J**a**ryeni na r**a**shpyeryeh

grocer's бакалейный магазин
bakal**yay**ni magaz**ee**n

ground: on the ground на
земле na zyeml**yeh**

ground floor первый этаж
p**ye**rvi et**a**sh

group группа gr**oo**p-pa

guarantee (*noun*) гарантия
garant**ee**-ya

guest (*male/female*) гость/

гостья gost/gostya

guesthouse дом для приезжих dom dlya pree-yeJ-jiн

guide (*noun: male/female*) гид geet

guidebook путеводитель pooteevadeetyel

guided tour экскурсия с гидом ekskoorsee-ya zgeedam

guitar гитара geetara

gum (in mouth) десна dyesna

gun (pistol) пистолет peestalyet

(rifle) ружьё roojyo

gym спортзал sportzal

gymnastics гимнастика geemnasteeka

H

hair волосы pl volasi

hairbrush щётка для волос sh-chotka dlya valos

haircut стрижка streeshka

hairdresser's парикмахерская pareeнмaнyerska-ya

hairdryer фен fyen

hair gel гель для волос gyel dlya valos

hair grips шпильки shpeelkee

hairspray лак для волос lak dlya valos

half половина palaveena

half an hour полчаса polchasa

half a litre пол-литра polleetra

about half that примерно половина от этого preemyerna

palaveena at etava

half board полупансион poloopansee-on

half-bottle полбутылки polbootiylkee

half fare половинный тариф palaveen-ni tareef

half-price полцены pol-tseniy

ham ветчина vyetcheena

hamburger гамбургер gamboorger

hand рука rooka

handbag сумочка soomachka

handbrake ручной тормоз roochnoy tormas

handkerchief носовой платок nasavoy platok

handle (on door, suitcase etc) ручка roochka

hand luggage ручная кладь roochna-ya klat

hangover похмелье ранmyelyeh

I've got a hangover я с похмелья уa spанmyelya

happen случаться/случиться sloochatsa/sloocheetsa

what's happening? что нового? shto novava?

what has happened? что случилось? shto sloocheelas?

happy счастливый sh-chastleevi

I'm not happy about this мне это не нравится mnyeh eta nyeh nraveetsa

harbour порт port

hard твёрдый tvyordi

(difficult) трудный troodni

hard-boiled egg яйцо вкрутую
yitso fkrootoo-yoo

hard currency валюта valyoota

hard lenses жёсткие линзы
Joskee-yeh leensi

hardly едва yedva

   hardly ever очень редко
   ochyen ryetka

hardware shop
хозяйственный магазин
Hazylstvyen-ni magazeen

hat шляпа shlyapa

   (with flaps) шапка shapka

Travel tip The main clothing bargains for visitors
are Russian linen and fur
hats and coats (if you've
no moral scruples about
fur), and brightly patterned
merino-wool shawls from
Pavlovskiy-Posad. Fake
fur hats make a popular
souvenir.

---

hate (*verb*) ненавидеть
nyenaveedyet

have иметь eemyet

   can I have...? можно,
   пожалуйста...? moJna,
   paJalsta...?

   do you have...? у вас
   есть...? oo vas yest...?

   what'll you have?
   что бы вы хотели? shto biy viy
   Hatyelee?

   I have to leave now мне
   нужно идти mnyeh nooJna eet-
   tee

do I have to...? нужно ли
мне...? nooJnalee mnyeh...?

can we have some...?
можно, пожалуйста...?
moJna, paJalsta...?

hayfever сенная лихорадка
syen-naya leeHaratka

hazelnuts фундук foondook

he он on

head голова galava

headache головная боль
galavna-ya bol

headlights фары fari

healthy здоровый zdarovi

hear слышать/услышать
sliyshat/oosliyshat

---

   can you hear me? вы
   меня слышите? viy myenya
   sliyshityeh?

   **I can't hear you, could
   you repeat that?** я вас
   не слышу, повторите,
   пожалуйста ya vas nyeh
   sliyshoo, paftareetyeh, paJalsta

---

hearing aid слуховой аппарат
slooHavoy aparat

heart сердце syertseh

heart attack сердечный
приступ syerdyechni preestoop

heartburn изжога eezJoga

heat жара Jara

heater (in room, car)
обогреватель abagryevatyel

heating отопление ataplyenee-yeh

heavy тяжёлый tyeJoli

heel (of foot) пятка p**ya**tka

(of shoe) каблук kabl**oo**k

please could you heel these? вы можете поставьте сюда набойки? viy m**o**Jetyeh pastav**ee**t syo**o**da nab**oy**kee?

heelbar мастерская по ремонту обуви mastyersk**a**-ya pa ryem**o**ntoo **o**boovee

height (of person) рост rost

(of mountain, building etc) высота vis**a**ta

helicopter вертолёт vyertal**yo**t

hello здравствуйте zdrastv**oo**ytyeh

(answer on phone) алло all**o**

helmet (for motorcycle) шлем shlyem

help (noun) помощь p**o**mash-ch
(verb) помогать/помочь pamag**a**t/pam**o**ch

help! помогите! pamag**ee**tyeh!

can you help me? вы можете мне помочь? viy m**o**Jetyeh mnyeh pam**o**ch?

thank you very much for your help большое спасибо за помощь balsh**o**-yeh spas**ee**ba za p**o**mash-ch

helpful полезный pal**ye**zni

hepatitis гепатит gyepat**ee**t

her: I haven't seen her (said by man/woman) я её не видел/видела ya yeh-**yo** nyeh v**ee**dyel/v**ee**dyela

to her ей yay

with her с ней snyay

for her для неё dlya nyeh-**yo**

that's her это она **e**ta an**a**

that's her towel это её полотенце **e**ta yeh-**yo** palat**ye**ntseh

herbal tea травяной чай travyan**oy** chi

herbs кухонные травы k**oo**Han-ni-yeh tr**a**vi

here здесь zdyes

here is/are... вот... vot...

here you are вот, пожалуйста vot, paJ**a**lsta

hers её yeh-**yo**

that's hers это её **e**ta yeh-**yo**

hey! эй! ay!

hi! (hello) привет! preev**ye**t!

hide (verb) прятаться/спрятаться pr**ya**tatsa/spr**ya**tatsa

high высокий vis**o**kee

highchair высокий детский стул vis**o**kee d**ye**tskee stool

highway (US) автострада aftastr**a**da

hill холм Holm

him: I haven't seen him (said by man/woman) я его не видел/видела ya yev**o** nyeh v**ee**dyel/v**ee**dyela

to him ему yem**oo**

with him с ним sneem

for him для него dlya nyev**o**

that's him это он **e**ta on

hip бедро byedr**o**

hire брать/взять напрокат brat/vzyat naprak**a**t

for hire напрокат naprak**a**t

where can I hire a bike? где я могу взять напрокат велосипед? gdyeh ya magoo vzyat naprakat vyelaseepyet?

his: it's his car это его машина eta yevo mashiyna

that's his это его eta yevo

hit (*verb*) ударять/ударить oodaryat/oodareet

hitch-hike путешествовать автостопом pootyeshestvavat aftastopam

hobby хобби Hob-bee

hockey хоккей Hakyay

hold (*verb*) держать/подержать dyerjat/padyerjat

hole дыра dira

holiday праздник prazneek

on holiday в отпуске votpooskyeh

> **Travel tip** National holidays (*prazneek*) have been contentious since the end of Communism. May Day, once a compulsory march nationwide, now sees only die-hard Communists and anarchists take to the streets, while National Unity Day (November 4), replacing the November 7 anniversary of the Bolshevick Revolution, has been hijacked by the far right.

Holland Голландия galandee-ya

home дом dom

at home (in my house etc) дома doma

(in my country) на родине na rodeenyeh

we go home tomorrow мы едем домой завтра miy yedyem damoy zaftra

honest честный chyesni

honey мёд myot

honeymoon медовый месяц myedovi myesyats

hood (US: of car) капот kapot

hope (*verb*) надеяться nadyeh-yatsa

I hope so надеюсь, что да nadyeh-yoos, shto da

I hope not надеюсь, что нет nadyeh-yoos, shto nyet

hopefully надо надеяться nada nadyeh-yatsa

horn (of car) гудок goodok

horrible ужасный ooJasni

horse лошадь loshat

horse riding верховая езда vyerHava-ya yezda

hospital больница balneetsa

hospitality гостеприимство gastyepree-eemstva

thank you for your hospitality спасибо за ваше гостеприимство spaseeba za vasheh gastyepree-eemstva

hot (water, food) горячий garyachee

(weather) жаркий Jarkee

(spicy) острый ostri

I'm hot мне жарко mnyeh Jarka

it's hot today сегодня жарко syev**o**dnya **J**arka

hotel гостиница gast**ee**neetsa

hotel room номер n**o**myer

hour час chas

house дом dom

hovercraft судно на воздушной подушке s**oo**dna na vazd**oo**shnı pad**oo**shkyeh

how как kak

how many? сколько? sk**o**lka?

how do you do? здравствуйте zdr**a**stvooytyeh

how are you? как дела? kak dyela?

fine, thanks, and you? хорошо, спасибо, а у вас? Harash**o**, spas**ee**ba, a oo vas?

how much is it? сколько это стоит? sk**o**lka eta st**o**-eet?

10,500 roubles десять тысяч пятьсот рублей d**ye**syat t**ii**ysyach pyats**o**t roobl**ya**y

I'll take it я возьму это ya vazm**oo** eta

humid влажный vl**a**Jnı

Hungary Венгрия v**ye**ngree-ya

hungry голодный gal**o**dnı

are you hungry? вы голодны? viy g**o**ladnı?

hurry (*verb*) спешить spyesh**ii**yt

I'm in a hurry я спешу ya spyesh**oo**

there's no hurry это не к спеху eta nyeh ksp**ye**hoo

hurry up! быстрее! bistr**yeh**-yeh

hurt (*verb*) причинять/ причинить боль preecheen**ya**t/ preecheen**ee**t bol

it hurts больно b**o**lna

it really hurts очень больно **o**chyen b**o**lna

husband муж moosh

hydrofoil судно на подводных крыльях s**oo**dna na padv**o**dnıh kr**ii**ylyaн

I я ya

ice лёд lyot

with ice со льдом sald**o**m

no ice, thanks безо льда, пожалуйста byez**a**lda, paJ**a**lsta

ice cream мороженое mar**o**Jena-yeh

ice-cream cone рожок ra**J**ok

ice lolly эскимо eskeem**o**

ice rink каток kat**o**k

ice skates коньки kank**ee**

ice skating катание на коньках katan**ee**-yeh na kankaн

icon икона eek**o**na

icy ледяной lyedyan**o**y

idea идея eed**yeh**-ya

idiot идиот eedee-**o**t

if если **yes**lee

ignition зажигание za**ji**ganee-yeh

ill: he/she is ill он болен/она
больна on b**o**lyen/ona baln**a**

   I feel ill мне плохо mnyeh
   pl**o** на

illness болезнь bal**yez**n

imitation (leather)
   искусственный
   eesk**oo**stvyen-ni
   (jewellery) подделка pad-d**yel**ka

immediately немедленно
   nyem**ye**dlyen-na

important важный **va**jni

   it's very important это очень
   важно **e**ta **o**chyen **va**jna

   it's not important это не
   важно **e**ta nyeh **va**jna

impossible: it's impossible
   это невозможно **e**ta
   nyevazm**o**jna

impressive впечатляющий
   fpyechatl**ya**-yoosh-chee

improve улучшать/улучшить
   ool**oo**chshat/ool**oo**chshit

in: it's in the centre это в
   центре **e**ta fts**e**ntryeh

   in my car в моей машине
   vma-**yay** mash**i**nyeh

   in Moscow в Москве
   vmaskv**yeh**

   in two days from now через
   два дня ch**ye**ryez dva dnya

   in five minutes через пять
   минут ch**ye**ryes pyat meen**oo**t

   in May в мае vma-yeh

in English по-английски
   pa-angl**ee**skee

in Russian по-русски
   pa-r**oo**skee

include включать/включить
   fkl**yoo**chat/fkl**yoo**cheet

   does that include meals?
   в это входит стоимость
   питания? **v**eta fh**o**deet sto-
   eemast peetanee-ya?

   is that included? это
   включено в стоимость? **e**ta
   fkl**yoo**chyen**o** fsto-eemast?

inconvenient неудобный nyeh-
   ood**o**bni

incredible поразительный
   paraz**ee**tyelni

Indian (adj) индийский
   eend**ee**skee

indicator указатель ookaz**a**tyel

indigestion несварение
   nyesvar**ye**nee-yeh

indoor pool закрытый бассейн
   zakr**i**ti bass**ya**yn

indoors в помещении fpamyesh-
   ch**ye**nee-ee

inexpensive дешёвый dyesh**o**vi

infection инфекция
   eenf**ye**ktsi-ya

infectious инфекционный
   eenfyektsi-**o**n-ni

inflammation воспаление
   vaspal**ye**nee-yeh

informal неофициальный nyeh-
   afeetsi-**a**lni

information информация
   eenfarm**a**tsi-ya

   **do you have any
   information about...?** у вас

есть какая-то информация о…? oo vas yest kaka-ya-ta eenfarmatsi-ya a…?

information desk справочный стол spravachni stol

injection инъекция eenyektsi-ya

injured раненый ranyeni

she's been injured она ранена ana ranyena

innocent: I'm innocent (said by man/woman) я не виновен/виновна ya nyeh veenovyen/veenovna

insect насекомое nasyekoma-yeh

insect bite укус насекомого ookoos nasyekomava

do you have anything for insect bites? у вас есть что-то от укусов насекомых? oo vas yest shto-ta at ookoosaf nasyekomiн?

insect repellent средство от насекомых sryetstva at nasyekomiн

inside внутри vnootree

inside the hotel в гостинице vgasteeneetseh

let's sit inside давайте сядем внутри davItyeh syadyem vnootree

insist настаивать nasta-eevat

I insist я настаиваю ya nasta-eeva-yoo

instant coffee растворимый кофе rastvareemi kofyeh

instead вместо vmyesta

give me that one instead дайте мне это взамен dItyeh mnyeh eta vzamyen

instead of… вместо… vmyesta…

insurance страховка straнofka

intelligent умный oomni

interested: I'm interested in… меня интересует… myenya eentyeryesoo-yet…

interesting интересный eentyeryesni

that's very interesting это очень интересно eta ochyen eentyeryesna

international международный myeJdoonarodni

Internet Интернет eenternet

interpreter (male/female) переводчик/переводчица pyeryevotcheek/pyeryevotcheetsa

intersection перекрёсток pyeryekryostak

interval (at theatre) антракт antrakt

into в v

I'm not into… я не увлекаюсь… ya nyeh oovlyeka-yoos…

Intourist Интурист eentooreest

introduce знакомить/познакомить znakomeet/paznakomeet

may I introduce…? разрешите представить… razryeshiIytyeh pryetstaveet…

invitation приглашение preeglashenee-yeh

invite приглашать/пригласить preeglashat/preeglaseet

Ireland Ирландия eerlandee-ya

Irish ирландский eerlantskee

I'm Irish (*male/female*) я ирландец/ирландка ya eerlandyets/eerlantka

iron (for ironing) утюг ootyook

can you iron these for me? вы не могли бы погладить это? viy nyeh magleebi pagladeet eta?

island остров ostraf

it это eta

it is… это… eta…

is it…? это…? eta…?

where is it? где это? gdyeh eta?

it's him это он eta on

Italian (*adj*) итальянский eetalyanskee

Italy Италия eetalee-ya

itch: it itches чешется chyeshetsa

J

jack (for car) домкрат damkrat

jacket куртка koortka

(tailored) пиджак peedjak

jam варенье varyenyeh

jammed: it's jammed заело za-yela

January январь yanvar

jar (*noun*) банка banka

jaw челюсть chyelyoost

jazz джаз djaz

jealous ревнивый ryevneevi

jeans джинсы djinsi

jellyfish медуза myedooza

jersey джерси djersee

jetty пристань preestan

jeweller's ювелирный магазин yoovyeleerni magazeen

jewellery ювелирные изделия pl yoovyeleerni-yeh eezdyelee-ya

Jewish еврейский yevrayskee

job работа rabota

jogging бег трусцой byek troostsoy

to go jogging бегать трусцой byegat troostsoy

joke шутка shootka

journey путешествие pootyeshestvee-yeh

have a good journey! счастливого пути! sh-chasleevava pootee!

jug кувшин koofshiyn

a jug of water кувшин воды koofshiyn vadiy

juice сок sok

July июль ee-yool

jump (*verb*) прыгать/прыгнуть priygat/priygnoot

jumper джемпер djempyer

junction (of roads) перекрёсток pyeryekryostak

(on motorway) развилка razveelka

June июнь ee-yoon

just (only) только tolka

just two только два
tolka dva

just for me только для меня
tolka dlya myenya

just here именно здесь
eemyen-na zdyes

not just now не сейчас nyeh
syechas

we've just arrived мы
только что приехали miy tolka
shto pree-yehalee

K

keep (*verb*) оставлять/оставить
astavlyat/astaveet

keep the change сдачи не
надо zdachee nyeh nada

can I keep it? я могу
оставить это себе? ya magoo
astaveet eta seebyeh?

please keep it пожалуйста,
оставьте это себе paJalsta,
astaftyeh eta seebyeh

ketchup кетчуп kyetchoop

kettle чайник chineek

key ключ klyooch

**the key for room 201,
please** ключ от номера
двести один, пожалуйста
klyooch at nomyera dvyestee
adeen, paJalsta

keyring кольцо для ключей
kaltso dlya klyoochyay

kidneys почки pochkee

kill (*verb*) убивать/убить
oobeevat/oobeet

kilo килограмм keelagram

kilometre километр keelamyetr

**how many kilometres is it
to...?** сколько километров
до... skolka keelamyetraf da...

kind (*generous*) добрый dobri

that's very kind вы очень
любезны viy ochyen lyoobyezni

which kind do you want?
какой именно вы хотите?
kakoy eemyen-na viy
Hateetyeh?

I want this/that kind вот
этот/тот, пожалуйста vot
etat/tot, paJalsta

kiosk киоск kee-osk

kiss (*noun*) поцелуй patselooy
(*verb*) целовать/поцеловать
tselavat/patselavat

kitchen кухня kooHnya

Kleenex бумажный носовой
платок boomaJni nasavoy platok

knee колено kalyena

knickers трусики trooseekee

knife нож nosh

knock (*verb*) стучать/постучать
stoochat/pastoochat

knock down сбивать/сбить
zbeevat/zbeet

**he's been knocked down
by a car** его сбила машина
yevo zbeela mashiyna

knock over (*object*)
опрокидывать/опрокинуть
aprakeedivat/aprakeenoot
(*pedestrian*) сбивать/сбить с
ног zbeevat/zbeet snok

know (somebody, something, a place) знать znat

  I don't know я не знаю ya nyeh zna-yoo

  I didn't know that (said by man/woman) я этого не знал/ знала ya **e**tava nyeh znal/zn**a**la

  do you know where I can find…? вы не знаете, где я могу найти…? viy nyeh zn**a**-yetyeh, gdyeh ya mag**oo** nit**ee**…?

Kremlin Кремль kryeml

L

label ярлык yarl**iy**k

ladies' room, ladies' toilets женский туалет Jenskee too-al**ye**t

ladies' wear женская одежда Jenska-ya ad**ye**Jda

lady дама d**a**ma

lager светлое пиво sv**ye**tla-yeh p**ee**va

lake озеро **o**zyera

lamb (meat) баранина bar**a**neena

lamp лампа l**a**mpa

lane (narrow street) переулок pyereyeh-**oo**lak

  (country road) дорожка dar**o**shka

  (motorway) ряд ryat

language язык yaz**iy**k

language course курсы иностранного языка k**oo**rsi eenastr**a**n-nava yaz**i**ka

laptop ноутбук no-ootb**oo**k

large большой balsh**oy**

last последний pasl**ye**dnee

  last week на прошлой неделе na pr**o**shli nyed**ye**lyeh

  last Friday в прошлую пятницу fpr**o**shloo-yoo p**ya**tneetsoo

  last night (evening) вчера вечером fch**ye**ra v**ye**chyeram

  what time is the last train to Omsk? когда отходит последний поезд в Омск? kagd**a** atH**o**deet pasl**ye**dnee p**o**-yest vomsk?

late: sorry I'm late извините за опоздание eezveen**ee**tyeh za apazd**a**nee-yeh

  the train was late поезд опоздал p**o**-yest apazd**a**l

  we must go, we'll be late нам нужно идти, а то опоздаем nam n**oo**Jna eet-t**ee**, a to apazd**a**-yem

  it's getting late становится поздно stan**o**veetsa p**o**zna

later позже p**o**J-Jeh

  I'll come back later я вернусь попозже ya vyern**oo**s pap**o**J-Jeh

  see you later пока! pak**a**!

  later on потом pat**o**m

latest последний pasl**ye**dnee

  by Wednesday at the latest не позднее среды nyeh pazn**ye**-yeh sryed**iy**

laugh (verb) смеяться/ засмеяться smyeh-**ya**tsa/ zasmyeh-**ya**tsa

launderette, laundromat прачечная

самообслуживания
prachyechna-ya
sama-apsloojivanee-ya

laundry (clothes) бельё byel**yo**

(place) прачечная pr**a**chyechna-
ya

lavatory туалет too-al**yet**

law закон zak**o**n

lawn газон gaz**o**n

lawyer юрист yoor**ee**st

laxative слабительное
slab**ee**tyelna-yeh

lazy ленивый lyen**ee**vi

lead (electrical) провод pr**o**vat

(*verb*) вести/привести vyest**ee**/
preevest**ee**

where does this lead to?
куда это ведёт? kood**a e**ta
vyed**yo**t?

leaf лист leest

leaflet брошюрка brash**oo**rka

leak течь tyech

the roof leaks крыша течёт
kr**i**ysha tyech**o**t

learn учиться ooch**ee**tsa

least: not in the least
нисколько neesk**o**lka

at least по крайней мере pa
kr**i**nyay m**ye**ryeh

leather кожа k**o**ja

leave (*verb*: by transport) уезжать/
уехать oo-yeJ-J**a**t/oo-**ye**Hat

(on foot) уходить/уйти
ooHad**ee**t/ooyt**ee**

I am leaving tomorrow я
уезжаю завтра ya oo-yeJJ**a**-yoo
z**a**ftra

he left yesterday он уехал
вчера on oo-**ye**Hal fch**ye**ra

may I leave this here?
можно это здесь оставить?
m**o**Jna **e**ta zdyes ast**a**veet?

I left my coat in the bar
(said by man/woman)
я оставил/оставила пальто в
баре ya ast**a**veel/ast**a**veela palt**o**
vb**a**ryeh

**when does the bus for
Vladimir leave?** когда
отходит автобус во
Владимир? kagd**a** at**H**odeet
aft**o**boos va vlad**ee**meer?

leek лук-порей look-par**yay**

left-handed левша lyefsh**a**

left левый l**ye**vi

on the left слева sl**ye**va

to the left налево nal**ye**va

turn left поверните налево
pavyern**ee**tyeh nal**ye**va

there's none left ничего

не осталось neechyevo nyeh astalas

left luggage (office) камера хранения kamyera нranyenee-ya

leg нога naga

lemon лимон leemon

lemonade лимонад leemanat

lemon tea чай с лимоном chї sleemonam

lend одолжить adalJiyt

will you lend me your pen? одолжите, пожалуйста, вашу ручку adalJiytyeh, paJalsta, vashoo roochkoo

lens (of camera) объектив abyekteef

lesbian лесбиянка lyezbee-yanka

less меньше myensheh

less than меньше, чем myensheh, chyem

less expensive менее дорогой myenyeh-yeh daragoy

lesson урок oorok

let (allow) позволять/позволить pazvalyat/pazvoleet

will you let me know? вы мне дадите знать? viy mnyeh dadeetyeh znat?

I'll let you know я дам вам знать ya dam vam znat

let's go for something to eat пойдёмте поедим pidyomtyeh pa-yedeem

to let сдаётся sda-yotsa

let off высаживать/высадить visaJivat/viysadeet

let me off at the corner я

выйду на углу ya viydoo na oogloo

letter письмо peesmo

do you have any letters for me? есть ли для меня письма? yestlee dlya myenya peesma?

letterbox почтовый ящик pachtovi yash-cheek

lettuce салат salat

lever (noun) рычаг richak

library библиотека beeblee-atyeka

licence (driver's) водительские права pl vadeetyelskee-yeh prava (permit) лицензия leetsenzee-ya

lid крышка kriyshka

lie (verb: tell untruth) лгать/солгать lgat/salgat

lie down лежать/лечь lyeJat/lyech

life жизнь Jizn

lifebelt спасательный пояс spasatyelni po-yas

lifeguard (male/female) спасатель spasatyel

life jacket спасательный жилет spasatyelni Jilyet

lift (in building) лифт leeft

could you give me a lift? вы не могли бы меня подвезти? viy nyeh magleebi menya padvyestee?

would you like a lift? вас подвезти? vas padvyestee?

light (noun) свет svyet (not heavy) лёгкий lyoнkee

do you have a light? (for

cigarette) нет ли у вас огонька? nyetlee oo vas aganka?

light green светло-зелёный svyetla-zyelyoni

light bulb лампочка lampachka

I need a new light bulb мне нужна новая лампочка mnyeh noojna nova-ya lampachka

lighter (cigarette) зажигалка zaJigalka

lightning молния molnee-ya

like: I like it мне это нравится mnyeh eta nraveetsa

I like going for walks я люблю гулять ya lyooblyoo goolyat

I like you вы мне нравитесь viy mnyeh nraveetyes

I don't like it мне это не нравится mnyeh eta nyeh nraveetsa

do you like…? вам нравится…? vam nraveetsa…?

I'd like a beer (said by man/woman) я бы выпил/выпила кружку пива ya biy viypeel/viypeela krooshkoo peeva

I'd like to go swimming (said by man/woman) я бы хотел/хотела поплавать ya biy Hatyel/Hatyela paplavat

would you like a drink? не хотите что-нибудь выпить? nyeh Hateetyeh shto-neeboot viypeet?

would you like to go for a walk? не хотите прогуляться? nyeh Hateetyeh

pragoolyatsa?

what's it like? на что это похоже? na shto eta paHoJeh?

I want one like this я такой же хочу ya takoyJeh Hachoo

lime лайм lIm

line линия leenee-ya

lips губы goobi

lip salve гигиеническая помада geegee-yeneecheeskaya pamada

lipstick губная помада goobnaya pamada

liqueur ликёр leekyor

listen слушать slooshat

litre литр leetr

a litre of milk литр молока leetr malaka

little маленький malyenkee

just a little, thanks чуть-чуть, спасибо choot-choot, spaseeba

a little milk немного молока nyemnoga malaka

a little bit more ещё немного yesh-cho nyemnoga

live (verb) жить Jit

we live together мы живём вместе miy Jivyom vmyestyeh

lively оживлённый aJivlyon-ni

liver (in body, food) печень pyechyen

loaf буханка booнanka

lobby (in hotel) вестибюль vyesteebyool

lobster омар amar

local местный myesni

can you recommend a local restaurant? вы можете порекомендовать местный ресторан? viy moJetyeh paryekamyendavat myesni ryestaran?

lock (*noun*) замок zamok

(*verb*) запирать/запереть zapeerat/zapyeryet

it's locked это заперто eta zapyerta

lock in запирать/запереть zapeerat/zapyeryet

lock out: I've locked myself out (said by man/woman) я случайно захлопнул/захлопнула дверь ya sloochIna zaнlopnool/zaнlopnoola dvyer

locker шкафчик shkafcheek

(for luggage etc) автоматическая камера хранения aftamateechyeska-ya kamyera Hranyenee-ya

lollipop леденец lyedeenyets

London Лондон london

long длинный dleen-ni

how long will it take to fix it? сколько времени займёт починка? skolka vryemeenee zimyot pacheenka?

how long does it take? сколько времени это занимает? skolka vryemeenee eta zaneema-yet?

a long time долго dolga

one day/two days longer ещё один день/два дня yesh-cho adeen dyen/dva dnya

long-distance call междугородный разговор myeJdoogarodni razgavor

look: I'm just looking, thanks я просто смотрю, спасибо ya prosta smatryoo, spaseeba

you don't look well вы неважно выглядите viy nyeh vaJna viyglyadeetyeh

look out! осторожно! astaroJna!

can I have a look? можно мне взглянуть? moJna mnyeh vzglyanoot?

look after ухаживать за ooнaJivat za

look at смотреть/посмотреть на smatryet/pasmatryet na

look for искать/поискать eeskat/pa-eeskat

I'm looking for... я ищу… ya eesh-choo…

look forward to с нетерпением ждать snyetyerpyenee-yem Jdat

I'm looking forward to it я с нетерпением жду этого ya snyetyerpyenee-yem Jdoo etava

loose (handle etc) расшатанный rasshatan-ni

lorry грузовик groozaveek

lose терять/потерять tyeryat/patyeryat

I've lost my way (said by man/woman) я заблудился/

заблудилась ya zabloodeelsya/
zabloodeelas

**I'm lost, I want to get
to...** (said by man/woman) я
заблудился/заблудилась, мне
нужно добраться до... ya
zabloodeelsa/zabloodeelas, mnyeh
nooJna dabratsa da...

I've lost my bag (said by man/
woman) я потерял/потеряла
сумку ya patyeryal/patyeryala
soomkoo

lost property (office) бюро
находок byooro naHodak

lot: a lot, lots много mnoga

not a lot немного nyemnoga

a lot of people много
народу mnoga narodoo

a lot bigger намного больше
namnoga bolsheh

I like it a lot мне очень
нравится mnyeh ochyen
nraveetsa

lotion лосьон lasyon

loud громкий gromkee

lounge (in house) гостиная
gasteena-ya

(in hotel) фойе fay-**yeh**

(in airport) зал ожидания zal
aJidanee-ya

love (*noun*) любовь lyoobof

(*verb*) любить lyoobeet

lovely замечательный
zamyechatyelni

low низкий neeskee

luck удача oodacha

good luck! желаю успеха!
Jila-yoo oospyeнa!

luggage багаж bagash

luggage trolley тележка для
багажа tyelyeshka dlya bagaJa

lunch обед abyet

lungs лёгкие lyoнkee-yeh

luxurious (hotel, furnishings)
роскошный raskoshni

luxury роскошь roskash

M

machine машина mashiyna

mad (insane) сумасшедший
soomashetshi

(angry) рассерженный
rassyerJen-ni

magazine журнал Joornal

maid (in hotel) горничная
gorneechna-ya

maiden name девичья
фамилия dyeveechya fameelee-
ya

mail (*noun*) почта pochta

(*verb*) отправлять/отправить
atpravlyat/atpraveet

is there any mail for me?
есть ли для меня почта?
yestlee dlya myenya pochta?

mailbox почтовый ящик
pachtovi yash-cheek

main главный glavni

main course основное блюдо
asnavno-yeh blyooda

main post office главпочтамт
glafpachtamt

main road (in town) главная
улица glavna-ya ooleetsa

(in country) главная дорога

glavna-ya daroga

make (brand name) марка marka

(*verb*) делать/сделать dyelat/sdyelat

I make it 130,000 roubles
по моим расчётам, сто тридцать тысяч рублей pa ma-**eem** rash-**cho**tam, sto **tree**tsat **tiy**syach roobl**ya**y

what is it made of? из чего это сделано? ees chy**e**vo eta zd**ye**lana?

make-up косметика kasm**ye**teeka

man мужчина moosh-ch**ee**na

manager (of hotel)
администратор admeeneestr**a**tar

(of company) менеджер m**e**nedjer

can I see the manager?
позовите администратора, пожалуйста pazav**ee**tyeh admeeneestr**a**tara, pa**J**alsta

manageress (in shop etc)
заведующая zav**ye**doosh-cha-ya

manual (with manual gears) с ручной коробкой передач srooc**hn**oy kar**o**pki pyeryed**a**ch

many многие mn**o**gee-yeh

not many немногие nyemn**o**gee-yeh

map (city plan) план plan

(road map, geographical) карта karta

network map схема sh**ye**ma

March март mart

margarine маргарин margar**ee**n

market рынок r**i**ynak

marmalade мармелад marmyel**a**t

married: I'm married (said by a man/woman) я женат/замужем ya Jen**a**t/z**a**moo**J**em

are you married? (to man/woman) вы женаты/замужем? viy Jen**a**ti/z**a**moo**J**em?

mascara тушь для ресниц toosh dlya ryesn**ee**ts

match (football etc) матч match

matches спички sp**ee**chkee

material (fabric) ткань tkan

matter: it doesn't matter
неважно nyev**a**Jna

what's the matter? в чём дело? fchom d**ye**la?

mattress матрас matr**a**s

May май mi

may: may I have another one? можно ещё один, пожалуйста? mo**J**na yesh-ch**o** ad**ee**n, pa**J**alsta

may I come in? можно войти? mo**J**na vit**ee**?

may I see it? можно мне взглянуть? mo**J**na mnyeh vzglyan**oo**t?

may I sit here? здесь свободно? zdyes svab**o**dna?

maybe может быть mo**J**et biyt

mayonnaise майонез mi-an**e**s

me: that's for me это для меня eta dlya myen**ya**

send it to me пошлите это мне pash**lee**tyeh eta mnyeh

me too я тоже ya to**J**eh

meal еда yed**a**

did you enjoy your meal?
понравилась ли вам еда?
panraveelaslee vam yeda?

it was excellent, thank you было очень вкусно,
спасибо b**i**yla **o**chyen
fk**oo**sna, spas**ee**ba

mean (*verb*) значить zn**a**cheet
what do you mean? что
вы имеете в виду? shto viy
eem**yeh**-yetyeh v-veed**oo**?

what does this word mean? что значит это
слово? shto zn**a**cheet **e**ta
sl**o**va?

it means... это значит... **e**ta
zn**a**cheet...

measles корь kor
German measles краснуха
krasn**oo**нa

meat мясо m**ya**sa

mechanic механик meх**a**neek

medicine медицина
myedeets**i**yna

medium (*adj*: size) средний
sr**ye**dnee

medium-dry полусухой p**o**loo-
soo**ho**y

medium-rare немного
недожаренный nyemn**o**ga
nyeda**ja**ryen-ni

medium-sized среднего
размера sr**ye**dnyeva razm**ye**ra

meet встречаться/встретиться

fstryech**a**tsa/fstr**ye**teetsa

nice to meet you приятно
познакомиться pree-**ya**tna
paznak**o**meetsa

where shall I meet you? где
мы встретимся? gdyeh miy
fstr**ye**teemsa?

meeting встреча fstr**ye**cha
(business, with more than one person) совещание savyesh-
ch**a**nee-yeh

(gathering) собрание sabr**a**nee-
yeh

meeting place место для
встречи m**ye**sta dlya fstr**ye**chee

melon дыня d**i**ynya

memory stick флешка fl**e**shka

men мужчины moosh-ch**ee**ni

mend чинить/починить
cheen**ee**t/pacheen**ee**t

could you mend this for me? вы не могли бы это
починить? viy nyeh magl**ee**bi **e**ta
pacheen**ee**t?

mens' room мужской туалет
mooshsk**o**y too-al**ye**t

menswear мужская одежда
m**oo**shska-ya ad**ye**Jda

mention (*verb*) упоминать/
упомянуть oopameen**a**t/
oopameen**oo**t

don't mention it не за что
ny**eh**-za-shta

menu меню myeny**oo**
may I see the menu, please? можно меню,
пожалуйста? m**o**Jna myeny**oo**,
pa**J**alsta

see **Menu Reader** p.233

message сообщение sa-apsh-chyenee-yeh

are there any messages for me? мне что-нибудь передавали? mnyeh shto-neeboot pyeryedavalee?

I want to leave a message for... вы не могли бы передать... viy nyeh magleebi pyeryedat...?

metal (*noun*) металл myetal

metre метр myetr

microwave oven высокочастотная печь visoka-chastotna-ya pyech

midday полдень poldyen

at midday в полдень fpoldyen

middle: in the middle в середине fsyereedeenyeh

in the middle of the night посреди ночи pasreedee nochee

the middle one средний sryednee

midnight полночь polnach

at midnight в полночь fpolnach

might: I might want to stay another day возможно я захочу остаться ещё на один день vazmoJna ya zaHachoo astatsa yesh-cho na adeen dyen

migraine мигрень meegryen

mild (weather) тёплый tyopli

(taste) неострый nyeh-ostri

milk молоко malako

milkshake молочный коктейль

malochni kaktyayl

millimetre миллиметр meeleemyetr

minced meat фарш farsh

mind: never mind не важно nyeh vaJna

I've changed my mind (said by man/woman) я передумал/ передумала ya pyeryedoomal/ pyeryedoomala

do you mind if I open the window? вы не возражаете, если я открою окно? viy nyeh vazraJa-yetyeh, yeslee ya atkro-yoo akno?

no, I don't mind нет, я не возражаю nyet, ya nyeh vazraJa-yoo

mine: it's mine это моё eta ma-yo

mineral water минеральная вода meenyeralna-ya vada

mints мятные конфеты myatni-yeh kanfyeti

minute минута meenoota

in a minute через минуту chyeryez meenootoo

just a minute минуточку meenootachkoo

mirror зеркало zyerkala

Miss девушка dyevooshka

miss: I missed the bus (said by a man/woman) я опоздал/ опоздала на автобус ya apazdal/apazdala na aftoboos

missing: one of my... is missing пропал один из моих... prapal adeen eez ma-**ee**н...

there's a suitcase missing одного чемодана не хватает adnavo chyemadana nyeh Hvata-yet

mist туман tooman

mistake (*noun*) ошибка ash**iy**pka

I think there's a mistake мне кажется, здесь ошибка mnyeh ka**j**etsa, zdyes ash**iy**pka

sorry, I've made a mistake (*said by a man/ woman*) извините, я ошибся/ ошиблась eezveen**ee**tyeh, ya ash**iy**psya/ash**iy**blas

mix-up: sorry, there's been a mix-up извините, произошла путаница eezveen**ee**tyeh, pra-eezashla p**oo**taneetsa

mobile phone мобильный телефон mab**ee**lni tyelyef**o**n

modern современный savryem**ye**n-ni

modern art gallery галерея современного искусства galyer**ye**h-ya savryem**ye**n-nava eesk**oo**stva

moisturizer увлажняющий крем oovlaJn**ya**-yoosh-chee kryem

moment: I won't be a moment минутку meen**oo**tkoo

monastery монастырь manast**iy**r

Monday понедельник panyed**ye**lneek

money деньги pl d**ye**ngee

month месяц m**ye**syats

monument памятник p**a**myatneek

moon луна loon**a**

more больше b**o**lsheh

can I have some more water, please? можно ещё воды, пожалуйста m**o**Jna yesh-ch**o** vad**iy**, pa**J**alsta

more expensive/interesting более дорогой/интересный b**o**lyeh-yeh darag**oy**/eentyery**e**sni

more than 50 больше пятидесяти b**o**lsheh pyat**ee**dyestee

more than that более того b**o**lyeh-yeh tav**o**

a lot more гораздо больше gar**a**zda b**o**lsheh

DIALOGUE

would you like some more? вы хотите ещё? viy Hat**ee**tyeh yesh-ch**o**?

no, no more for me, thanks нет, спасибо, мне больше не надо nyet, spas**ee**ba, mnyeh b**o**lsheh nyeh n**a**da

how about you? а вы? a viy?

I don't want any more, thanks спасибо, я больше не хочу spas**ee**ba, ya b**o**lsheh nyeh Hach**oo**

morning утро **oo**tra

this morning сегодня утром syev**o**dnya **oo**tram

in the morning утром **oo**tram

Moscow Москва maskva

mosquito комар kama**r**

mosquito repellent средство
от комаров sr**ye**tstva at kama**r**of

**most: I like this one most
of all** мне больше всего
нравится вот это mnyeh
b**o**lsheh fsye**vo** n**ra**veetsa vot **e**ta

most of the time большую
часть времени b**o**lshoo-yoo
chast vr**ye**myenee

most tourists большинство
туристов balshinstv**o** too**r**eestaf

mostly главным образом
gl**a**vnim **o**brazam

mother мать mat

mother-in-law (wife's mother)
тёща t**yo**sh-cha

(husband's mother) свекровь
svyek**r**of

motorbike мотоцикл
matats**i**ykl

motorboat моторная лодка
mat**o**rna-ya l**o**tka

motorway автострада aftast**ra**da

mountain гора ga**ra**

in the mountains в горах
vga**ra**н

mountaineering альпинизм
alpeen**ee**zm

mouse мышь m**i**ysh

moustache усы pl **oo**s**iy**

mouth рот rot

mouth ulcer язвочка во рту
yazvachka vart**oo**

move (verb) двигать/подвинуть
dv**ee**gat/padv**ee**noot

**he's moved to another
room** он перешёл в другую
комнату on pye**r**yesh**o**l
vdroog**oo**-yoo k**o**mnatoo

**could you move up a
little?** вы не могли бы
подвинуться? viy nyeh magl**ee**bi
padv**ee**nootsa?

where has it moved to? где
это теперь находится? gdyeh
eta tyep**ye**r na**нo**deetsa?

movie кинофильм keenaf**ee**lm

movie theater (US) кинотеатр
keenatyeh-**a**tr

MP3 format формат MP3
fa**r**mat empetr**ee**

Mr господин gaspad**ee**n

Mrs/Ms госпожа gaspa**ja**

much много mn**o**ga

much better/worse гораздо
лучше/хуже ga**ra**zda l**oo**chsheh/
нooJeh

much hotter гораздо жарче
ga**ra**zda **Ja**rchyeh

not much немного nyemn**o**ga

not very much не очень
много nyeh **o**chyen mn**o**ga

I don't want very much я
не хочу много ya nyeh нach**oo**
mn**o**ga

mud грязь gryas

mug (for drinking) кружка
kr**oo**shka

I've been mugged меня
ограбили men**ya**
agra**bee**lee

mum мама m**a**ma

mumps свинка sv**ee**nka

museum музей moo**zyay**
mushrooms грибы greeb**iy**
music музыка **moo**zika
musician (*male/female*)
музыкант/музыкантша
moo**zi**kant/moozi**kan**tsha
Muslim (*adj*) мусульманский
moosool**man**skee
mussels мидии m**ee**dee-ee
must: I must (said by a man/
woman) я должен/
должна ya do**l**Jen/dal**J**na
  I mustn't drink alcohol мне
не следует пить алкоголь
mnyeh nyeh sl**ye**doo-yet peet
alka**gol**
mustard горчица gar**chee**tsa

my мой moy
  my sister моя сестра ma-**ya**
sy**e**stra
myself: I'll do it myself (said
by a man/woman) я сам/сама
это сделаю ya sam/sam**a e**ta
zd**ye**la-yoo
  by myself (said by man/woman)
один/одна a**deen**/ad**na**

N

nail (finger) ноготь **no**gat
  (metal) гвоздь gvost
nailbrush щёточка для ногтей
sh-ch**o**tachka dlya nakt**yay**
nail varnish лак для ногтей lak

dlya nakt**yay**

name имя **ee**mya

my name's... меня зовут... men**ya** zav**oo**t...

what's your name? как вас зовут? kak vas zav**oo**t?

what is the name of this street? как называется эта улица kak naziva-yetsa **e**ta **oo**leetsa?

napkin салфетка s**a**lfyetka

nappy пелёнка pyel**yo**nka

narrow узкий **oo**skee

nasty (weather, person) скверный skv**ye**rni

(accident) тяжёлый tya**J**oli

national национальный natsi-an**a**lni

nationality национальность natsi-an**a**lnast

natural натуральный nat**oo**ralni

nausea тошнота tashn**a**ta

navy (blue) тёмно-синий t**yo**mna-s**ee**nee

near рядом r**ya**dam

is it near the city centre? это недалеко от центра города? **e**ta nyedal**e**ko at ts**e**ntra g**o**rada?

do you go near the Winter Palace? вы не проезжаете Зимний дворец? viy nyeh pra-ye**JJ**a-yetyeh z**ee**mnee dvar**ye**ts?

where is the nearest...? где ближайший...? gdyeh blee**J**ishi...?

nearby поблизости pabl**ee**zastee

nearly почти pacht**ee**

necessary необходимый nyeh-apʜad**ee**mi

neck шея sh**e**h-ya

necklace ожерелье aʌer**ye**h-lyeh

necktie галстук g**a**lstook

need: I need... мне надо... mnyeh n**a**da...

do I need to pay? нужно ли мне заплатить? n**oo**ʌnalee mnyeh zaplat**ee**t

needle иголка eeg**o**lka

negative (film) негатив nyegat**ee**f

neither: neither (one) of them ни один из них nee ad**ee**n eez neeʜ

neither... nor... ни... ни... nee... nee...

nephew племянник plyem**ya**n-neek

net (in tennis) сетка s**ye**lka

(in football) ворота var**o**ta

Netherlands Нидерланды n**ee**derlandi

never никогда neekagd**a**

have you ever been to Pskov? вы когда-нибудь были в Пскове? viy kagda-neeb**o**t b**i**ylee fpsk**o**vyeh?

no, never, I've never been there (said by man/woman) нет, я там никогда не был/не была nyet, ya tam neekagd**a** n**ye**bil/nyeh bil**a**

new новый n**o**vi

news (radio, TV etc) новости pl n**o**vastee

newsagent's (kiosk) газетный
киоск gaz**ye**tni kee-**o**sk

newspaper газета gaz**ye**ta

newspaper kiosk газетный
киоск gaz**ye**tni kee-**o**sk

New Year Новый год n**o**vi got

Happy New Year! с Новым
годом! sn**o**vim g**o**dam!

New Year's Eve новогодняя
ночь navag**o**dnya-ya noch

New Zealand Новая Зеландия
n**o**va-ya zyeland**ee**-ya

**New Zealander: I'm a New
Zealander** (*male/female*) я
новозеландец/новозеландка
ya novazyel**a**ndyets/novazyel**a**ntka

next следующий sl**ye**doosh-chee

the next turning on the left
следующий поворот налево
sl**ye**doosh-chee pavar**o**t nal**ye**va

at the next stop на
следующей остановке na
sl**ye**doosh-chyay astan**o**fkyeh

next week на следующей
неделе na sl**ye**doosh-chyay
nyed**ye**lyeh

next to рядом с r**ya**dam s

nice (food) вкусный fk**oo**sni

(looks, view etc) красивый
kras**ee**vi

(person) приятный pree-**ya**tni

niece племянница plyem**ya**n-
neetsa

night ночь noch

at night ночью n**o**chyoo

good night спокойной ночи
spak**oy**ni n**o**chee

DIALOGUE

**do you have a single room
for one night?** у вас есть
одноместный номер на
одни сутки? oo vas yest
adnam**ye**stni n**o**myer na adn**ee**
s**oo**tkee?

yes, madam да, есть da, yest

how much is it per night?
сколько это стоит в сутки?
sk**o**lka **e**ta st**o**-eet fs**oo**tkee?

**it's 300,000 roubles for
one night** триста тысяч
рублей в сутки tr**ee**sta
t**i**ysyach roobl**ya**y fs**oo**tkee

OK, I'll take it хорошо, это
меня устраивает Harash**o**,
eta myen**ya** oostra-eeva-yet

nightclub ночной клуб nachn**oy**
kloop

nightdress ночная рубашка
nachn**a**-ya roob**a**shka

night porter ночной портье
nachn**oy** part**ye**h

no нет nyet

I've no change у меня
нет мелочи oo myen**ya** nyet
m**ye**lachee

there's no... left... больше
нет b**o**lsheh nyet

no way! ни за что! nee-za-
sht**o**!

nobody никто neekt**o**

there's nobody there там
никого нет tam neekav**o** nyet

noise шум shoom

noisy: it's too noisy слишком
шумно sl**ee**shkam sh**oo**mna

non-alcoholic безалкогольный byezalkag**o**lni

none ничего neechyev**o**

nonsmoking compartment купе для некурящих koop**eh** dlya nyekoor**ya**sh-chee**n**

noon полдень p**o**ldyen

  at noon в полдень fp**o**ldyen

no-one никто neekt**o**

nor: nor do I я тоже нет ya t**o**Jeh nyet

normal нормальный narm**a**lni

north север s**ye**vyer

  in the north на севере na s**ye**vyeryeh

  to the north на север na s**ye**vyer

  north of Moscow к северу от Москвы ks**ye**vyeroo at maskv**i**y

northeast северо-восточный s**ye**vyera-vast**o**chni

northern северный s**ye**vyerni

Northern Ireland Северная Ирландия s**ye**vyerna-ya eerl**a**ndee-ya

northwest северо-западный s**ye**vyera-z**a**padni

Norway Норвегия narv**ye**gee-ya

Norwegian (adj) норвежский narv**ye**shskee

nose нос nos

not не nyeh

  I'm not hungry (said by man/ woman) я не голоден/голодна ya nyeh g**o**ladyen/galadn**a**

  I don't want any, thank you

я не хочу, спасибо ya nyeh Hach**oo**, spas**ee**ba

  it's not necessary в этом нет необходимости v**e**tam nyet nyeh-apHad**ee**mastee

  I didn't know that (said by man/ woman) я этого не знал/ знала ya **e**tava nyeh znal/znal**a**

  not that one, this one не тот, а этот nyeh tot, a **e**tat

note (banknote) банкнота bankn**o**ta

notebook блокнот blakn**o**t

notepaper (for letters) почтовая бумага pacht**o**va-ya boom**a**ga

nothing ничего neechyev**o**

  nothing for me, thanks мне ничего, спасибо mnyeh neechyev**o**, spas**ee**ba

  nothing else больше ничего b**o**lsheh neechyev**o**

novel роман ram**a**n

November ноябрь na-**ya**br

now сейчас seech**a**s

number (room, telephone etc) номер n**o**myer

  (figure) число chees**l**o

  I've got the wrong number (said by man/woman) я не туда попал/попала ya nyeh tood**a** pap**a**l/pap**a**la

  what is your phone number? какой ваш номер телефона? kak**oy** vash n**o**myer tyelyef**o**na?

number plate номерной знак namyern**oy** znak

nurse (male/female) медбрат/

медсестра myedbrat/myetsyestra

nut (for bolt) гайка g**i**ka

nuts орехи ar**ye**hee

O

occupied (toilet/telephone) занято
z**a**nyata

o'clock: it's 3 o'clock три часа
tree chas**a**

October октябрь akt**ya**br

odd (strange) странный stran-ni

off (lights) выключено
v**iy**klyoochyena

   it's just off Pushkin Square
   это рядом с Пушкинской
   площадью **eta** r**ya**dam
   sp**oo**shkeenski plosh-chad**yoo**

   we're off tomorrow мы
   уезжаем завтра m**iy** oo-yeJ-J**a**-
   yem z**a**ftra

offensive (language, behaviour)
оскорбительный askarb**ee**tyelni

office (place of work) офис **o**fees

often часто ch**a**sta

   not often нечасто
   nyech**a**sta

   how often are the buses?
   как часто ходят автобусы?
   kak ch**a**sta H**o**dyat aft**o**boosi?

oil масло m**a**sla

ointment мазь maz

OK хорошо Har**a**sho

   are you OK? с вами всё
   в порядке? sv**a**mee fsyo
   fpar**ya**tkyeh?

   is that OK with you? вы не

возражаете? viy nyeh vazraJ**a**-
yetyeh?

is it OK to…? можно…?
m**o**Jna…?

that's OK thanks ничего,
спасибо neechy**e**vo,
spas**ee**ba

I'm OK мне ничего, спасибо
mnyeh neechy**e**vo, spas**ee**ba

(I feel OK) со мной всё
в порядке sa mnoy fsyo
fpar**ya**tkyeh

is this train OK for…? этот
поезд идёт до…? **e**tat po-yest
eed**yo**t da…?

I said I'm sorry, OK? (said
by man/woman) я же уже
извинился/извинилась!
ya Jeh ooJ**eh** eezveen**ee**lsya/
eezveen**ee**las

old старый st**a**ri

how old are you? сколько
вам лет? sk**o**lka vam lyet?

I'm 25 мне двадцать пять
mnyeh dv**a**tsat pyat

and you? а вам? a vam?

old-fashioned старомодный
staram**o**dni

old town (old part of town) старая
часть города st**a**ra-ya chast
g**o**rada

   in the old town в старой
   части города fst**a**ri ch**a**stee
   g**o**rada

omelette омлет aml**ye**t

on на na

on the street/beach на улице/пляже na **oo**leetseh/ pl**ya**Jeh

is it on this road? это на этой дороге? **e**ta na **e**ti dar**o**gyeh?

on the plane на самолёте na samal**yo**tyeh

on Saturday в субботу fsoob**o**too

on television по телевизору pa tyelyev**ee**zaroo

I haven't got it on me у меня его нет с собой oo men**ya** yev**o** nyet s-sab**oy**

this one's on me (drink) этот за мой счёт **e**tat za moy sh-chot

the light wasn't on свет не горел svyet nyeh gar**ye**l

what's on tonight? что идёт сегодня? shto eed**yo**t syev**o**dnya?

once (one time) один раз ad**ee**n ras

at once (immediately) сразу же sr**a**zooJeh

one один ad**ee**n

the white one белый b**ye**li

one-way ticket билет в один конец beel**ye**t vad**ee**n kan**ye**ts

onion лук look

online (book, check) онлайн anl**i**n

only только t**o**lka

only one только один t**o**lka ad**ee**n

it's only 6 o'clock сейчас только шесть часов syech**a**s t**o**lka shest chas**o**f

I've only just got here (said

by man/woman) я только что пришёл/пришла ya t**o**lka shto preesh**o**l/preeshl**a**

on/off switch выключатель viklyooch**a**tyel

open (adj) открытый atkr**i**ti

(verb: door) открывать/ открыть atkr**i**vat/atkr**i**yt

when do you open? когда вы открываетесь? kagd**a** viy atkr**i**va-yetyes?

I can't get it open я не могу это открыть ya nyeh mag**oo** **e**ta atkr**i**yt

in the open air на открытом воздухе na atkr**i**tam v**o**zdooнyeh

opening times время открытия vr**ye**mya atkr**i**ytee-ya

open ticket билет с открытой датой beel**ye**t satkr**i**yti d**a**ti

opera опера **o**pyera

operation (medical) операция apyer**a**tsi-ya

operator (telephone: man/woman) телефонист/телефонистка tyelyefan**ee**st/tyelyefan**ee**stka

opposite: in the opposite direction в противоположном направлении fprateevapal**o**Jnam napravl**ye**nee-ee

the bar opposite бар напротив bar napr**o**teef

opposite my hotel напротив моей гостиницы napr**o**teef ma-**ya**y gast**ee**neetsi

optician оптика **o**pteeka

or или **ee**lee

orange (fruit) апельсин apyel**seen**

(colour) оранжевый ar**a**njevi

fizzy orange газированный апельсиновый напиток gazeer**o**van-ni apyels**ee**navi nap**ee**tak

orange juice апельсиновый сок apyels**ee**navi sok

orchestra оркестр ark**ye**str

order: can we order now? (in restaurant) можно заказать сейчас? m**o**jna zakaz**a**t syech**a**s?

I've already ordered, thanks (said by man/woman) я уже заказал/заказала, спасибо ya ooj**e**h zakaz**a**l/zak**a**zala, spas**ee**ba

I didn't order this (said by man/woman) я этого не заказывал/заказывала ya **e**tava nyeh zak**a**zival/zak**a**zivala

out of order не работает nyeh rab**o**ta-yet

ordinary обычный ab**i**ychni

Orthodox православный pravasl**a**vni

other другой droog**o**y

the other one другой droog**o**y

the other day на днях na dnyaн

I'm waiting for the others я жду остальных ya Jdoo astaln**i**yн

do you have any others? у вас нет других? oo vas nyet droog**ee**н?

otherwise иначе een**a**chyeh

our/ours наш nash

our mother наша мать n**a**sha mat

out: he's out его нет yev**o** nyet

three kilometres out of town в трёх километрах от города ftryoн keel**a**m**ye**traн at g**o**rada

outdoors на открытом воздухе na atkr**i**ytam v**o**zdooнyeh

outside снаружи snar**oo**ji

can we sit outside? можно сесть снаружи? m**o**jna syest snar**oo**ji?

oven духовка dooн**o**fka

over: over here вот здесь vot zdyes

over there вон там von tam

over 500 свыше пятисот sv**i**ysheh pyatees**o**t

our holidays are over наш отпуск кончился nash **o**tpoosk k**o**ncheelsa

overcharge: you've overcharged me вы с меня слишком много взяли viy smen**ya** sl**ee**shkam mn**o**ga vz**ya**lee

overcoat пальто pal**to**

overlooking: I'd like a room overlooking the courtyard (said by man/woman) я хотел/хотела бы номер с окнами во двор ya нat**ye**l/нat**ye**la biy n**o**myer s **o**knamee va dvor

overnight (travel) ночной nachn**o**y

overtake обогнать/обогнать abganya**t/**abagn**a**t

owe: how much do I owe you? (said by man/woman) сколько я вам должен/должна? sk**o**lka ya vam d**o**lJen/dalJn**a**?

own: my own... мой

собственный… moy s**o**pstvyen-
ni…

are you on your own? (to
man/woman) вы один/одна? viy
ad**ee**n/adn**a**?

I'm on my own (said by man/
woman) я один/одна ya ad**ee**n/
adn**a**

owner (*male/female*) владелец/
владелица vlad**ye**lyets/
vlad**ye**leetsa

P

pack (*verb*) складывать/
сложить вещи skl**a**divat/sla**J**iyt
v**ye**sh-chee

a pack of… пачка… p**a**chka

package (parcel) посылка
pas**i**ylka

package holiday
организованный отдых
arganeez**o**van-ni **o**d-diH

packet: a packet of cigarettes
пачка сигарет p**a**chka seegar**ye**t

padlock висячий замок
vees**ya**chee zam**o**k

page (of book) страница
stran**ee**tsa

could you page Mr…?
вызовите, пожалуйста,
господина… v**i**yzaveetyeh,
pa**J**alsta gaspad**ee**na…

pain боль bol

I have a pain here у меня
здесь болит oo myen**ya** zdyes
bal**ee**t

painful болезненный

bal**ye**znyen-ni

painkillers болеутоляющие
bolyeh-ootal**ya**-yoosh-chee-yeh

paint (*noun*) краска kr**a**ska

painting (occupation) живопись
J**i**yvapees

(picture) картина kart**ee**na

pair: a pair of… пара… p**a**ra…

Pakistani (*adj*) пакистанский
pakeest**a**nskee

palace дворец dvar**ye**ts

pale бледный bl**ye**dni

pale blue светло-голубой
sv**ye**tla-galoob**oy**

pan кастрюля kastr**yoo**lya

pancakes блины bleen**i**y

panties (women's) трусики
tr**oo**seekee

pants (underwear: men's) трусы
troos**i**y

(women's) трусики tr**oo**seekee

(US: trousers) брюки br**yoo**kee

pantyhose колготки pl kalg**o**tkee

paper бумага boom**a**ga

(newspaper) газета gaz**ye**ta

a piece of paper листок
бумаги leest**o**k boom**a**gee

paper handkerchiefs
бумажные носовые платки
boom**a**Jni-yeh nasav**i**y-yeh platk**ee**

parcel посылка pas**i**ylka

pardon (me)? (didn't understand/
hear) простите? prast**ee**tyeh?

parents родители rad**ee**tyelee

park (*noun*) парк park

(*verb*) парковаться/
припарковаться parkav**a**tsa/

preeparkav**a**tsa

can I park here? можно
здесь припарковаться? mo**J**na
zdyes preeparkav**a**tsa?

parking lot стоянка sta-**ya**nka

part часть chast

partner (boyfriend, girlfriend) друг/
подруга dr**oo**k/padr**oo**ga

party (group) группа gr**oo**p-pa

(celebration) вечеринка
vyechyer**ee**nka

pass (in mountains) перевал
pyeryev**a**l

passenger (*male/female*)
пассажир/пассажирка
pasa**J**iyr/pasa**J**iyrka

passport паспорт p**a**spart

password пароль par**o**l

past: in the past в прошлом
fpr**o**shlam

just past the post office
сразу за почтой sr**a**zoo za p**o**chti

path тропинка trap**ee**nka

---

patronymic отчество **o**chyestva

pattern узор ooz**o**r

pavement тротуар tratoo-**a**r

on the pavement на
тротуаре na tratoo-**a**ryeh

pay (*verb*) платить/заплатить
plat**ee**t/zaplat**ee**t

can I pay, please? можно
заплатить? mo**J**na zaplat**ee**t?

it's already paid for это уже
оплачено **e**ta oo**J**eh apl**a**chyena

who's paying? кто платит?
kto plat**ee**t?

I'll pay я заплачу ya zaplach**oo**

**no, you paid last time,
it's my turn now** нет,
вы платили в прошлый
раз, теперь моя очередь
nyet, viy plat**ee**lee fpr**o**shli ras,
tyep**ye**r ma-**ya o**chyeryet

DIALOGUE

payphone телефон-автомат
tyelyef**o**n-aftam**a**t

peaceful мирный m**ee**rni

peach персик p**ye**rseek

peanuts арахис ar**a**hees

pear груша gr**oo**sha

peas горох gar**o**н

peculiar странный str**a**n-ni

pedestrian crossing
пешеходный переход
pyeshe**H**odni pyeryeu**e**not

peg (for washing) прищепка
preesh-ch**ye**pka

(for tent) колышек k**o**lishek

pen ручка r**oo**chka

pencil карандаш karand**a**sh

penfriend (*male/female*) знакомый/знакомая по переписке znak**o**mi/znak**o**ma-ya pa pyeryepe**e**skyeh

penicillin пенициллин pyeneetsil**ee**n

penknife перочинный ножик pyerach**ee**n-ni n**o**jik

pensioner (*male/female*) пенсионер/пенсионерка pyensee-an**ye**r/pyensee-an**ye**rka

people люди l**yoo**dee

the other people in the hotel другие люди в гостинице droog**ee**-yeh l**yoo**dee vgast**ee**neetse

too many people слишком много народу sl**ee**shkam mn**o**ga nar**o**doo

pepper (spice, vegetable) перец p**ye**rets

peppermint (sweet) мятная конфета m**ya**tna-ya kanf**ye**ta

per: per night за ночь z**a**nach

how much per day? сколько стоит в сутки? sk**o**lka st**o**-eet fs**oo**tkee?

per cent процент prats**e**nt

perfect идеальный eede**e**-alni

perfume духи pl doon**ee**

perhaps может быть m**o**Jet biyt

perhaps not может быть, нет m**o**Jet biyt, nyet

period (of time) период pyer**ee**-ot

(menstruation) месячные pl m**ye**syachni-yeh

perm перманент pyerman**ye**nt

permit (*noun*) разрешение razryesh**e**nee-yeh

person человек chyelav**ye**k

personal stereo плейер pl**a**y-yer

petrol бензин byenz**ee**n

petrol can канистра для бензина kan**ee**stra dlya byenz**ee**na

petrol station бензоколонка byenzakal**o**nka

pharmacy аптека apt**ye**ka

phone (*noun*) телефон tyelyef**o**n

(verb) звонить/позвонить zvan**ee**t/pazvan**ee**t

phone book телефонный справочник tyelyef**o**n-ni spr**a**vachneek

phone box телефонная будка tyelyef**o**n-na-ya b**oo**tka

phone call звонок zvan**o**k

phonecard карточка для телефона-автомата k**a**rtachka dlya tyelyef**o**na-aftam**a**ta

phone charger зарядное устройство для телефона zar**ya**dna-yeh oostr**oy**stva dlya tyelyef**o**na

phone number номер телефона n**o**myer tyelyef**o**na

photo фотография fatagraf**ee**-ya

excuse me, could you take a photo of us? извините, пожалуйста, вы не могли бы нас сфотографировать? eezveen**ee**tyeh, paJ**a**lsta, viy nyeh magl**ee**bi nas sfatagraf**ee**ravat?

phrasebook разговорник razgav**o**rneek

piano пианино pee-aneena

pickpocket (*male/female*) вор/
воровка-карманник vor/
varofka-karman-neek

**pick up: will you pick me
up?** вы заедете за мной? viy
za-yedeeteh za mnoy?

picnic пикник peekneek

picture (painting) картина
karteena

(photo) фотография fatagrafee-
ya

pie пирог peerok

piece кусок koosok

a piece of... кусок...
koosok...

pill таблетка tablyetka

I'm on the pill я принимаю
противозачаточные таблетки
ya preeneema-yoo proteeva-
zachatachni-yeh tablyetkee

pillow подушка padooshka

pillow case наволочка
navalachka

pin булавка boolafka

pineapple ананас ananas

pineapple juice ананасовый
сок ananasavi sok

pink розовый rozavi

pipe (for smoking) трубка troopka

(for water) трубопровод
troobapravot

pity: it's a pity жаль Jal

place (*noun*) место myesta

at your place у вас oo vas

at his place у него oo nyevo

plain (not patterned) однотонный

adnaton-ni

plane самолёт samalyot

by plane самолётом
samalyotam

plant растение rastyenee-yeh

plasters пластыри plastiree

plastic пластмассовый plasmas-
savi

plastic bag пластиковый пакет
plasteekavi pakyet

plate тарелка taryelka

platform платформа platforma

**which platform is it for
Sergiev Posad?** с какой
платформы идут поезда
до сергиева посада? skakoy
platformi eedoot po-yezda da
syergee-yeva pasada?

play (*verb*) играть/сыграть
eegrat/sigrat

(*noun*: in theatre) пьеса
pyesa

playground детская площадка
dyetska-ya plash-chatka

pleasant приятный pree-yatni

please пожалуйста paJalsta

yes please да, спасибо da,
spaseeba

could you please...? вы
не могли бы...? viy nyeh
magleebi...?

please don't пожалуйста, не
надо paJalsta, nyeh nada

**pleased: pleased to meet
you** очень приятно ochyen
pree-yatna

pleasure: my pleasure
пожалуйста paJalsta

plenty: plenty of... много...
mnoga...

we have plenty of time у нас
много времени oo nas mnoga
vryemyenee

that's plenty, thanks
достаточно, спасибо
dastatachna, spaseeba

pliers плоскогубцы plaskagooptsi

plug (electrical) штепсельная
вилка shtepsyelna-ya veelka

(for car) свеча svyecha

(in sink) пробка propka

> Travel tip Electricity con-
> forms to the standard
> Continental 220 volts AC;
> most European appliances
> should work as long as
> you have an adaptor for
> two-pin round plugs. North
> Americans will need this,
> plus a transformer.

plumber сантехник santyeнneek

pm: 2pm два часа дня dva chasa
dnya

10pm десять часов вечера
dyesyat chasof vyechyera

poached egg яйцо-пашот
yitso-pashot

pocket карман karman

point: two point five две целых
пять десятых dvyeh tseliн pyat
dyesyatiн

there's no point нет смысла
nyet smiysla

poisonous ядовитый yadaveeti

Poland Польша polsha

police милиция meeleetsi-ya

call the police! вызовите
милицию! viyzaveetyeh
meeleetsi-yoo!

policeman милиционер
meeleetsi-anyer

police station отделение
милиции addyelyenee-yeh
meeleetsee-ee

policewoman женщина-
милиционер
Jensh-cheena-meeleetsi-anyer

Polish польский polskee

polish (for shoes) крем для обуви
kryem dlya oboovee

polite вежливый vyeJleevi

polluted загрязнённый
zagryaznyon-ni

pool (for swimming) бассейн
basyayn

poor (not rich) бедный byedni

(quality) низкокачественный
neeska-kachyestvyen-ni

pop music поп-музыка pop
moozika

pop singer (male/female) поп-
певец/певица pop pyevyets/
pyeveetsa

popular популярный papoolyarni

pork свинина sveeneena

port (for boats) порт port

(drink) портвейн partvyayn

porter (in hotel) швейцар
shvyaytsar

portrait портрет partryet

posh шикарный shikarni

possible возможный vazmoJni

is it possible to...?
возможно ли...? vazm**o**lnalee

as soon as possible как
можно быстрее как м**o**лна
bistr**yeh**-yeh

post (*noun*: mail) почта

pochta

(*verb*) отправлять/
отправить atpravl**yat**/
atpr**a**veet

could you post this for me?
вы не могли бы отправить

это? viy nyeh mag**lee**bi atpra**veet**
eta

postbox почтовый ящик
pachtovi **ya**sh-cheek

postcard открытка atk**riy**tka

postcode почтовый индекс
pachtovi **een**deks

poster плакат pla**kat**

poste restante до
востребования
da vastr**ye**bavanee-ya

post office почта **po**chta

potato картофель kar**to**fyel

pots and pans кухонная
посуда **koo**Han-na-ya
pa**soo**da

pottery керамика kye**ra**meeka

pound (money) фунт стерлингов
foont st**ye**rleengaf

power cut отключение
электричества atklyooch**ye**nee-
yeh elyekt**ree**chyestva

power point розетка ra**zye**tka

**practise: I want to practise
my Russian** я хочу
поупражняться в
русском языке ya Hach**oo**
pa-ooprajn**ya**tsa vr**oo**skam
yazik**yeh**

prawns крсветки kreev**vye**tkee

prefer: I prefer... я
предпочитаю... ya
pryetpacheet**a**-yoo...

pregnant беременная
byer**ye**myen-na-ya

prescription (for medicine)
рецепт ryets**ye**pt

present (gift) подарок pad**a**rak

president (of country) президент
pryezeed**ye**nt

pretty симпатичный
seempat**ee**chni

it's pretty expensive это
довольно дорого **e**ta dav**o**lna
d**o**raga

price цена tsen**a**

priest священник
svyash-ch**ye**n-neek

prime minister премьер-
министр pry**em**yer mee**nee**str

printed matter печатный
материал pech**a**tni matyer**ya**l

prison тюрьма tyoor**ma**

private частный ch**a**sni

private bathroom отдельная
ванная add**ye**lna-ya
v**a**n-na-ya

probably вероятно vyer**a**-**ya**tna

problem проблема prabl**ye**ma

no problem! нет проблем!
nyet prabl**ye**m

program(me) программа
pra**gra**m-ma

promise: I promise я обещаю
ya abyesh-cha-yoo

**pronounce: how is this
pronounced?** как это
произносится? kak **e**ta pra-
eezn**o**seetsa?

properly (repaired, locked etc) как
следует kak sl**ye**doo-yet

protection factor (of suntan
lotion) защитный фактор zash-
ch**ee**tni f**a**ktar

Protestant протестантский
pratyest**a**ntskee

public holiday официальный праздник afeetsalni prazneek

public toilet туалет too-alyet

pudding (*dessert*) десерт dyesyert

pull тянуть/потянуть tyanoot/ patyanoot

pullover свитер sveeter

puncture (*noun*) прокол prakol

purple фиолетовый fee-alyetavi

purse (*for money*) кошелёк kashelyok

(*US: handbag*) сумочка soomachka

push толкать/толкнуть talkat/ talknoot

pushchair детская коляска dyetska-ya kalyaska

put класть/положить klast/ palaJiyt

where can I put…? куда мне положить…? kooda mnyeh palaJiyt…?

could you put us up for the night? нельзя ли нам переночевать у вас? nyelzyalee nam pyeryenacheevat oo vas?

pyjamas пижама peeJama

Q

quality качество kachyestva

quarantine карантин karanteen

quarter четверть chyetvyert

question вопрос vapros

queue (*noun*) очередь ochyeryet

quick быстрый biystri

what's the quickest way

there? как туда побыстрее добраться? kak tooda pabistryeh-yeh dabratsa?

fancy a quick drink? не хотите пропустить стаканчик? nyeh Hateetyeh prapoosteet stakancheek?

quickly быстро biystra

quiet (*place, hotel*) тихий teeнее

quiet! тише! teesheh!

quite: that's quite right совершенно верно savyershen-na vyerna

quite a lot довольно много davolna mnoga

R

rabbit кролик kroleek

race (*for cars*) гонки pl gonkee

(*for runners*) забег zabyek

(*for horses*) скачки pl skachkee

racket (*tennis, squash*) ракетка rakyetka

radiator (*in room*) батарея bataryeh-ya

(*in car*) радиатор radee-atar

radio радио radee-o

on the radio по радио pa radee-o

rail: by rail поездом po-yezdam

railway железная дорога Jelyezna-ya daroga

rain (*noun*) дождь dosht

in the rain под дождём pad daJdyom

it's raining идёт дождь eedyot

dosht

raincoat плащ plash-ch

rape (*noun*) изнасилование eeznaseelavanee-yeh

rare (uncommon) редкий ryetkee

(steak) с кровью skrovyoo

rash (on skin) сыпь siyp

raspberry малина maleena

rat крыса kriysa

rate (for changing money) курс koors

rather: it's rather good очень неплохо ochyen nyeploha

I'd rather... (said by man/ woman) я предпочёл/ предпочла бы... ya pryetpachol/pryetpachla biy...

razor бритва breetva

razor blades лезвия бритвы lyezvee-ya breetvi

read читать/прочесть cheetat/ prachyest

ready готовый gatovi

are you ready? вы готовы? viy gatovi?

I'm not ready yet (said by man/ woman) я ещё не готов/готова ya yesh-cho nyeh gatof/gatova

when will it be ready? когда это будет готово? kagda eta boodyet gatova?

it should be ready in a couple of days это будет готово через пару дней eta boodyet gatova chyeryes paroo dnyay

real настоящий

nasta-yash-chee

really действительно dyestveetyelna

I'm really sorry я очень сожалею ya ochyen saJalyeh-yoo

that's really great! это замечательно! eta zamyechatyelna!

really? (doubt) серьёзно? syeryozna?

(polite interest) да? da?

rear lights задние фары zadnee-ee fari

rearview mirror зеркало заднего вида zyerkala zadnyeva veeda

reasonable (prices etc) умеренный oomyeryen-ni

receipt квитанция kveetantsi-ya

recently недавно nyedavna

reception (in hotel) служба размещения slooJba razmyesh-chyenee-ya

at reception в службе размещения fslooJbyeh razmyesh-chyenee-ya

reception desk конторка дежурного администратора kantorka dyeJoornava admeeneestratara

receptionist дежурный администратор dyeJoorni admeeneestratar

recognize узнать ooznat

recommend: could you recommend...? вы можете

порекомендовать…? viy
mo**j**etyeh paryekamyendava**t**…?

record (music) пластинка
plast**ee**nka

red красный kr**a**sni

red wine красное вино kr**a**sna-
yeh veen**o**

refund возмещение vazmyesh-
ch**ye**nee-yeh

   can I have a refund? могу
   я получить обратно деньги?
   mag**oo** ya palooch**ee**t abr**a**tna
   d**ye**ngee?

region область **o**blast

registered: by registered mail
заказной почтой zakazn**oy**
p**o**chti

registration number номер
машины n**o**myer mash**ii**ni

relative (*male/female*)
родственник/родственница
r**o**tstvyen-neek/
r**o**tstvyen-neetsa

religion религия rye**lee**egee-ya

remember: I don't remember
я не помню ya nyeh p**o**mnyoo

   I remember я помню ya
   p**o**mnyoo

   do you remember? вы
   помните? viy p**o**mneetyeh?

rent (*noun*: for apartment)
квартирная плата kvart**ee**rna-
ya pl**a**ta

   (*verb*: car etc) брать/взять
   напрокат brat/vzyat naprak**a**t

rented car взятая напрокат
машина vz**ya**ta-ya naprak**a**t
mash**ii**na

repair (*verb*) чинить/починить
cheen**ee**t/pacheen**ee**t

   can you repair it? вы
   можете это починить? viy
   mo**j**etyeh **e**ta pacheen**ee**t?

repeat повторять/
повторить paftar**ya**t/
paftar**ee**t

   could you repeat that?
   повторите, пожалуйста
   paftar**ee**tyeh, pa**j**alsta

reservation предварительный
заказ pryedvar**ee**tyelni zak**a**s

   **I'd like to make a
   reservation** (at hotel/theatre:
   said by a man/woman) я хотел/
   хотела бы заказать номер/
   билет ya нat**ye**l/нat**ye**la biy
   zakaz**a**t n**o**myer/beel**ye**t

> **I have a reservation** (at
> hotel/theatre) у меня заказан
> номер/билет oo myen**ya**
> zak**a**zan n**o**myer/beel**ye**t
>
> **what name please?** ваше
> имя, пожалуйста v**a**sheh
> **ee**mya, pa**j**alsta

DIALOGUE

reserve (*verb*) заказывать/
заказать заранее zak**a**zivat/
zakaz**a**t zar**a**nyeh-yeh

> **can I reserve a table for
> tonight?** могу я заказать
> столик на сегодня
> вечером? mag**oo** ya
> zakaz**a**t st**o**leek na syev**o**dnya
> v**ye**chyeram
>
> **yes madam, for how many**

DIALOGUE

people? да, пожалуйста, на сколько человек? da, paJalsta, na skolka chyelavyek?

for two на двоих na dva-eeH

and for what time? на какое время? na kako-yeh vryemya?

for eight o'clock на восемь часов na vosyem chasof

and could I have your name please? ваше имя, пожалуйста vasheh eemya, paJalsta

see **Basics** for spelling

---

rest: I need a rest мне нужно отдохнуть mnyeh nooJna ad-daHnoot

the rest of the group остальные члены группы astalniy-yeh chlyeni groop-pi

restaurant ресторан ryestaran

restaurant car вагон-ресторан vagon-ryestaran

rest room туалет too-alyet

retired: I'm retired я на пенсии ya na pyensee-ee

return: a return to... туда и обратно до... tooda ee abratna da...

return ticket обратный билет abratni beelyet

see **ticket**

reverse charge call разговор, оплачиваемый вызываемым лицом razgavor, aplacheeva-yemi viziva-yemim leetsom

reverse gear задний ход zadnee Hot

revolting отвратительный atvrateetyelni

rib ребро ryebro

rice рис rees

rich (person) богатый bagati

(food) жирный Jiyrni

ridiculous нелепый nyelyepi

right (correct) правильный praveelni

(not left) правый pravi

you were right вы были правы viy biylee pravi

that's right правильно praveelna

this can't be right не может такого быть nyeh moJet takova biyt

right! хорошо Harasho

is this the right road for...? я доеду по этой дороге до...? ya da-yedoo pa eti darogyeh da...?

on the right справа sprava

to the right направо naprava

turn right поверните направо pavyerneetyeh naprava

right-hand drive вождение по правой стороне vaJdyenee-yeh pa pravi staranyeh

ring (on finger) кольцо kaltso

I'll ring you я вам позвоню ya vam pazvanyoo

ring back перезвонить pyeryezvaneet

ripe (fruit) зрелый zryeli

rip-off: it's a rip-off это
обдираловка eta abdeera**lofka**

   rip-off prices грабительские
цены grab**ee**tyelskee-yeh ts**e**ni

risky рискованный reesk**o**van-ni

river река ry**e**ka

road дорога da**ro**ga

   is this the road for…? это
дорога до…? eta da**ro**ga da…?

   it's just down the road это
совсем близко отсюда eta
safs**yem** bl**ee**ska ats**yoo**da

road accident дорожная
катастрофа da**ro**Jna-ya
katastr**o**fa

road map дорожная карта
da**ro**Jna-ya k**a**rta

roadsign дорожный знак
da**ro**Jni znak

rob: I've been robbed меня
ограбили men**ya** agrabeelee

rock скала skal**a**

   (music) рок rok

   on the rocks (with ice) со
льдом sald**om**

roll (bread) булочка b**oo**lachka

Romania Румыния room**i**ynee-ya

roof крыша kr**i**ysha

room (in hotel) номер n**o**myer

   (in house) комната k**o**mnata

   in my room в моём номере
vma-**yom** n**o**myeryeh

room service обслуживание
в номере apsl**oo**Jivanee-yeh
vn**o**myeryeh

rope канат kan**a**t

rosé (wine) розовое вино r**o**zava-
yeh veen**o**

roughly (approximately)
приблизительно
preebleez**ee**tyelna

round: it's my round моя
очередь ma-**ya o**chyeryet

roundabout (for traffic) круговое
движение kroogav**o**-yeh
dvee**J**enee-yeh

route маршрут marshr**oo**t

   what's the best route to…?
как лучше добраться до…?
kak l**oo**chsheh dabr**a**tsa da…?

rubber (material) резина ry**e**z**ee**na

   (eraser) ластик l**a**steek

rubber band резинка ry**e**z**ee**nka

rubbish (waste) мусор m**oo**sar

   (poor quality goods) барахло
bar**a**Hlo

   rubbish! (nonsense) чепуха!
chyep**oo**Ha!

rucksack рюкзак ry**oo**kzak

rude грубый gr**oo**bi

ruins развалины razv**a**leeni

rum ром rom

   rum and Coke кока-кола с
ромом koka-k**o**la sr**o**mam

run (verb: person) бежать/
побежать bye**J**at/pabye**J**at

   **how often do the buses
run?** как часто ходят
автобусы? kak ch**a**sta H**o**dyat
aft**o**boosi?

   I've run out of money у
меня кончились деньги oo
men**ya** k**o**ncheelees dy**e**ngee

Russia Россия rass**ee**-ya

Russian (adj, man) русский
r**oo**skee

(woman) русская rooska-ya

(language) русский язык rooskee yaziyk

the Russians русские rooskee-yeh

S

sad грустный groosni

saddle (for bike, horse) седло syedlo

safe (not in danger) в безопасности vbyezapasnastee

(not dangerous) безопасный byezapasni

safety pin английская булавка angleeska-ya boolafka

sail (*verb*) плавать/плыть plavat/pliyt

sailing (sport) парусный спорт paroosni sport

salad салат salat

salad dressing заправка к салату zaprafka ksalatoo

salami салями salyamee

sale: for sale продаётся prada-yotsa

salmon лосось lasos

salt соль sol

same: the same то же самое toJeh sama-yeh

the same as this такой же как этот takoyJeh kak etat

the same again, please то же самое, пожалуйста toJeh sama-yeh, paJalsta

it's all the same to me мне

всё равно mnyeh fsyo ravno

sand песок pyesok

sandals сандали sandalee

sandwich бутерброд booterbrot

sanitary napkins/towels гигиенические прокладки geegee-yeneechyeskee-yeh praklatkee

Saturday суббота soobota

sauce соус so-oos

saucepan кастрюля kastryoolya

saucer блюдце blyootseh

sauna сауна sa-oona

sausage (salami) колбаса kalbasa

(frankfurter) сосиска saseeska

say говорить/сказать gavareet/skazat

how do you say… in Russian? как по-русски…? kak pa-rooskee…?

what did he say? что он сказал? shto on skazal?

she said… она сказала… ana skazala…

could you say that again? повторите, пожалуйста paftareetyeh, paJalsta

scarf (for neck) шарф sharf

(for head) платок platok

scenery пейзаж pyayzash

schedule (US: timetable) расписание raspeesanee-yeh

scheduled flight рейсовый полёт ryaysavi palyot

school школа shkola

scissors: a pair of scissors ножницы pl noJneetsi

scooter мотороллер matar**o**l-lyer

scotch виски v**ee**skee

Scotch tape клейкая лента kl**yay**ka-ya l**ye**nta

Scotland Шотландия shatl**a**ndee-ya

Scottish шотландский shatl**a**ntskee

I'm Scottish (*male/female*) я шотландец/шотландка ya shatl**a**ndyets/shatl**a**ntka

scrambled eggs яичница-болтунья ya-**ee**shneetsa-balt**oo**nya

scratch (*noun*) царапина tsar**a**peena

screw (*noun*) винт veent

screwdriver отвёртка atv**yo**rtka

sea море m**o**ryeh

by the sea у моря oo m**o**rya

seafood морские продукты marsk**ee**-yeh prad**oo**kti

search (*verb*) искать eesk**a**t

seasick: I feel seasick меня укачало men**ya** ookach**a**la

I get seasick меня укачивает men**ya** ook**a**cheeva-yet

seaside: by the seaside на море na m**o**ryeh

seat место m**ye**sta

is this seat taken? это место свободно? **e**ta m**ye**sta svab**o**dno?

seat belt ремень ryem**ye**n

secluded уединённый oo-yedeen**yo**n-ni

second (*adj*) второй ftar**oy**

(in time) секунда syek**oo**nda

just a second! секундочку! syek**oo**ndachkoo!

second class (travel etc) второй класс ftar**oy** klas

second floor третий этаж tr**ye**tee et**a**sh

(US) второй этаж ftar**oy** et**a**sh

second-hand подержанный pad**ye**rJan-ni

second-hand bookshop букинистический магазин bookeeneest**ee**chyeskee magaz**ee**n

see видеть/увидеть v**ee**dyet/oov**ee**dyet

can I see? можно посмотреть? m**o**Jna pasmatr**ye**t?

have you seen...? вы не видели...? viy nyeh v**ee**dyelee...?

I saw him this morning (said by man/woman) я видел/видела его сегодня утром ya v**ee**dyel/v**ee**dyela yev**o** syev**o**dnya **oo**tram

see you! пока! pak**a**!

I see (I understand) понятно pan**ya**tna

self-service самообслуживание sama-apsl**oo**Jivanee-yeh

sell продавать/продать pradav**a**t/prad**a**t

do you sell...? у вас продаётся...? oo vas prada-**yo**tsa...?

Sellotape клейкая лента kl**yay**ka-ya l**ye**nta

send посылать/послать pasil**a**t/pasl**a**t

I want to send this to England я хочу послать это в Англию ya nachoo paslat eta vanglee-yoo

senior citizen (*male/female*) пожилой человек/пожилая женщина paдiloy chyelavyek/ paдila-ya дensh-cheena

separate (*adj*) отдельный ad-dyelni

separated: we're separated мы разошлись miy razashlees

separately (pay, travel) отдельно ad-dyelna

September сентябрь syentyabr

septic септический syepteechyeskee

serious серьёзный syeryozni
(illness) опасный apasni

service charge плата за обслуживание plata za apslooJivanee-yeh

service station (for repairs) станция техобслуживания stantsi-ya tyeнapslooJivanee-ya
(for petrol) бензоколонка byenzakalonka

serviette салфетка salfyetka

set menu комплексный обед komplyeksni abyet

several несколько nyeskolka

sew шить/сшить shiyt/s-shiyt
could you sew this back on? вы не могли бы пришить это viy nyeh magleebi preeshiyt eta

sex секс seks

sexy привлекательный preevlyekatyelni

shade: in the shade в тени ftyenee

shake: to shake hands пожимать/пожать руку paдimat/paдat rookoo

shallow мелкий myelkee

shame: what a shame! как жаль! kak Jal!

shampoo шампунь shampoon
shampoo and set мытьё и укладка волос mityo ee ooklatka valos

share: to share a room жить в одной комнате Jiyt vadnoy komnatyeh
to share a table сидеть за одним столом seedyet za adneem stalom

sharp острый ostri

shattered: I'm shattered я совершенно без сил ya savyershen-na byes seel

shaver бритва breetva

shaving foam пена для бритья pyena dlya breetya

shaving point розетка для электробритвы razyetka dlya elyektrabreetvi

shawl шаль shal

she она ana
is she here? она здесь? ana zdyes?

sheet (for bed) простыня prastinya

shelf полка polka

shellfish моллюск malyoosk

sherry херес Hyeryes

ship корабль karabl

by ship на корабле na karablyeh

shirt рубашка roobashka

shit! чёрт! chort!

shock шок shok

I got an electric shock меня ударило током menya oodareela tokam

shocking ужасный ooJasni

shoe (man's/woman's) ботинок/ туфля bateenak/tooflya

a pair of shoes ботинки/ туфли bateenkee/tooflee

shoelaces шнурки shnoorkee

shoe polish крем для обуви kryem dlya oboovee

shoe repairer's мастерская по ремонту обуви mastyerska-ya pa ryemontoo oboovee

shop магазин magazeen

shopping: I'm going shopping я иду за покупками ya eedoo za pakoopkamee

shopping centre торговый центр targovi tsentr

shop window витрина veetreena

shore берег byeryek

short (person) невысокий nyevisokee

(time, journey) короткий karotkee

shortcut кратчайший путь kratchIshi poot

shorts шорты shorti

should: what should I do? что

мне делать? shto mnyeh dyelat?

you should… вам следует… vam slyedoo-yet…

you shouldn't… вам не следует… vam nyeh slyedoo-yet…

he should be back soon он должен скоро вернутся on dolJen skora vyernootsa

shoulder плечо plyecho

shout (verb) кричать/ крикнуть kreechat/kreeknoot

show (in theatre) представление pryetstavlyenee-yeh

could you show me? покажите, пожалуйста pakaJIytyeh, paJalsta

shower (of rain) ливень leevyen

(in bathroom) душ doosh

with shower с душем sdooshem

shower gel гель для душа gyel dlya doosha

shut (verb) закрывать/ закрыть zakrivat/zakriyt

when do you shut? когда вы закрываетесь? kagda viy zakriva-yetyes?

they're shut они закрыты anee zakriyti

I've shut myself out я не могу попасть внутрь ya nyeh magoo papast vnootr

shut up! замолчите! zamalcheetyeh!

shutter (on camera) затвор zatvor

(on window) ставень stavyen

shy застенчивый

zast**ye**ncheevi

sick (ill) больной baln**oy**

   I'm going to be sick (vomit)
   меня сейчас стошнит myen**ya**
   syech**a**s stashn**ee**t

   I feel sick меня тошнит
   men**ya** tashn**ee**t

side сторона staran**a**

   on the other side of the
   street на другой стороне
   улицы na droog**oy** staran**yeh**
   ooleetsi

side lights подфарники
   patf**a**rneekee

side street переулок pyer**ye**h-
   oolak

sidewalk тротуар tratoo-**ar**

   on the sidewalk на тротуаре
   na tratoo-**a**ryeh

sight: the sights of...
   достопримечательности
   ... dastapreemyech**a**tyelnastee...

sightseeing: we're going
   sightseeing мы идём
   осматривать
   достопримечательности
   miy eed**yo**m asm**a**treevat
   dastapreemyech**a**tyelnastee

sightseeing tour экскурсия
   eksk**oo**rsee-ya

sign (roadsign etc) знак znak

signature подпись p**o**tpees

signpost указатель ookaz**a**tyel

silence тишина teesh**i**na

silk шёлк sholk

silly глупый gl**oo**pi

silver серебро syeryebr**o**

similar похожий pah**o**Ji

simple (easy) простой prast**oy**

since: since last week с
   прошлой недели spr**o**shlı
   nyed**ye**lee

   since I got here (said by
   man/woman) с тех пор,
   как я приехал/приехала
   styeн por, kak ya pree-**ye**нal/
   pree-**ye**нala

sing петь/спеть pyet/spyet

singer (*male/female*) певец/
   певица pyev**ye**ts/pyev**ee**tsa

single: a single to... билет
   в один конец до... beel**ye**t
   vad**ee**n kan**ye**ts da...

   I'm single (said by man/woman)
   я не женат/замужем ya nyeh
   Jen**a**t/z**a**mooJem

single bed односпальная
   кровать adnasp**a**lna-ya krav**a**t

single room одноместный номер adnam**ye**sni **no**myer

single ticket билет в один конец beel**ye**t vad**ee**n kan**ye**ts

sink (in kitchen) раковина rak**a**veena

sister сестра syestr**a**

sister-in-law (wife's sister) своячениɕа sva-**ya**chyeneetsa (husband's sister) золовка zal**o**fka

sit: can I sit here? можно здесь сесть? m**o**ʝna zdyes syest?

is anyone sitting here? здесь кто-нибудь сидит? zdyes kto-neeboot seed**ee**t?

sit down садится/сесть sad**ee**tsa/syest

please, sit down садитесь, пожалуйста sad**ee**tyes, paʐ**a**lsta

size размер razm**ye**r

skate (*verb*) кататься на коньках kat**a**tsa na kank**a**н

skates коньки kank**ee**

skating rink каток kat**o**k

ski (*verb*) кататься на лыжах kat**a**tsa na l**iy**ʝaн

skin кожа k**o**ʝa

skinny тощий t**o**sh-chee

skirt юбка **yoo**pka

skis лыжи l**iy**ʝi

sky небо n**ye**ba

sleep (*verb*) спать/поспать spat/ paspat

did you sleep well? вам хорошо спалось? vam нar**a**sho spal**o**s?

sleeper (on train) спальный вагон sp**a**lni vag**o**n

sleeping bag спальный мешок sp**a**lni myesh**o**k

sleeping car спальный вагон sp**a**lni vag**o**n

sleeping pills снотворные таблетки snatv**o**rni-yeh tabl**ye**tkee

sleepy: I'm feeling sleepy меня клонит ко сну mye**ya** kl**o**neet ka snoo

sleeve рукав rook**a**f

slide (photographic) слайд slid

slippers тапочки t**a**pachkee

slippery скользкий sk**o**lskee

Slovakia Словакия slav**a**kee-ya

slow медленный m**ye**dlyen-ni

slow down! помедленнее, пожалуйста pam**ye**dleen-nyeh-yeh, paʐ**a**lsta

slowly медленно m**ye**dlyen-na

very slowly очень медленно **o**chyen m**ye**dlyen-na

could you speak more slowly? вы не могли бы говорить помедленнее? viy nyeh magl**ee**bi gavar**ee**t pam**ye**dleenyeh-yeh?

small маленький m**a**lyenkee

smell: it smells (smells bad) плохо пахнет pl**o**нa p**a**ннyet

smile (*verb*) улыбаться/ улыбнуться ool**i**batsa/ oolibn**oo**tsa

smoke (*noun*) дым diym

do you mind if I smoke? вы не возражаете, если я закурю? viy nyeh vazra**ʝa**-yetyeh, **ye**slee ya zakoor**yoo**?

I don't smoke я не курю ya
nyeh koor**yoo**

do you smoke? вы курите?
viy **koo**reetyeh?

snack: I'd just like a snack
(said by man/woman) я хотел/
хотела бы слегка перекусить
ya hat**yel**/hat**ye**la biy sl**ye**нka
pyeryekoos**eet**

sneeze (*verb*) чихать/
чихнуть chee**na**t/cheeHn**oot**

snorkel дыхательная трубка
di**na**tyelna-ya tr**oo**pka

snow снег snyek

it's snowing снег идёт snyek
eed**yot**

snowstorm метель myet**yel**

so так tak

this wine is so good
очень хорошее вино **o**chyen
Har**o**sheh-yeh veen**o**

it's so expensive это так
дорого **e**ta tak d**o**raga

not so much не так много
nyeh tak mn**o**ga

not so bad не так уж плохо

nyeh tak oosh pl**o**Ha

so am I, so do I я тоже ya
t**o**Jeh

so-so так себе tak seeb**yeh**

**soaking solution (for contact
lenses)** раствор для линз
rastv**o**r dlya leenz

soap мыло m**i**yla

soap powder стиральный
порошок steer**a**lni parash**o**k

sober трезвый tr**ye**zvi

sock носок nas**o**k

socket (electrical) розетка
raz**ye**tka

soda (water) газированная
вода gazeer**o**van-na-ya vad**a**

sofa диван deev**a**n

soft (material etc) мягкий m**ya**Hkee

soft-boiled egg яйцо всмятку
yits**o** fsm**ya**tkoo

soft drink безалкогольный
напиток byezalkag**o**lni nap**ee**tak

soft lenses мягкие линзы
m**ya**Hkee-yeh l**ee**nzi

soldier солдат sald**a**t

sole (of foot) ступня stoop**n**ya

(of shoe) подошва pad**o**shva

could you put new soles on these? вы не могли бы поставить сюда новые подмётки? viy nyeh mag**lee**bi pastav**ee**t syood**a** n**o**vi-yeh padm**yot**keh?

some: can I have some? дайте мне, пожалуйста d**i**tyeh mnyeh, paJ**a**lsta

can I have some water/ bread? дайте мне, пожалуйста воды/хлеба d**i**tyeh mnyeh, paJ**a**lsta, vad**iy**/Hl**ye**ba

somebody, someone кто-то kt**o**-ta

something что-нибудь sht**o**-neeboot

something to eat что-нибудь поесть sht**o**-neeboot pa-**ye**st

sometimes иногда eenagd**a**

somewhere где-нибудь gd**yeh**-neeboot

son сын siyn

song песня p**ye**snya

son-in-law зять zyat

soon скоро sk**o**ra

I'll be back soon я скоро вернусь ya sk**o**ra vyern**oos**

as soon as possible как можно скорее kak m**o**Jna skar**yeh**-yeh

sore: it's sore болит bal**ee**t

sore throat: I've got a sore throat у меня болит горло oo myen**ya** bal**ee**t g**o**rla

sorry: I'm sorry прошу прощения prash**oo** prash-ch**ye**nee-ya

sorry! извините! eezveen**ee**tyeh!

sorry? (didn't understand) простите? prast**ee**tyeh?

sort: what sort of...? какой...? kak**oy**...?

this sort такой tak**oy**

soup суп soop

sour (taste) кислый k**ee**sli

soured cream сметана smet**a**na

south юг yook

in the south на юге na **yoo**gyeh

South Africa Южная Африка **yoo**Jna-ya **a**freeka

South African (adj) южно-африканский **yoo**Jna-afreek**a**nskee

I'm South African я из Южной Африки ya eez **yoo**Jni **a**freekee

southeast юго-восточный yooga-vast**o**chni

southern южный **yoo**Jni

southwest юго-западный yooga-z**a**padni

souvenir сувенир soovyen**ee**r

Soviet советский sav**ye**tskee

Soviet Union Советский Союз sav**ye**tskee sa-**yoos**

spade лопата lap**a**ta

Spain Испания eesp**a**nee-ya

Spanish (adj) испанский eesp**a**nskee

spanner гаечный ключ
ga-yechni klyooch

spare part запчасть zapchast

spares запчасти zapchastee

spare tyre запасная шина
zapasna-ya shiyna

speak: do you speak English?
вы говорите по-английски?
viy gavareetyeh pa-angleeskee?

I don't speak Russian я не
говорю по-русски ya nyeh
gavaryoo pa-rooskee

can I speak to Nikolai?
можно Николая,
пожалуйста? moJna
neekala-ya, paJalsta?

who's calling? кто
говорит? kto gavareet?

it's Patricia это Патриша
eta patreesha

**I'm sorry, he's not in,
can I take a message?**
извините, его нет, вы
хотите что-нибудь
передать? eezveeneetyeh,
yevo nyet, viy Hateetyeh shto-
neeboot pyeryedat?

**no thanks, I'll call back
later** нет, спасибо, я
перезвоню попозже nyet,
spaseeba, ya pyeryezvanyoo
papoJ-Jeh

please tell him I called
пожалуйста, передайте
ему, что я звонила
paJalsta, pyeryedltyeh yemoo,
shto ya zvaneela

spectacles очки achkee

speed (*noun*) скорость skorast

speed limit максимальная
скорость makseemalna-ya
skorast

spell: how do you spell it? как
это пишется по буквам? kak
eta peeshetsa pa bookvam?

see **alphabet**

spend тратить/потратить
trateet/patrateet

spider паук pa-ook

spin-dryer центробежная
сушилка tsentrabyeJna-ya
sooshiylka

spoon ложка loshka

sport спорт sport

> **Travel tip** It's widely believed
> in Russia that baseball
> (*baysbol*) derives from the
> ancient Russian game of *lapta*
> – which might explain the
> success of the national team
> on the European circuit, and
> the excellence of Moscow
> teams such as Balashikha
> Tornado and TsKA. The
> season runs from April to
> October, with the Russian
> Championship in July.

sprain: I've sprained my...
(said by man/woman) я
растянул/растянула... ya
rastyanool/rastyanoola...

spring (of car, seat) рессора
ryes-sora

(season) весна vyesna

in the spring весной vyesnoy

square (in town) площадь plosh-chat

stairs лестница lyesneetsa

stale несвежий nyesvyeji

stalls партер parter

stamp (*noun*) марка marka

DIALOGUE

how much is a stamp for England? сколько стоит марка для Англии? skolka sto-eet marka dlya anglee-ee?

what are you sending? что вы посылаете shto viy pasila-yetyeh?

this postcard эту открытку etoo atkriytkoo

star звезда zvyezda

start (*noun*) начало nachala

(*verb*) начинать/начать nacheenat/nachat

when does it start? когда начало? kagda nachala?

my car won't start моя машина не заводится ma-ya mashiyna nyeh zavodeetsa

starter (food) закуска zakooska

starving: I'm starving я умираю от голода ya oomeera-yoo at golada

state (country) государство gasoodarstva

(*adj*) государственный gasoodarstvyen-ni

the States штаты shtati

station (rail) вокзал vakzal

(underground, bus) станция stantsi-ya

stationery канцелярские принадлежности kantselyarskee-yeh preenadlyeJnastee

statue статуя statoo-ya

stay: where are you staying? где вы остановились? gdyeh viy astanaveelees?

I'm staying at... (said by man/woman) я остановился/остановилась в... ya astanaveelsa/astanaveelas v...

I'd like to stay another two nights (said by man/woman) я бы хотел/хотела остаться ещё на пару суток yabi hatyel/hatyela astatsa yesh-cho na paroo sootak

steak бифштекс beefshteks

steal красть/украсть krast/ookrast

my bag has been stolen у меня украли сумку oo menya ookralee soomkoo

steep (hill) крутой krootoy

step: on the steps на ступеньках na stoopyenkaH

stereo стерео styeryeh-o

sterling фунт стерлингов foont styerleengaf

steward (on plane) стюард styoo-art

stewardess стюардесса styoo-ardes-sa

still: I'm still here я ещё здесь ya yesh-cho zdyes

is he still there? он ещё здесь? on yesh-cho zdyes?

keep still! не двигайтесь!

nyeh dveegityes!

sting: I've been stung by a wasp меня укусила оса menya ookooseela asa

stockings чулки choolkee

stomach желудок Jeloodak

stomach ache: I have stomach ache у меня болит живот oo menya baleet Jivot

stone (rock) камень kamyen

stop (*verb*) останавливать/остановить astanavleevat/astanaveet

stop here, please (to taxi driver etc) пожалуйста, остановитесь здесь paJalsta, astanaveetyes zdyes

do you stop near...? вы останавливаетесь у...? viy astanavleeva-yetyes oo...?

stop it! прекратите! pryekrateetyeh!

stopover остановка (в пути) astanofka (fpootee)

storm буря boorya

St Petersburg Санкт-Петербург sankt-peetyerboork

straight прямой pryamoy

(whisky etc) неразбавленный nyerazbavlyen-ni

it's straight ahead это прямо eta pryama

straightaway немедленно nyemyedlyen-na

strange (odd) странный stran-ni

stranger (*male/female*) незнакомец/незнакомка nyeznakomyets/nyeznakomka

I'm a stranger here (said by man/woman) я здесь чужой/чужая ya zdyes chooJoy/chooJa-ya

strap (on watch, suitcase) ремешок ryemyeshok

(on dress) бретелька bryetelka

strawberry клубника kloobneeka

stream ручей roochay

street улица ooleetsa

on the street на улице na ooleetseh

streetmap план города plan gorada

string верёвка vyeryofka

strong (person, material, taste) сильный seelni

(drink) крепкий kryepkee

stuck: it's stuck застряло zastryala

student (male/female) студент/студентка stoodyent/stoodyentka

stupid глупый gloopi

suburb пригород preegarat

subway подземный переход padzyemni pyeryeHot

(US: underground) метро myetro

suede замша zamsha

sugar сахар saнar

suit (*noun*) костюм kastyoom

it doesn't suit me (jacket etc) мне это не идёт mnyeh eta nyeh eedyot

it suits you вам это идёт vam eta eedyot

suitcase чемодан chyemadan

summer лето lyeta

in the summer летом l**y**etam

sun солнце s**o**ntseh

in the sun на солнце na s**o**ntseh

out of the sun в тени vt**y**en**ee**

sunbathe загорать zagar**a**t

sunblock средство против загара sr**y**etstva pr**o**teef zag**a**ra

sunburn солнечный ожог s**o**lnyechni aj**o**k

sunburnt (burnt) обгорелый abgar**y**eli

Sunday воскресенье vaskryes**y**enyeh

sunglasses очки от солнца achk**ee** at s**o**ntsa

sunny: it's sunny солнечно s**o**lnyechna

sunset закат zak**a**t

sunshade зонтик от солнца z**o**nteek at s**o**ntsa

sunshine солнечный свет s**o**lnyechni sv**y**et

sunstroke солнечный удар s**o**lnyechni **oo**dar

suntan загар zag**a**r

suntan lotion лосьон для загара las**y**on dlya zag**a**ra

suntanned загорелый zagar**y**eli

suntan oil масло для загара m**a**sla dlya zag**a**ra

super замечательный zam**y**ech**a**tyelni

supermarket универсам oon**ee**vyers**a**m, супермаркет soop**y**ermark**y**et

supper ужин **oo**jin

supplement (extra charge)

доплата dapl**a**ta

sure: are you sure? вы уверены? viy oov**y**er**y**eni?

I'm sure (said by man/woman) я уверен/уверена ya oov**y**er**y**en/ oov**y**er**y**ena

sure! конечно! kan**y**eshna!

surname фамилия fam**ee**lee-ya

sweater свитер sv**ee**ter

sweatshirt спортивная майка sport**ee**vna-ya m**i**ka

Sweden Швеция shv**y**etsi-ya

Swedish (adj) шведский shv**y**etskee

sweet (taste) сладкий sl**a**tkee

(noun: dessert) десерт dyes**y**ert

sweets конфеты kanf**y**eti

swelling опухоль **o**poo**H**al

swim (verb) плавать/ поплавать pl**a**vat/papl**a**vat

I'm going for a swim я иду плавать ya eed**oo** pl**a**vat

let's go for a swim пойдём поплаваем pid**y**om papl**a**va-yem

swimming costume купальник koop**a**lneek

swimming pool бассейн bas**y**ayn

swimming trunks плавки pl**a**fkee

Swiss швейцарский shv**y**ets**a**rskee

switch (noun) выключатель vikly**o**ch**a**tyel

switch off выключать/ выключить vikly**o**ch**a**t/ v**i**ykly**o**och**ee**t

switch on включать/включить

fklyoochat/fklyoocheet

Switzerland Швейцария
shvyetsaree-ya

swollen распухший raspooHshi

T

table стол stol

a table for two столик на
двоих stoleek na dva-eeH

tablecloth скатерть skatyert

table tennis настольный
теннис nastolni tenees

table wine столовое вино
stalova-yeh veeno

tailor портной partnoy

take (verb: lead) брать/взять
brat/vzyat

(accept) принимать/принять
preeneemat/preenyat

can you take me to the…?
вы можете отвезти меня в…?
viy moJetyeh atvestee menya
v…?

do you take credit cards?
вы принимаете кредитные
карточки? viy
preeneema-yetyeh kryedeetni-yeh
kartachkee?

fine, I'll take it хорошо, я
возьму это Harasho, ya vazmoo
eta

can I take this? (leaflet etc)
можно это взять? moJna eta
vzyat?

how long does it take?
сколько времени это займёт?
skolka vryemyenee eta zimyot?

it takes three hours это
займёт три часа eta zimyot tree
chasa

is this seat taken? это
место свободно? eta myesta
svabodna?

hamburger to take away
гамбургер на вынос
gamboorgyer na viynas

can you take a little off
here? (to hairdresser) вы
можете немного подстричь
здесь viy moJetyeh nyemnoga
patstreech zdyes?

talcum powder тальк tallk

talk (verb) говорить/
поговорить gavareet/
pagavareet

tall высокий visokee

tampons тампоны tamponi

tan загар zagar

to get a tan загореть zagaryet

tap кран kran

tape measure рулетка roolyetka

tape recorder магнитофон
magneetafon

taste (noun) вкус fkoos

can I taste it? можно
попробовать? moJna
paprobavat?

taxi такси taksee

will you get me a taxi?
вызовите для меня такси,
пожалуйста viyzaveetyeh dlya
myenya taksee, paJalsta

where can I find a taxi? где
можно поймать такси? gdyeh
moJna pimat taksee?

to the airport/to the... Hotel, please в аэропорт/ в гостиницу..., пожалуйста va-eraport/ vgasteeneetsoo..., paｊalsta

how much will it be? сколько это будет стоить? skolka eta boodyet sto-eet?

60,000 roubles шестьдесят тысяч рублей shezdyesyat tiysyach rooblyay

that's fine right here thanks я выйду здесь, спасибо ya viydoo zdyes, spaseeba

taxi driver таксист takseest

taxi rank стоянка такси sta-yanka taksee

tea (drink) чай chｊ

one tea/two teas, please один чай/два чая, пожалуйста adeen chｊ/dva cha-ya, paｊalsta

tea with milk чай с молоком chｊ smalakom

tea with lemon чай с лимоном chｊ sleemonam

teabags чайные пакетики chｊni-yeh pakyeteekee

teach: could you teach me? вы могли бы меня научить...? viy magleebi menya na-oocheet...?

teacher (male/female) учитель/ учительница oocheetyel/ oocheetyelneetsa

team команда kamanda

teaspoon чайная ложка chｊna-ya loshka

tea towel чайное полотенце chｊna-yeh palatyentseh

teenager подросток padrostak

telephone телефон tyelyefon
see **phone**

television (set) телевизор tyelyeveezar

(medium) телевидение tyelyeveedyenyeh

tell: could you tell him...? скажите ему, пожалуйста... skaｊiytyeh yemoo, paｊalsta...

could you tell me where...? вы не скажете, где...? viy nyeh skaｊityeh, gdyeh...?

temperature (weather) температура tyempyeratoora

tennis теннис ten-nees

tent палатка palatka

term (at university, school) семестр syemyestr

terminus (rail, underground) конечная станция kanyechna-ya stantsi-ya

(bus, tram) конечная остановка kanyechna-ya astanofka

terrible ужасный ooｊasni

terrific замечательный zamyechatyelni

text (verb) отправлять/ отправить SMS atpravlyat/ atpraveet

text (message) SMS, смс es-em-es

than чем chyem

smaller than... меньше, чем... m**ye**nsheh, chyem...

thank: thank you/thanks спасибо spas**ee**ba

thank you very much большое спасибо balsh**o**-yeh spas**ee**ba

thanks for the lift спасибо, что подвезли spas**ee**ba, shto padvyezl**ee**

no, thanks нет, спасибо nyet, spas**ee**ba

thanks спасибо spas**ee**ba
that's OK, don't mention it не за что n**ye**zashto

that тот tot, та ta, то to

that boy тот мальчик tot m**a**lcheek

that girl та девочка ta d**ye**vachka

that one тот tot, та ta, то to

I hope that... я надеюсь, что... ya nad**yeh**-yoos, shto...

that's great отлично atl**ee**chna

is that...? это...? **e**ta...?

that's it (that's right) точно t**o**chna

thaw (*noun*) оттепель **o**t-tyepyel

the Russian has no word for 'the'

theatre театр tyeh-**a**tr

their/theirs их eeн

them: I'll tell them я им скажу ya eem ska**J**oo

I know them я их знаю ya eeн zna-yoo

for them для них dlya neeн

with them с ними sn**ee**mee

to them им eem

who? -- them кто? – они kto? - an**ee**

then (at that time) тогда tagd**a**

(after that) потом pat**o**m

there там tam

over there вон там von tam

up there там, наверху tam, navyerн**oo**

is there/are there...? есть ли...? **ye**stlee...?

there you are (giving something) вот, пожалуйста vot, pa**J**alsta

thermometer термометр tyerm**o**myetr

Thermos flask термос t**e**rmas

these эти **e**tee

I'd like these (said by man/ woman) я бы хотел/хотела вот эти **ya**bi нat**ye**l/нat**ye**la vot **e**tee

they они an**ee**

thick густой goost**oy**

(stupid) тупой toop**oy**

thief (*male/female*) вор/воровка vor/var**o**fka

thigh бедро byedr**o**

thin (person) худой нood**oy**

(thing) тонкий t**o**nkee

thing вещь vyesh-ch

my things мои вещи ma-**ee** v**ye**sh-chee

think думать/подумать d**oo**mat/ pad**oo**mat

I think so думаю, да d**oo**ma-yoo, da

I don't think so я так не думаю ya tak nyeh dooma-yoo

I'll think about it я подумаю об этом ya padooma-yoo ab etam

third третий tryetee

thirsty: I'm thirsty мне хочется пить mnyeh Hochyetsa peet

this этот etat, эта eta, это eto

this boy этот мальчик etat malcheek

this girl эта девочка eta dyevachka

this one этот etat, эта eta, это eta

this is my wife это моя жена eta ma-ya Jena

is this...? это...? eta...?

those те tyeh

which ones? – those какие? – те kakee-yeh? – tyeh

thread (noun) нитка neetka

throat горло gorla

throat pastilles пастилки для горла pasteelkee dlya gorla

through через chyeryes

does it go through...? (train, bus) он проезжает через...? on pra-yeJ-Ja-yet chyeryes...?

throw бросать/бросить brasat/broseet

throw away выбрасывать/выбросить vibrasivat/viybraseet

thumb большой палец balshoy palyets

thunderstorm гроза graza

Thursday четверг chyetvyerk

ticket билет beelyet

(for bus) талон talon

DIALOGUE

a return to Sergiev Posad обратный билет до сергиева посада abratni beelyet da syergee-yeva pasada

coming back when? когда обратно? kagda abratna?

today/next Tuesday сегодня/в следующий вторник syevodnya/fslyedoosh-chee ftorneek

that will be 10,000 roubles (это будет) десять тысяч рублей (eta boodyet) dyesyat tiysyach rooblyay

ticket office билетная касса beelyetna-ya kas-sa

ticket punch компостер kampostyer

tie (necktie) галстук galstook

tight (clothes etc) тесный tyesni

it's too tight тесновато tyesnavata

tights колготки kalgotkee

till касса kas-sa

time время vryemya

what's the time? который час? katori chas?

this time в этот раз vetat ras

last time в прошлый раз fproshli ras

next time в следующий раз fslyedoosh-chee ras

three times три раза tree raza

timetable расписание raspeesanee-yeh

tin (can) консервная банка kanservna-ya banka

tinfoil оловянная фольга alavyan-na-ya falga

tin-opener консервный нож kanservni nosh

tiny крошечный kroshechni

tip (to waiter etc) чаевые pl cha-yeviy-yeh

tired усталый oostali

  I'm tired (said by man/woman) я устал/устала ya oostal/oostala

tissues бумажные носовые платки boomaлni-yeh nasaviy-yeh platkee

to: **to Moscow/London** в Москву/в Лондон vmaskvoo/vlondan

  to Russia/England в Россию/Англию vrassee-yoo/vanglee-yoo

  to the post office на почту na pochtoo

toast (bread) гренок gryenok

tobacco табак tabak

today сегодня syevodnya

toe палец ноги palyets nagee

together вместе vmyestyeh

  we're together (in shop etc) мы вместе miy vmyestyeh

toilet туалет too-alyet

  where is the toilet? где туалет? gdyeh too-alyet?

  I have to go to the toilet мне нужно в туалет mnyeh nooлna ftoo-alyet

toilet paper туалетная бумага too-alyetna-ya boomaga

token жетон лeton

tomato помидор pameedor

tomato juice томатный сок tamatni sok

tomato ketchup кетчуп kyetchoop

tomorrow завтра zaftra

  tomorrow morning завтра утром zaftra ootram

  the day after tomorrow послезавтра poslyezaftra

toner (cosmetic) тонизирующий лосьон taneezeeroo-yoosh-chee lasyon

tongue язык yazik

tonic (water) тоник toneek

tonight сегодня вечером syevodnya vyechyeram

tonsillitis тонзиллит tanzeeleet

too (excessively) слишком sleeshkam

  (also) тоже toлeh

  too hot слишком жарко sleeshkam лarka

  too much слишком много sleeshkam mnoga

  me too я тоже ya toлeh

tooth зуб zoop

toothache зубная боль zoobna-ya bol

toothbrush зубная щётка zoobna-ya sh-chotka

toothpaste зубная паста zoobna-ya pasta

top: **on top of...** на... na...

  at the top наверху navyerhoo

top floor верхний этаж vyerнnee

etash

topless с обнажённой грудью sabnaJon-ni gr**oo**dyoo

torch фонарик fan**a**reek

total (*noun*) итог eet**o**g

tour (*noun*) экскурсия eksk**oo**rsee-ya

   is there a tour of...? есть ли экскурсия по...? y**e**stlee eksk**oo**rsee-ya pa...?

tour guide (*male/female*) экскурсовод eksk**oo**rsav**o**t

tourist (*male/female*) турист/туристка toor**ee**st/toor**ee**stka

tour operator бюро путешествий by**oo**ro pootyesh**e**stvee

towards к k

towel полотенце palat**ye**ntseh

town город g**o**rat

   in town в городе vg**o**radyeh

   just out of town за городом z**a**garadam

town centre центр города tsentr g**o**rada

town hall мэрия m**e**ree-ya

toy игрушка eegr**oo**shka

track (US: platform) платформа platf**o**rma

tracksuit тренировочный костюм tryeneer**o**vachni kast**yoo**m

traditional традиционный tradeetsi-**o**n-ni

traffic движение dvee**J**enee-yeh

traffic jam пробка pr**o**pka

traffic lights светофор svyetaf**o**r

train поезд p**o**-yest

   by train поездом p**o**-yezdam

DIALOGUE

   is this the train for Ufa? это поезд до Уфы? **e**ta p**o**-yest da oof**i**y?

   sure да да

   no, you want that platform there нет, вам нужна та платформа nyet, vam n**oo**Jna ta platf**o**rma

trainers (shoes) кроссовки kras**o**fkee

train station железнодорожная станция Jelyeznadar**o**Jna-ya st**a**ntsi-ya

tram трамвай tramv**I**

translate переводить/перевести pyeryevad**ee**t/pyeryeh-vyest**ee**

   would you translate that? переведите это, пожалуйста pyeryeh-vyed**ee**tyeh **e**ta, pa**J**alsta

translator (*male/female*) переводчик/переводчица pyeryev**o**tcheek/pyeryev**o**tcheetsa

trash мусор m**oo**sar

trash can мусорное ведро m**oo**sarna-yeh vyedr**o**

travel путешествовать pootyesh**e**stvavat

   we're travelling around мы путешествуем miy pootyesh**e**stvoo-yem

travel agent's бюро путешествий by**oo**ro pootyesh**e**stvee

traveller's cheque дорожный чек daroJni chyek

tray поднос padnos

tree дерево dyereva

tremendous (large) огромный agromni

(splendid) замечательный zamyechatyelni

trendy модный modni

trim: just a trim please (to hairdresser) немного подровняйте, пожалуйста nyemnoga padravnyItyeh, paJalsta

trip (excursion) экскурсия ekskoorsee-ya

I'd like to go on a trip to… я хочу съездить в…ya Hachoo syezdeet v…

trolley тележка tyelyeshka

trolley bus троллейбус tralyayboos

trouble неприятность nyepree-yatnast

I'm having trouble with… у меня проблемы с… oo menya prablyemi s…

trousers брюки bryookee

true верно vyerna

that's not true это неправда eta nyepravda

trunk (US: of car) багажник bagaJneek

trunks (swimming) плавки plafkee

try (verb) пробовать/ попробовать probavat/ paprobavat

can I try it? можно я попробую moJna ya paproboo-yoo

try on мерить/померить myereet/pamyereet

can I try it on? можно померить? moJna pamyereet?

T-shirt футболка footbolka

Tuesday вторник ftorneek

tuna тунец toonyets

tunnel туннель toonel

turn: turn left/right повернуть налево/направо pavyernoot nalyeva/naprava

turn off: where do I turn off? где мне надо свернуть? gdyeh mnyeh nada svyernoot?

can you turn the heating off? вы можете выключить отопление? viy moJetyeh viyklyoocheet ataplyenee-yeh?

turn on: can you turn the heating on? вы можете включить отопление? viy moJetyeh fklyoocheet ataplyenee-yeh?

turning (in road) поворот pavarot

TV (set) телевизор tyelyeveezar

(medium) телевидение tyelyeveedyenyeh

tweezers пинцет peentset

twice дважды dvaJdi

twice as much в два раза больше vdva raza bolsheh

twin beds две односпальные кровати dvyeh adnaspalni-yeh kravatee

twin room номер с двумя

кроватями nomyer sdvoomya
kpavatyemee

**twist: I've twisted my
ankle** (said by man/woman) я
подвернул/подвернула ногу ya
padvyernool/padvyernoola nogoo

type (*noun*) тип teep

another type of…… другого
типа… droogova teepa

typical типичный teepeechni

tyre шина shiyna

ugly некрасивый nyekraseevi

UK Соединённое Королевство
sa-yedeenyon-na-yeh karalyefstva

Ukraine Украина ookra-eena

Ukrainian (*adj*) украинский
ookra-eenskee

ulcer язва yazva

umbrella зонтик zonteck

uncle дядя dyadya

uncomfortable неудобный
nyeh-oodobni

unconscious без сознания byes
saznanee-ya

under (in position) под pot
(less than) меньше myensheh

underdone (meat)
недожаренный
nyedaJaryen-ni

underground (railway) метро
myetro

underpants трусы troosiy

understand: I understand я
понимаю ya paneema-yoo

I don't understand я не
понимаю ya nyeh paneema-yoo

do you understand? вы
понимаете? viy paneema-
yetyeh?

unemployed безработный
byezrabotni

unfashionable немодный
nyemodni

United States Соединённые
Штаты sa-yedeenyon-ni-yeh
shtati

university университет
ooneevyerseetyet

unleaded petrol
неэтилированный бензин
nyeh-eteeleeravan-ni byenzeen

unlimited mileage
неограниченный
километраж nyeh-
agraneechyen-ni keelamyetrash

unlock открывать/открыть
atkrivat/atrkriyt

unpack распаковывать/
распаковать raspakovivat/
raspakavat

until до do

unusual необыкновенный
nyeh-abiknavyen-ni

up вверх v-vyerн

up there там наверху tam
navyerнoo

he's not up yet он ещё не
встал on yesh-cho nyeh fstal

what's up? в чём дело? fchom
dyela?

upmarket элитарный eleetarni

upset stomach расстройство

желудка rastr**oy**stva Jel**oo**tka

upside-down вверх дном
v-vyerн dnom

upstairs наверху navyerн**oo**

up-to-date современный
savryem**y**en-ni

urgent срочный sr**o**chni

us мы miy

with us с нами sn**a**mee

for us для нас dlya nas

USA США seh-sheh-**a**

use (*verb*) пользоваться/
воспользоваться p**o**lzavatsa/
vasp**o**lzavatsa

may I use your pen? можно
воспользоваться вашей
ручкой? m**o**Jna vasp**o**lzavatsa
v**a**shay r**oo**chkI?

useful полезный pal**y**ezni

usual обыкновенный
abiknav**y**en-ni

the usual (*drink etc*) то, что
обычно to, shto ab**i**ychna

usually обычно ab**i**ychna

V

**vacancy: do you have any
vacancies?** у вас есть
свободные номера? oo vas yest
svab**o**dni-yeh namyer**a**?

vacation отпуск **o**tpoosk

on vacation в отпуске
v**o**tpooskyeh

vaccination прививка
preev**ee**fka

vacuum cleaner пылесос

pilyes**o**s

valid (*ticket etc*)
действительный
dyaystv**ee**tyelni

how long is it valid for?
на сколько времени он
действителен? na sk**o**lka
vr**y**emyenee on
dyaystv**ee**tyelyen?

valley долина dal**ee**na

valuable (*adj*) ценный ts**e**n-ni

**can I leave my valuables
here?** можно оставить здесь
ценные вещи? m**o**Jna ast**a**veet
zdyes ts**e**n-ni-yeh v**y**esh-chee?

value ценность ts**e**n-nast

van фургон foorg**o**n

vanilla ваниль van**ee**l

a vanilla ice cream
ванильное мороженое
van**ee**lna-yeh mar**o**Jena-yeh

vase ваза v**a**sa

veal телятина tyel**y**ateena

vegetables овощи **o**vash-chee

vegetarian (*noun: male/female*)
вегетарианец/вегетарианка
vyegeetaree-**a**nyets/vyegeetaree-
anka

vending machine (торговый)
автомат (t**a**rgovi) aftam**a**t

very очень **o**chyen

very little for me совсем
чуть-чуть для меня safs**y**em
choot-choot dlya myen**ya**

I like it very much мне
очень нравится mnyeh **o**chyen
nr**a**veetsa

vest (*under shirt*) майка m**I**ka

via через ch**ye**ryes

video (*noun:* film) видео v**ee**dee-o

view вид veet

village деревня dyer**ye**vnya

vinegar уксус **oo**ksoos

visa виза v**ee**za

visit (*verb*) посещать/посетить pasyesh-chat/pasyet**ee**t

> **I'd like to visit…** (said by man/ woman) я хотел/хотела бы посетить… ya нat**ye**l/нat**ye**la biy pasyet**ee**t…

vital: it's vital that… абсолютно необходимо, чтобы… apsal**yoo**tna nyeh-apнad**ee**ma, sht**o**bi…

vodka водка v**o**tka

> Travel tip Vodka is the national drink – its name means something like "a little drop of water". Normally served chilled, vodka is drunk neat in one gulp, followed by a mouthful of food, such as pickled herring, cucumber or mushrooms; many people inhale deeply before tossing the liquor down their throats.

voice голос g**o**las

voltage напряжение napreeJ**ye**nee-yeh

vomit тошнить/стошнить tashn**ee**t/stashn**ee**t

W

waist талия t**a**lee-ya

waistcoat жилет Jil**ye**t

wait ждать/подождать Jdat/ padaJd**a**t

> **wait for me** подождите меня padaJd**ee**tyeh men**ya**

> **don't wait for me** не ждите меня nyeh Jd**ee**tyeh myen**ya**

> **can I wait until my wife/ my friend gets here?** я могу подождать до прихода моей жены/моего друга? ya mag**oo** padaJd**a**t da preeн**o**da ma-**yay** Jen**iy**/ma-yev**o** dr**oo**ga?

> **can you do it while I wait?** вы можете это сделать при мне? viy m**o**Jetyeh **e**ta zd**ye**lat pree mnyeh?

> **could you wait here for me?** вы можете меня здесь подождать? viy m**o**Jetyeh myen**ya** zdyes padaJd**a**t?

waiter официант afeetsi-**a**nt

> **waiter!** официант! afeetsi-**a**nt!

waiting room (doctor's etc) приёмная pree-**yo**mna-ya (station) зал ожидания zal aJid**a**nee-ya

waitress официантка afeetsi-**a**ntka

> **waitress!** девушка! d**ye**vooshka!

wake: can you wake me up at 5.30? пожалуйста, разбудите меня в половине шестого

paɹalsta, razbood**ee**tyeh men**ya**
fpalav**ee**nyeh shest**o**va

wake-up call телефонный
будильник tyelyef**o**n-ni
bood**ee**lneek

Wales Уэльс oo-**e**ls

walk: is it a long walk? это
далеко пешком? **e**ta dalyek**o**
pyeshk**o**m?

it's only a short walk это в
нескольких шагах отсюда
eta vn**ye**skalkeeн shag**a**н
atsy**oo**da

I'll walk я пойду пешком ya
pid**oo** pyeshk**o**m

I'm going for a walk я
иду прогуляться ya eed**oo**
pragool**ya**tsa

wall стена styen**a**

wallet бумажник boomaɹneek

**wander: I like just wandering
around** я люблю бродить ya
lyoobl**yoo** brad**ee**t

want: I want… я хочу… ya
Hach**oo**…

I don't want any… я не
хочу… ya nyeh Hach**oo**…

I want to go home я хочу
пойти домой ya Hach**oo** pit**ee**
dam**oy**

I don't want to я не хочу ya
nyeh Hach**oo**

he wants to… он хочет… oп
H**o**chyet…

what do you want? что вы
хотите? shto viy Hat**ee**tyeh?

ward (in hospital) палата pal**a**ta

warm тёплый t**yo**pli

I'm so warm мне жарко
mnyeh ɹ**a**rka

was: he was он был… oп
biyl…

she was она была… oпa
bil**a**…

it was это было… **e**ta b**i**yla…

wash (verb: hands etc) мыть/
помыть miyt/pam**i**yt

(clothes) стирать/постирать
steer**a**t/pasteer**a**t

can you wash these? вы
можете это постирать? viy
m**o**ɹetyeh **e**ta pasteer**a**t?

washhand basin раковина
rak**a**veena

washing (clothes) бельё byel**yo**

washing machine стиральная
машина steer**a**lna-ya mash**i**yna

washing powder стиральный
порошок steer**a**lni par**a**shok

**washing-up: to do the
washing-up** мыть/помыть
посуду miyt/pam**i**yt pas**oo**doo

washing-up liquid жидкость
для мытья посуды ɹ**i**ytkast
dlya mit**ya** pas**oo**di

wasp оса as**a**

watch (wristwatch) часы pl chas**i**y

**will you watch my things
for me?** присмотрите,
пожалуйста, за моими
вещами preesmatr**ee**tyeh,
paɹ**a**lsta, za ma-**ee**mee vyesh-
cham**ee**

watch strap ремешок для
часов ryemyesh**o**k dlya chas**o**f

water вода vad**a**

**may I have some
water?** можно мне воды,
пожалуйста? m**o**Jna mnyeh
vad**iy**, paJ**a**lsta?

waterproof (*adj*)
непромокаемый nyepramak**a**-
yemi

water-skiing воднолыжный
спорт vadna-l**iy**Jni sport

way: it's this way в эту
сторону v**e**too st**o**ranoo

it's that way в ту сторону
ftoo st**o**ranoo

is it a long way to…?
далеко ли до…? dalyek**o**lee
da…?

no way! ни в коем случае!
nee fk**o**-yem sl**oo**cha-yeh!

**could you tell me the
way to…?** скажите,
пожалуйста, как дойти
до…? skaJ**iy**tyeh, paJ**a**lsta,
kak d**i**tyeh da…?

**go straight on until
you reach the traffic
lights** идите прямо, до
светофора eed**ee**tyeh
pr**ya**ma, da svyetaf**o**ra

turn left сверните налево
svyern**ee**tyeh nal**ye**va

**take the first turn on the
right** первый поворот
направо p**ye**rvi pavar**o**t
napr**a**va

see **where**

we мы miy

weak слабый sl**a**bi

weather погода pag**o**da

**what's the weather
forecast?** какой прогноз
погоды? kak**oy** pragn**o**s
pag**o**di?

it's going to be fine будет
хорошая погода b**oo**dyet
Har**o**sha-ya pag**o**da

it's going to rain будет
дождливо b**oo**dyet daJdl**ee**va

it'll brighten up later
обещают просветление
позже abyesh-ch**a**-yoot
prasvyetl**ye**nee-yeh poJ-Jeh

website веб-сайт vyep-s**i**t

wedding свадьба sv**a**dba

wedding ring обручальное
кольцо abrooch**a**lna-yeh kalts**o**

Wednesday среда sryed**a**

week неделя nyed**ye**lya

a week (from) today ровно
через неделю r**o**vna ch**ye**ryes
nyed**ye**lyoo

a week (from) tomorrow
через неделю, считая с
завтрашнего дня ch**ye**ryes
nyed**ye**lyoo, sh-cheet**a**-ya
z-z**a**ftrashnyeva dnya

weekend конец недели kan**ye**ts
nyed**ye**lee

at the weekend в субботу-
воскресенье vsoob-b**o**too-
vaskryes**ye**nyeh

weight вес vyes

weird странный str**a**n-ni

welcome: welcome to…
добро пожаловать dabr**o**

paJalavat

you're welcome (don't mention it) не за что nyezashta

well: I don't feel well мне нехорошо mnyeh nyeHarasho

she's not well ей нехорошо yay nyeHarasho

you speak English very well вы очень хорошо говорите по-английски viy ochyen Harasho gavareetyeh pa-angleeskee

well done! молодец! maladyets

this one as well этот тоже etat toJeh

well well! ну и ну! noo ee noo!

how are you? как вы поживаете? kak viy paJiva-yetyeh?

very well, thanks, and you? спасибо, хорошо, а вы? spaseeba, Harasho, a viy?

well-done (meat) хорошо прожаренный harasho praJaryen-ni

Welsh уэльский oo-elskee

I'm Welsh я из Уэльса ya eez oo-elsa

were: we were мы были… miy biylee…

you were вы были… viy biylee…

they were они были… anee biylee…

West: the West Запад zapat

west запад zapat

in the west на западе na zapadyeh

western западный zapadni

West Indian (adj) вест-индский vyest-eentskee

wet мокрый mokri

what? что? shto?

what's that? что это? shto-eta?

what should I do? что мне делать? shto mnyeh dyelat?

what a view! вот это вид! voteta veet!

what bus do I take? на какой автобус мне надо сесть? na kakoy aftoboos mnyeh nada syest?

wheel колесо kalyeso

wheelchair инвалидная коляска eenvaleedna-ya kalyaska

when? когда? kagda?

when we get back когда мы вернёмся kagda miy vyernyomsya

when's the train? когда поезд? kagda po-yest?

where? где? gdyeh?

I don't know where it is я не знаю, где это ya nyeh zna-yoo, gdyeh-eta

where is the cathedral? где собор? gdyeh sabor?

it's over there вон там von tam

could you show me where

it is on the map? вы можете показать это на карте? viy mojetyeh pakazat eta na kartyeh?

it's just here вот здесь vot zdyes

see **way**

which: which bus? какой автобус? kakoy aftoboos?

which one? какой из них? kakoy eez neen?

that one тот tot

this one? этот? etat?

no, that one нет, тот nyet, tot

while: while I'm here пока я здесь paka ya zdyes

whisky виски veeskee

white белый byeli

white wine белое вино byela-yeh veeno

who? кто? kto?

who is it? кто там? kto tam?

the man who... человек, который... chyelavyek, katori...

whole: the whole week всю неделю vsyoo nyedyelyoo

the whole lot всё fsyo

whose: whose is this? чьё это? chyo eta?

why? почему? pacheemoo?

why not? почему бы нет? pacheemoobi nyet?

wide широкий shirokee

wife жена Jena

Wi-Fi Wi-Fi vi-fi

will: will you do it for me? вы это сделаете для меня? viy eta sdyela-yetyeh dlya myenya?

wind (*noun*) ветер vyetyer

window окно akno

near the window у окна oo akna

in the window (of shop) в витрине v-veetreenyeh

window seat место у окна myesta oo akna

windscreen ветровое стекло vyetravo-yeh styeklo

windscreen wipers стеклоочистители styekla-acheesteetyelee, дворники dvorneekee

windsurfing виндсёрфинг veentsyorfeenk

windy ветреный vyetryen-ni

wine вино veeno

can we have some more wine? можно ещё вина, пожалуйста moJna yesh-cho veena, paJalsta

wine list карта вин karta veen

winter зима zeema

in the winter зимой zeemoy

winter holiday зимний отпуск zeemnee otpoosk

wire проволока provalaka

(electric) провод provat

wish: best wishes с наилучшими пожеланиями sna-eeloochshimee paJilanee-yamee

with c s

I'm staying with... я живу
у... ya Jiv**oo** oo...

without без byes

witness (*male/female*) свидетель/
свидетельница sveed**ye**tyel/
sveed**ye**tyelneetsa

**will you be a witness
for me?** (to man/woman)
вы можете быть моим
свидетелем/моей
свидетельницей? viy m**o**Jetyeh
biyt ma-**eem** sveed**ye**tyel-yem/
ma-**yay** sveed**ye**tyelneetsay?

woman женщина
J**e**nsh-cheena

wonderful замечательный
zamyech**a**tyelni

won't: it won't start не
заводится nyeh zav**o**deetsa

wood (*material*) дерево d**ye**ryeva
(*forest*) лес lyes

wool шерсть sherst

word слово sl**o**va

work (*noun*) работа rab**o**ta
(*verb*) работать rab**o**tat

it's not working это не
работает **e**ta nyeh rab**o**ta-yet

I work in... я работаю в... ya
rab**o**ta-yoo v...

world мир meer

worry: I'm worried
я беспокоюсь
ya byespak**o**-yoos

worse: it's worse это хуже **e**ta
H**oo**Jeh

worst самый плохой
s**a**mi plaH**oy**

worth: is it worth a visit?
стоит ли туда ехать? st**o**-eetlee
t**oo**da **ye**Hat?

**would: would you give
this to...?** передайте это,
пожалуйста... pyeryed**i**tyeh **e**ta,
pa**J**alsta...

wrap: could you wrap it up?
заверните, пожалуйста
zavyern**ee**tyeh, pa**J**alsta

wrapping paper обёрточная
бумага ab**yo**rtachna-ya
boom**a**ga

wrist запястье zap**ya**styeh

write писать/написать pees**a**t/
napees**a**t

could you write it down?
запишите, пожалуйста
zapeesh**i**ytyeh, pa**J**alsta

how do you write it? как это
пишется? kak **e**ta p**ee**shetsa?

writing paper почтовая бумага
pacht**o**va-ya boom**a**ga

wrong неправильно
nyepr**a**veelna

it's the wrong key
это не тот ключ **e**ta nyeh tot
kly**oo**ch

this is the wrong train вы не
на том поезде viy nyeh na tom
p**o**-yezdyeh

the bill's wrong счёт
ошибочный sh-chot
ash**i**ybachni

sorry, wrong number (said
by man/woman) извините,
я не туда попал/попала
eezveen**ee**tyeh, ya nyeh t**oo**da
pap**a**l/pap**a**la

sorry, wrong room (said by man/woman) извините, я ошибся/ошиблась номером eezveen**ee**tyeh, ya ash**i**ypsya/ ash**i**yblas n**o**myeram

there's something wrong with... что-то не так с... sht**o**-ta nyeh tak s...

what's wrong? в чём дело? fchom d**ye**la?

X

X-ray рентгеновский снимок ryentg**ye**nafskee sn**ee**mak

Y

yacht яхта y**a**Hta

yard двор dvor

year год got

yellow жёлтый J**o**lti

yes да da

yesterday вчера fch**ye**ra

    yesterday morning вчера утром fch**ye**ra **oo**tram

    the day before yesterday позавчера paz**a**fchera

yet ещё yesh-ch**o**

    is it here yet? оно ещё не пришло? an**o** yesh-ch**o** nyeh preeshl**o**?

    no, not yet нет ещё nyet yesh-ch**o**

    you'll have to wait a little longer yet вам придётся

ещё немного подождать vam preed**yo**tsa yesh-ch**o** nyemn**o**ga pad**a**Jdat

yoghurt йогурт y**o**goort

you (sing pol or pl) вы viy

    (sing, fam) ты tiy

    this is for you это для вас **e**ta dlya vas

    with you с вами sv**a**mee

young молодой malad**oy**

your/yours (sing pol or pl) ваш vash

    (sing, fam) твой tvoy

    your sister ваша/твоя сестра v**a**sha/tva-**ya** s**ye**stra

    is this yours? это ваше/твоё **e**ta v**a**sheh/tva-**yo**?

youth hostel молодёжная гостиница malad**yo**Jna-ya gast**ee**neetsa

Z

zero нуль nool

    below zero ниже нуля n**ee**Jeh nool**ya**

zip молния m**o**lnee-ya

    could you put a new zip on? вставьте, пожалуйста, новую молнию fst**a**ftyeh, paJ**a**lsta, n**o**voo-yoo m**o**lnee-yoo

zip code почтовый индекс pacht**o**vi **ee**ndeks

zoo зоопарк zo-op**a**rk

RUSSIAN
→ **ENGLISH**

Colloquialisms

The following are words you may well hear. You shouldn't be tempted to use any of the stronger ones unless you are sure of your audience.

алкаш alkash wino, boozer

баксы baksi dollars

безобразие! byezabrazee-yeh! it's disgraceful!

блин! bleen! damn!

выпивка viypeefka bevvy, drink

деревянные dyeryevyan-ni-yeh roubles

дура/дурак doora/doorak idiot, thickhead

ёлки-палки! yolkee-palkee! bloody hell!

ерунда! eroonda! nonsense!

здорово! zdorava! great!

иди к чёрту! eedee kchortoo! go to hell!

козёл! kazyol! idiot!

какого чёрта…? kakova chorta…? what the hell…?

какой ужас! kakoy ooJas! that's awful!

класс! klass! great!, brilliant!

клёвый! klyovi! knockout!, brill!, fantastic!

кретин kryeteen twit

к черту! kchortoo! to hell with it!

лимон leemon a million

молодец! maladyets! well done!

ничего себе! neechyevo syebyeh! not bad!

отвяжись! atvyaJiys! get lost!

парень paryen bloke

пошёл ты! pashol tiy! get lost!

псих pseeн nutter

ребята ryebyata (the) lads, (the) guys

сволочь svolach bastard

с приветом spreevyetam crackers, nuts

хреновый Hryenovi rotten, lousy

хрен с ним! Hryen sneem! to hell with it!

чёрт! chort! damn!, shit!

чёрт знает что chort zna-yet shto God only knows

чёрт с тобой! chort staboy! to hell with you!

чокнутый choknooti barmy

ужасно! ooJasna! it's awful!, it's ghastly!

штука shtooka a thousand

это обдираловка eta abdeeralafka it's a rip-off

A

A bus stop

авария avaree-ya accident; breakdown

август avgoost August

авиакомпания avee-a-kampanee-ya airline

авиапочта avee-a-pochta airmail
  авиапочтой avee-a-pochtı by airmail

Австралия afstralee-ya Australia

Австрия afstree-ya Austria

автобус aftoboos bus

автовокзал aftavakzal bus station

автоматический aftamateechyeskee automatic

автомобилист aftamabeeleest car driver

автомобиль aftamabeel car

автоответчик afta-atvyetcheek answering machine

автостоянка aftasta-yanka car park, parking lot

автострада aftastrada motorway, freeway, highway

агентство agyenstva agency

адвокат advakat lawyer

администратор admeeneestrator manager

адрес adryes address

адресат adryesat addressee

адресная книга adryesna-ya kneega address book

Азербайджан azyerbidjan Azerbaijan

аккумулятор ak-koomoolyatar battery (for car)

акселератор aksyelyeratar accelerator

акцент aktsent accent

алкоголь alkagol alcohol

аллергия al-lyergee-ya allergy

алмаз almas diamond

Америка amyereeka America

американский amyereekanskee American

амперный: 13-и амперный ampyerni 13-amp

английская булавка angleeska-ya boolafka safety pin

английский angleeskee English

английский язык angleeskee yaziyk English (language)

англичане angleechanyeh the English

англичанин angleechaneen Englishman

англичанка angleechanka English woman

Англия anglee-ya England

антигистамин anteegeestameen antihistamine

антикварная вещь anteekvarna-ya vyesh-ch antique

антикварный anteekvarni antiquarian; antique

антикварный магазин anteekvarni magazeen antique shop

аппендицит ap-pyendeetsiyt appendicitis

аппетит ap-pyeteet appetite

апрель apryel April

аптека apt**ye**ka chemist, pharmacy

арестовать aryest**o**vat to arrest

Армения arm**ye**nee-ya Armenia

аромат aram**a**t flavour

Архангельск arнangyelsk Archangel

аспирин aspeer**ee**n aspirin

Афганистан afgan**ee**stan Afghanistan

афиша af**ee**sha poster

аэропорт a-erap**o**rt airport

Аэрофлот a-eraf**lo**t Aeroflot

Travel tip The Russian bathhouse or *banya* is a world unto itself, and the preferred cure for the complaint known as "feeling heavy" – which encompasses everything from having flu to feeling depressed. For a truly Russian experience, a visit to the *banya* is a must.

Б

бабушка bab**oo**shka grandmother

багаж bag**a**sh luggage, baggage

багажник bagaлneek boot (of car), (US) trunk

бак bak tank

бакалея bakal**yeh**-ya groceries

балалайка balal**i**ka balalaika

балкон balk**o**n balcony

Балтийское море balt**ee**ska-yeh m**o**ryeh Baltic Sea

бальзам для волос b**a**lzam dlya v**a**los conditioner

бампер b**a**mpyer bumper, (US) fender

банк bank bank

банкнота bankn**o**ta banknote, (US) bill

банкомат bankam**a**t cash dispenser, ATM

баня b**a**nya bathhouse

бар bar bar

бармен b**a**rmyen barman

бассейн bas**ya**yn swimming pool

батарейка batar**ya**yka battery

батарея batar**yeh**-ya radiator

башня b**a**shnya tower

бегать/бежать b**ye**gat/byeлat to run

бегать/бежать трусцой b**ye**gat/byeлat troosts**oy** to jog

беда by**e**da trouble; misfortune

бедный b**ye**dni poor

бедро byedr**o** thigh; hip

бежать byeлat to run

бежевый b**ye**лevi beige

без byez without

без двадцати два byez dvatsat**ee** dva twenty to two

безопасность byezap**a**snast safety

в безопасности fbyezap**a**snastee safe

безработный byezrab**o**tni unemployed

белокурый byelak**oo**ri blond

Белорусь byelar**oos** Belarus

белый b**ye**li white

Бельгия byelgee-ya Belgium

бельё byelyo washing; underwear

бензин byenzeen petrol, gasoline

берег byeryek coast; shore

на берегу моря na byeryegoo morya at the seaside

берегись… byeryegees… beware of…

беременная byeryemyen-na-ya pregnant

бесплатный byesplatni free of charge

беспокоиться byespako-eetsa to worry about

бесполезный byespalyezni useless

беспорядок byesparyadak mess

беспошлинный byesposhleen-ni duty-free

библиотека beeblee-atyeka library

бизнес beeznes business

билет beelyet ticket

билет в один конец beelyet vadeen kanyets single ticket, one-way ticket

билетная касса beelyetna-ya kas-sa ticket office

билеты beelyeti tickets

бить/побить beet/pabeet to hit, to beat

благодарить/поблагодарить blagadareet/pablagadareet to thank

благодарный blagadarni grateful

бланк blank form

ближайший bleeJIshi nearest

ближе bleeJeh nearer

близкий bleeskee near, close

близнецы bleeznyetsiy twins

близорукий bleezarookee shortsighted

А
Б
В
Г
Д
Е
Ё
Ж
З
И
Й
К
Л
М
Н
О
П
Р
С
Т
У
Ф
Х
Ц
Ч
Ш
Щ
Ъ
Ы
Ь
Э
Ю
Я

блокнот blaknot notebook

блоха blaha flea

блузка blooska blouse

блюдо blyooda dish

блюдце blyoodtseh saucer

бог boн God

богатый bagati rich

Болгария balgaree-ya Bulgaria

более bolyeh-yeh more

болезнь balyezn disease; illness

болеть/заболеть balyet/
zabalyet to be ill; to fall ill; to be
sore, to ache, to hurt

болеутоляющее средство
bolyeh-ootalyayoosh-chyeh
sryetstva painkiller

боль bol ache; pain

боль в желудке bol vлelootkyeh
stomach ache

больница balneetsa hospital

больной balnoy ill, (US) sick;
sore; patient

больше bolsheh more

большинство balshinstvo most
(of); majority

большой balshoy big, large

бомж bomJ homeless
person

борода barada beard

борт-проводник bort-
pravadneek steward

боюсь: я боюсь ya bayoos I'm
afraid

бояться ba-yatsa to be afraid
(of)

браслет braslyet bracelet

брат brat brother

бриллиант breel-lee-ant diamond

британский breetanskee British

бритва breetva razor

бритвенное лезвие breetvyen-
na-yeh lyezvee-yeh razor blade

бриться/побриться breetsa/
pabreetsa to shave

бровь brof eyebrow

бросать/бросить brasat/broseet
to throw

брошь brosh brooch

брошюра brashoora brochure;
leaflet

брюки bryookee trousers, (US)
pants

будет boodyet he will; she will;
it will; he will be; she will be;
it will be

будете boodyetyeh you will; you
will be

будешь boodyesh you will; you
will be

будильник boodeelneek alarm
clock

будить/разбудить boodeet/
razboodeet to wake

буду boodoo I will; I will be

будут boodoot they will; they
will be

будущее boodoosh-chyeh-yeh
future

будьте здоровы! boodtyeh
zdarovi! bless you!

буква bookva letter (of alphabet)

букинист bookeeneest
secondhand bookseller

букинистический магазин
bookeeneesteechyeskee

magaz**ee**n secondhand bookshop/bookstore

булавка boola**f**ka pin

булочная b**oo**lachna-ya bakery

бульвар boolv**a**r boulevard

бумага boom**a**ga paper

бумажник boom**aл**neek wallet

бумажные носовые платки boom**aл**ni-yeh nasav**iy**-yeh platk**ee** tissues, Kleenex

буря b**oo**rya storm

бутылка boot**iy**lka bottle

буфет boof**ye**t snack bar, café

бы: я хотел бы… ya hat**ye**l biy… I would like…

бывать/побывать biv**a**t/ pabiv**a**t to be; to frequent

бывший b**iy**fshi former

был biyl, **была** bil**a** was; were

были b**iy**lee were

было b**iy**la was

быстрее! bistr**yeh**-yeh! hurry up!

быстро b**iy**stra quickly, fast

быстрый b**iy**stri quick, fast

бытовая химия bitav**a**-ya **н**eem**ee**-ya household cleaning materials

быть biyt to be

бюро byoor**o** office

бюро находок byoor**o** na**н**od**o**k lost property office

бюро обслуживания byoor**o** apsl**oo**Jivanee-ya service bureau

бюро путешествий byoor**o** pootyesh**e**stvee travel agent's

бюстгальтер byoostg**a**ltyer bra

В

в v in

вагон vag**o**n carriage

вагон-ресторан vag**o**n-ryestar**a**n dining car

важный v**a**Jni important

ваза v**a**za vase

валюта val**yoo**ta foreign currency

вам vam (to) you

вами v**a**mee (by) you

ванна v**a**n-na bath

ванная v**a**n-na-ya bath; bathroom

вас vas you; of you

вата v**a**ta cotton wool, absorbent cotton

ваш vash, **ваша** v**a**sha, **ваше** v**a**sheh your; yours

вашего v**a**sheva (of) your; (of) yours

ваше здоровье! v**a**sheh zdar**o**vyeh! cheers!

вашей v**a**shay your; yours; of your; of yours; to your; to yours; by your; by yours

вашем v**a**shem your; yours

вашему v**a**shemoo (to) your; (to) yours

ваши v**a**shi your; yours

вашим v**a**shim your; yours; by your; by yours; to your; to yours

вашими v**a**shimee (by) your; (by) yours

ваших v**a**shi**н** (of) your; (of) yours

А
Б
В
Г
Д
Е
Ё
Ж
З
И
Й
К
Л
М
Н
О
П
Р
С
Т
У
Ф
Х
Ц
Ч
Ш
Щ
Ъ
Ы
Ь
Э
Ю
Я

вашу vashoo your; yours

в воскресенья и праздничные дни v-vaskryesyenya ee prazneechni-yeh dnee Sundays and public holidays

вдова vdava widow

вдовец vdavyets widower

вдруг vdrook suddenly

веб-сайт vyep-sIt website

вегетарианец vyegyetaree-anyets vegetarian

Travel tip While fish eaters will find plenty on offer, strict vegetarians often have to fall back on *blini* stuffed with mushrooms or cabbage, mushrooms cooked with onions and sour cream, or the cold summer soup *okroshka*; there are often veggie dishes from other ethnic cuisines on offer, from Georgian to Italian.

ведро vyedro bucket

вежливый vyeJleevi polite

везде vyezdyeн everywhere

век vyek century

вёл vyol, **вела** vyela led; was leading

вели vyelee led; were leading

Великобритания vyeleekabreetanee-ya Britain

великолепный vyeleekalyepni terrific, magnificent, splendid

велосипед vyelaseepyet bicycle

велосипедная трасса vyelaseepyedna-ya tras-sa cycle path

Венгрия vyengree-ya Hungary

веник vyeneek bunch of birch twigs; broom

вентилятор vyenteelyatar fan

верёвка vyeryofka string; rope

верить/поверить vyereet/pavyereet to believe

вернуть vyernoot to give back, to return

вернуться vyernootsa to get back, to come back, to return

верный vyerni true

вероятно vyera-yatna probably

верхний этаж vyerнnee etash upper floor

верховая езда vyerнava-ya yezda horse riding

вес vyes weight

веселиться: веселитесь! vyesyeleetyes! have fun!

весёлый vyesyoli cheerful

весна vyesna spring

весной vyesnoy in spring

вести vyestee to drive; to lead

весь vyes all; the whole

весь день vyes dyen all day

ветер vyetyer wind

вечер vyechyer evening

добрый вечер dobri vyechyer good evening

11 часов вечера chasof vyechyera 11 pm

вешалка vyeshalka peg; rack; stand; coathanger

вещи vyesh-chee things, belongings

вещь vyesh-ch thing

взбешённый vzbyeshon-ni furious

вздор vzdor rubbish, nonsense

взлёт vzlyot take-off

взрослые vzrosli-yeh adults

взрослый vzrosli adult

взять vzyat to take

взять напрокат vzyat naprakat to rent

вид veet view; appearance; form

видео veedyeh-o video

видеомагнитофон veedyeh-omagneetafon video recorder

видеть/увидеть veedyet/ ooveedyet to see

видоискатель veeda-eeskatyel viewfinder

виза veeza visa

визит veezeet visit

визитка veezeetka, **визитная карточка** veezeetna-ya kartachka business card

вилка veelka fork

Вильнюс veelnyoos Vilnius

винный магазин veen-ni magazeen wine and spirits shop

вираж veerash bend

витамины veetameeni vitamins

витрина veetreena shop window

включать/включить fklyoochat/ fklyoocheet to switch on

включён fklyoochon on, switched on; included

включено в цену fklyoochyeno ftsenoo included in the price

включить fklyoocheet to switch on

вкус fkoos taste

вкусный fkoosni nice; delicious, tasty

владелец vladyelyets owner

Владивосток vladeevastok Vladivostok

вместе vmyestyeh together

вместо vmyesta instead of

внешний vnyeshnee outward; external; foreign

вниз vnees down, downwards

внизу vneezoo downstairs

внимание vneemanee-yeh attention

внутренние рейсы vnootryen-nee-yeh ryaysi domestic flights

внутренний vnootryen-nee inner; inside; internal; domestic; inland

внутри vnootree inside

во время va vryemya during

вовремя vovryemya on time

вода vada water

водитель vadeetyel driver

водительские права vadeetyelskee-yeh prava driving licence

водить/вести vadeet/vyestee to drive; to lead

водопад vadapat waterfall

возвращать/вернуть vazvrash-chat/vyernoot to give back, to return

возвращаться/вернуться vazvrash-chatsa/vyernootsa to get back, to come back, to return

воздух vozdooH air

А
Б
В
Г
Д
Е
Ё
Ж
З
И
Й
К
Л
М
Н
О
П
Р
С
Т
У
Ф
Х
Ц
Ч
Ш
Щ
Ъ
Ы
Ь
Э
Ю
Я

вокзал vakzal station (railway)

Волгоград valgagrat Volgograd

волосы volasi hair

вон: вон! von! get out!

    вон там von tam over there

вонь von stink

вообще va-apsh-chyeh at all; on the whole, generally

вопрос vapros question

вор vor thief

вор-карманник var-karman-neek pickpocket

ворота varota gate

воротник varatneek collar

восемнадцатый vasyemnatsati eighteenth

восемнадцать vasyemnatsat eighteen

восемь vosyem eight

восемьдесят vosyemdyesyat eighty

восемьсот vasyemsot eight hundred

воскресенье vaskryesyenyeh Sunday

восток vastok east

    к востоку от k vastokoo ot east of

восьмой vasmoy eighth

вот vot here is; that's

    вот и всё vot ee fsyo that's all

    вот, пожалуйста vot, paJalsta here is, here are; here you are

    вот эти vot etee these

    вот этот vot etat this one

вперёд vpyeryot forwards; in future; in advance

воздушный шар vazdooshni shar balloon

возместить vazmyesteet to refund

возможно vazmoJna possible; perhaps

возражать: вы не возражаете если я…? viy nyeh vazraJa-yetyeh yeslee ya…? do you mind if I…?

возраст vozrast age

возьмите тележку/корзину vazmeetyeh tyelyeshkoo/karzeenoo please take a trolley/basket

войдите! videetyeh! come in!

война vina war

войти vitee to enter, to go in

впереди fpyeryed**ee** in front, ahead; in front of; before; in future

врач vrach doctor

вредить/повредить vryed**ee**t/ pavryed**ee**t to damage

время vr**ye**mya time

время года vr**ye**mya g**o**da season

время отправления vr**ye**mya atpravl**ye**nee-ya departure time

все fsyeh everyone; all

всё fsyo everything; all

всё вместе fsyo vm**ye**styeh altogether

всегда fsyegd**a** always

всего fsyev**o** in all, only

всё-таки vsy**o**-takee anyway

вспомнить fsp**o**mneet to remember, to recall

вспышка fsp**iy**shka flash

вставать/встать fstav**a**t/fstat to get up

встретить fstr**ye**teet to meet

встреча fstr**ye**cha appointment; meeting

встречать/встретить fstryech**a**t/fstr**ye**teet to meet

всякий fs**ya**kee any

вторник ft**o**rneek Tuesday

второй ftar**oy** second

второй этаж ftar**oy** et**a**sh first floor, (US) second floor

вход fHot entrance, way in

вход бесплатный fHot byespl**a**tni admission free

вход воспрещён fHot vaspryesh-ch**o**n no admittance

вход свободный fHot svab**o**dni admission free

входите fHad**ee**tyeh come in

входить/войти fHad**ee**t/v**i**t**ee** to enter, to go in

вчера fchyer**a** yesterday

вчера вечером fchyer**a** v**ye**chyeram last night (before midnight)

вчера днём fchyer**a** dnyom yesterday afternoon

вчера ночью fchyer**a** n**o**chyoo last night (after midnight)

вы viy you

выбирать/выбрать vibeer**a**t/ v**iy**brat to choose

выбросить v**iy**braseet to throw away

выглядеть v**iy**glyadyet to look; to seem

выдача багажа v**iy**dacha bagaJ**a** baggage claim

выдача покупок v**iy**dacha pak**oo**pak purchase collection point

выиграть v**iy**-eegrat to win

выйти v**iy**tee to go out; to get off

выключатель viklyooch**a**tyel switch

выключать/выключить viklyooch**a**t/v**iy**klyoocheet to switch off

выключен v**iy**klyoochyen off, switched off

выключить v**iy**klyoocheet to switch off

вылет v**iy**lyet departure

вылетать/вылететь vilyet**a**t/

А
Б
В
Г
Д
Е
Ё
Ж
З
И
Й
К
Л
М
Н
О
П
Р
С
Т
У
Ф
Х
Ц
Ч
Ш
Щ
Ъ
Ы
Ь
Э
Ю
Я

взlyetyet to take off

выпить **vi**peet to drink

высокий vi**so**kee tall; high

высота visa**ta** height, altitude

выставка **vi**stafka exhibition

выставочный зал **vi**stavachni zal exhibition hall

высший **vi**s-shee higher; highest

выхлопная труба vih**lap**na-ya tr**oo**ba exhaust pipe

выход **vi**Hat way out, exit; gate (at airport)

выход в город **vi**Hat vg**o**rat exit

выходить/выйти vih**a**deet/ **vi**ytee to go out; to get off

выход на посадку **vi**Hat na pas**a**tkoo gate

выходной день… vihadn**oy** dyen… closed on…

выходные vihadn**iy**-yeh weekend

выше **vi**sheh higher

вьюга vy**oo**ga snowstorm

Г

г. town/city

газ gas gas

газета gaz**ye**ta newspaper

газетный киоск gaz**ye**tni kee-**o**sk newsagent

газон gaz**o**n lawn

галантерея galantyer**yeh**-ya haberdashery

галерея galyer**yay**-a gallery

галстук g**a**lstook tie, necktie

гараж gar**a**sh garage

гарантия gar**a**ntee-ya guarantee, warranty

гардероб gardyer**o**p cloakroom

гастроном gastran**o**m food store

гвоздь gvost nail (in wall)

где? gdyeh? where?

где-нибудь gd**yeh**-neeboot somewhere; anywhere

где-то gd**yeh**-ta somewhere

г-жа gaspa**Ja** Mrs; Ms; Miss

гигиеническая прокладка geegee-yen**ee**chyeska-ya prakl**a**tka sanitary towel/napkin

гид geet guide

главный gl**a**vni main, principal

гладить/погладить gl**a**deet/ pagl**a**deet to iron

глаз glas eye

глубокий gloob**o**kee deep

глупый gl**oo**pi stupid

глухой gloo**Hoy** deaf

г-н gaspad**ee**n Mr

гнилой gneel**oy** rotten

говорить/сказать gavar**ee**t/ skaz**a**t to say; to speak

вы говорите по-… vi gavar**ee**tyeh pa-… do you speak…?

год got year

годовщина gadafsh-ch**ee**na anniversary

Голландия gal-l**a**ndee-ya Holland

голова galav**a** head

головная боль galavn**a**-ya bol headache

голодный gal**o**dni hungry

голос g**o**las voice

голый goli naked

гомосексуалист gomaseksoo-aleest gay, homosexual

гора gara mountain

гораздо garazda much more

гордый gordi proud

гореть/сгореть garyet/zgaryet to burn

горло gorla throat

горничная gorneechna-ya maid; cleaner

город gorat town; city

городской garadskoy town, city, urban

горький gorkee bitter

горячий garyachee hot

господин gaspadeen Mr; Sir

госпожа gaspaJa Miss; Mrs; Madam; Ms

гостеприимство gastyepree-eemstva hospitality

> **Travel tip** If you get the opportunity to stay with a Russian family, you'll be well looked after. Your introduction to cosy domesticity will be a pair of *tapachkee* – the slippers Russians wear indoors – followed by a cup of tea or a shot of vodka.

гостиная gasteena-ya lounge, living room

гостиница gasteeneetsa hotel

гость gost/**гостья** gostya guest (male/female)

государство gasoodarstva state

готовить/приготовить

gatoveet/preegatoveet to cook; to prepare

готовый gatovi ready

град grat hail

градус gradoos degree

грамматика gram-mateeka grammar

граммпластинки gramplasteenkee records

граница graneetsa border

   за границей za graneetsay abroad

гребная шлюпка gryebna-ya shlyoopka rowing boat

Греция gryetsi-ya Greece

грипп greep flu

гроза graza thunderstorm

гром grom thunder

громкий gromkee loud

громче gromchyeh louder

грубый groobi rude; coarse

грудная клетка groodna-ya klyetka chest

грудь groot breast; chest

грузинский groozeenskee Georgian

Грузия groozee-ya Georgia

грузовик groozaveek lorry, truck

группа groopa group

группа крови groopa krovee blood group

грустный groostni sad

грязное бельё gryazna-yeh byelyo dirty laundry, washing

грязный gryazni dirty

губа gooba lip

губная помада goobna-ya

pamaдa lipstick

гулять/погулять goolyat/
pagoolyat to go for a walk

густой goostoy thick

Д

д. house

да da yes

давай(те)… davI(tyeh)…
let's…

давать/дать davat/dat to give

давление в шинах davIyenee-
yeh fshIynaH tyre pressure

давно davno long ago; for a long
time; long since

дадим dadeem we will give

дадите dadeetyeh you will give

дадут dadoot they will give

даже daJeh even

даже если daJeh yeslee even if

далёкий dalyokee far, far away

далеко dalyeko far, far away

дальше dalsheh further

дам dam I will give

дама dama lady

Дания danee-ya Denmark

дарить/подарить dareet/
padareet to give (present)

даст dast he will give; she will
give; it will give

дать dat to give

дача dacha house/cottage in the
country

дашь dash you will give

два dva two

двадцатый dvatsati twentieth

двадцать dvatsat twenty

две dvyeh two

две недели dvyeh nyedyelee
fortnight, two weeks

двенадцатый dvyenatsati twelfth

двенадцать dvyenatsat twelve

дверь dvyer door

двести dvyestee two hundred

двойной dvInoy double

дворец dvaryets palace

дворник dvorneek windscreen
wiper; janitor; street cleaner

двухместный номер dvooH-
myesni nomyer double room

двухразовое питание
dvooHrazava-yeh peetanee-yeh
half board

дебютант dyebyootant beginner

деверь dyevyer brother-in-law
(husband's brother)

девичья фамилия dyeveechya
fameelee-ya maiden name

девочка dyevachka girl (child)

девушка dyevooshka girl (young
woman)

девяносто dyevyanosta ninety

девятнадцатый dyevyatnatsati
nineteenth

девятнадцать dyevyatnatsat
nineteen

девятый dyevyati ninth

девять dyevyat nine

девятьсот dyevyatsot nine
hundred

дедушка dyedooshka grandfather

дежурная dyeJoorna-ya

concierge

дежурная аптека dyeJoorna-ya
aptyeka duty pharmacist

**дезинфицирующее
средство** dyezeenfeetseeroo-
yoosh-chyeh sryetstva antiseptic;
disinfectant

дезодорант dyezadarant
deodorant

действительно dyaystveetyelna
really, indeed

действительный
dyaystveetyelni valid

декабрь dyekabr December

делать/сделать dyelat/zdyelat to
do; to make

делиться/поделиться
dyeleetsa/padyeleetsa to share

дело dyela matter, business

в самом деле fsamam dyelyeh
really

как дела? kak dyela? how are
you?, how are things?

день dyen day

деньги dyengee money

день рождения dyen raJdyenee-
ya birthday

деревня dyeryevnya countryside;
village

дерево dyeryeva tree; wood

из дерева eez dyeryeva wooden

держать dyerJat to hold; to keep;
to support

держитесь левой стороны
dyerJeetyes lyevi staraniy keep
to the left

десятый dyesyati tenth

десять dyesyat ten

дети dyetee children

детская коляска dyetska-ya
kalyaska pram, baby carriage

детская кроватка dyetska-ya
kravatka cot

детская порция dyetska-ya
portsi-ya children's portion

дешевле dyeshevlyeh cheaper

дешёвый dyeshovi cheap

джинсы dJeensi jeans

диабетик dee-abyeteek diabetic

диета dee-yeta diet

дизель deezyel diesel

дикий deekee wild

директор deeryektar director

дискотека deeskatyeka disco

длина dleena length

длинный dleen-ni long

для dlya for

для вас/меня dlya vas/myenya for you/me

для некурящих dlya nyekooryash-cheeн non-smoking

дневник dnyevneek diary

днём dnyom in the afternoon; p.m.

дно dno bottom

на дне na dnyeh at the bottom of

до do up to, as far as; before; until

доброе утро dobra-yeh ootra good morning

добрый dobri good; kind

добрый вечер dobri vyechyer good evening

добрый день dobri dyen good afternoon

довольно davolna quite; fairly

довольно хорошо davolna нarasho pretty good

довольный davolni pleased

до востребования da vastryebavanee-ya poste restante, general delivery

договор dagavor contract

дождик doJdeek shower

дождливый daJdleevi rainy

дождь dosht rain

идёт дождь eedyot dosht it's raining

документ dakoomyent document

долго dolga a long time

должен: я/он должен ya/on dolJen I/he must

должна: я/она должна ya/ana dalJna I/she must

долина daleena valley

дом dom house; home

дома doma at home

он дома? on doma? is he in?

доплата daplata supplement

дорога daroga road

дорогой daragoy expensive, dear

дороже daroJeh dearer

дорожные работы daroJni-yeh raboti roadworks

дорожный чек daroJni chyek traveller's cheque/check

досадно dasadna annoying

до свидания da sveedanya goodbye

доставать/достать dastavat/dastat to get, to obtain

достаточно dastatachna enough

достать dastat to get, to obtain

дочь doch daughter

драка draka fight

древний dryevnee ancient

друг drook friend; boyfriend

другой droogoy other; another,

а different

в другом месте vdroogom myestyeh elsewhere

что-то другое shto-ta droogoy-yeh something else

думать/подумать doomat/ padoomat to think

я думаю, что… ya dooma-yoo, shto… I think that…

духи dooнee perfume

духовка dooнofka oven

душ doosh shower

дым diym smoke

дыра dira hole

дышать dishat to breathe

дядя dyadya uncle

Е

еврейский yevryayskee Jewish

Европа yevropa Europe

европейский yevrapyayskee European

его yevo him; it; of him; of it; his; its

еда yeda food; meal

едим yedeem we eat

единый билет yedeeni beelyet monthly season ticket

едите yedeetyeh you eat

едят yedyat they eat

её yeh-yo her; it; of her; of it; hers; its

ездить yezdeet to go (by transport); to ride; to drive; to travel

ей yay her; to her; by her

ем yem I eat

ему yemoo him; it; to him; to it

если yeslee if

ест yest he eats; she eats; it eats

естественный yestyestvyen-ni natural

есть yest there is; there are

здесь есть…? zdyes yest…? is there… here?

у меня есть…? oo myenya yest… I have…

есть/съесть yest/syest to eat

ехать/ездить yeнat/yezdeet to go (by transport); to ride; to drive; to travel

ешь yesh you eat; eat

ешьте yeshtyeh eat

ещё yesh-cho still; another; another one; more

ещё более… yesh-cho bolyeh-yeh… even more…

ещё не yesh-cho nyeh not yet

ещё одно пиво yesh-cho adno peeva another beer

Ж

Ж ladies' toilets, ladies' room

жаловаться Jalavatsa to complain

жаль Jal pity; it's a pity

как жаль kak Jal what a pity

жара Jara heat

жарить Jareet to fry; to grill

жвачка Jvachka chewing gum

ждать/подождать Jdat/
padaJdat to wait

подождите меня!
padaJdeetyeh myenya! wait for
me!

железная дорога Jelyezna-ya
daroga railway

железо Jelyeza iron (metal)

жёлтый Jolti yellow

желудок Jeloodak stomach

жена Jena wife

женат Jenat married (man)

не женат nyeh Jenat single

жених Jeneeн fiancé;
bridegroom

женская одежда Jenska-ya
adyeJda ladies' clothing

женский зал Jenskee zal ladies'
hairdresser

женский отдел Jenskee ad-dyel
ladies' department

женский туалет Jenskee
too-alyet ladies' toilet, ladies'
room

женщина Jensh-cheena
woman

жетон Jeton token

живой Jivoy alive; living

живот Jivot stomach; belly

животное Jivotna-yeh
animal

жидкость для снятия лака
Jeetkast dlya snyatee-ya laka nail
polish remover

жизнь Jiyzn life

жильё Jilyo accommodation

жир Jiyr grease, fat

жирный Jiyrni greasy, fatty; rich

жить Jiyt to live

жить в палатках Jiyt fpalatkaн
to camp

журнал Joornal magazine

3

за za behind

забавный zabavni funny,
amusing

заблудиться zabloodeetsa to
lose one's way

заболеть zabalyet to be ill; to fall
ill; to be sore

забор zabor fence

забота zabota worry; bother

**заботиться/позаботиться
о** zaboteetsa/pazaboteetsa o to
take care of

забывать/забыть zabivat/
zabiyt to forget

заведующий zavyedooyoosh-
chee manager

завернуть zavyernoot to wrap

зависеть: это зависит eta
zaveeseet it depends

завод zavot factory, plant

завтра zaftra tomorrow

до завтра da zaftra see you
tomorrow

завтра вечером zaftra
vyechyeram tomorrow night

завтра утром zaftra ootram
tomorrow morning

завтрак zaftrak breakfast

загар zagar suntan

загорать/загореть zagarat/
zagar**yet** to get sunburnt, to tan

загораться/загореться
zagar**a**tsa/zagar**yet**sa to catch fire

загружать/загрузить
zagroo**J**at/zagroo**zeet** to
download

загрязнённый zagryazn**yon**-ni
polluted

зад zat bottom (of body)

задержка zad**yer**shka delay

задние фары zadnee-yeh f**a**ri
rear lights

задний z**a**dnee back; reverse

задний ход z**a**dnee Hot reverse
gear

задняя часть z**a**dnya-ya chast
back, back part

зажечь za**J**ech to light

зажигалка za**J**ig**a**lka lighter

зажигание za**J**ig**a**nee-yeh
ignition

зажигать/зажечь za**J**ig**a**t/
za**J**ech to light

заказ zak**a**s order; reservation

заказано zak**a**zana reserved

заказное письмо zakazn**o**-yeh
peesm**o** registered mail

заказывать/заказать
zak**a**zivat/zakaz**a**t to order; to
book

закат zak**a**t sunset

закон zak**o**n law

закричать zakreech**a**t to shout

закрывать/закрыть zakriv**a**t/
zakr**iy**t to close

закрыто zakr**iy**ta closed

закрыто на ремонт zakr**iy**ta na
ryem**o**nt closed for repairs

закрыто на учёт zakr**iy**ta na
ooch**o**t closed for stocktaking

закрыть zakr**iy**t to close

закурить zakoor**eet** to smoke

закуска zak**oo**ska snack; hors
d'oeuvre, appetizer

зал ожидания zal a**J**id**a**nee-
ya waiting room; departure
lounge

замечательный zamyech**a**telni
remarkable, wonderful

замок z**a**mok lock

замок z**a**mak castle

замороженный zamar**o**Jen-ni
frozen

замужем z**a**moo**J**em married

не замужем nyeh z**a**moo**J**em
single

замшевый z**a**mshevi suede

занавеска zanav**ye**ska curtain

занимать/занять zaneem**a**t/
zan**ya**t to borrow; to occupy;
to take up

заниматься/заняться
zaneem**a**tsa/zan**ya**tsa to occupy
oneself with; to study; to
begin to

занято z**a**nyata, **занятый**
z**a**nyati engaged, occupied;
engaged, busy

занять zan**ya**t to borrow

запад z**a**pat west

к западу от k z**a**padoo at west
of

запасной выход zapasn**o**y
v**iy**Hat emergency exit

запах za**pa**н smell

запирать/запереть za**pee**rat/
za**pyer**yet to lock

записная книжка-календарь
za**pees**na-ya kn**ee**shka-ka**lyen**dar
diary; planner

заплатить za**pla**teet to pay

заполнить za**pol**neet to fill in

запор za**po**r bar; bolt; lock;
constipation

заправочная станция
za**pra**vachna-ya st**a**ntsi-ya petrol/
gas station; garage

запрещено za**pryesh**-chyen**o**
prohibited, forbidden

запчасти za**p**chastee spare parts

запястье za**pya**styeh wrist

зарабатывать/заработать
za**ra**bativat/za**ra**botat to earn

заработок za**ra**batak salary

заражение za**ra**Jenee-yeh
infection; contamination

заранее za**ra**nyeh-yeh in advance

зарядное устройство для

телефона za**rya**dna-yeh
oost**ro**ystva dlya tye**lye**fona phone
charger

засмеяться za**smyeh**-**ya**tsa to
laugh

засоренный za**so**ryen-ni blocked

**застегните привязные
ремни** za**stye**gn**ee**tyeh
pree**vya**zn**iy**-yeh rye**mn**ee fasten
seatbelts

застёжка-молния za**styo**shka-
molnee-ya zip

застенчивый za**stye**ncheevi shy

затвор объектива za**tvo**r
abyek**tee**va shutter **(on camera)**

затормозить za**ta**rmaz**ee**t to
brake

защищать/защитить zash-
che**esh**-ch**at**/zash-ch**ee**te**et** to
protect, to defend

звать/позвать zvat/paz**va**t to
call

как вас зовут? kak vas
za**voo**t? what's your name?

меня зовут… mye**nya**

zavoot… my name is…

звезда zvyezda star

звонить/позвонить zvaneet/
pazvaneet to ring; to phone

звонок zvanok bell; phone call

здание zdanee-yeh building

здесь zdyes here

здоровый zdarovi healthy; huge

здоровье zdarovyeh health

за ваше здоровье! za vasheh
zdarovyeh! your health!, cheers!

здравствуйте zdrastvooytyeh
hello; how do you do?

зелёный zyelyoni green

земля zyemlya earth; world;
ground

зеркало zyerkala mirror

зима zeema winter

зимой zeemoy in winter

> **Travel tip** During the long
> Russian winter, anyone stay-
> ing more than a month can
> easily get run-down, owing
> to a lack of vitamins, and
> depressed by the darkness
> and ice. According to a
> survey of Moscow's ex-pat
> community, the chief prob-
> lems are alcoholism, nervous
> breakdowns and sexually
> transmitted diseases.

змея zmyeh-ya snake

знакомить/познакомить
znakomeet/paznakomeet to
introduce

знакомиться/познакомиться
znakomeetsa/paznakomeetsa

to get to know, to become
acquainted with, to meet

знать znat to know

я не знаю ya nyeh zna-yoo I
don't know

значить znacheet to mean

что это значит? shto eta
znacheet? what does it mean?

золовка zalofka sister-in-law
(husband's sister)

золото zolata gold

зонтик zonteek umbrella

зоопарк za-apark zoo

зрелый zryeli ripe

зуб zoop tooth

зубная боль zoobna-ya bol
toothache

зубная паста zoobna-ya pasta
toothpaste

зубная щётка zoobna-ya
sh-chotka toothbrush

зубной врач zoobnoy vrach
dentist

зубной протез zoobnoy prates
dentures

зуд zoot itch

зять zyat son-in-law

И

и ee and

иголка eegolka needle

игра eegra game

играть/сыграть eegrat/sigrat
to play

игрушка eegrooshka toy

идея eedyeh-ya idea

идти/ходить eet-**tee**/Ha**deet** to go (on foot), to walk; to suit

известный eez**vyes**ni famous

извините! eezvee**nee**tyeh! excuse me!, sorry!

извините, пожалуйста eezvee**nee**tyeh, pa**жal**sta excuse me

извиняться/извиниться eezvee**nya**tsa/eezvee**nee**tsa to apologize

я очень извиняюсь ya **o**chyen eezvee**nya**-yoos I'm really sorry

из-за eez-za because of

изнасиловать eeznа**see**lavat to rape

икона ee**ko**na icon

или ee**lee** or

или… или… ee**lee**… ee**lee**… either… or…

им eem him; it; by him; by it; them; to them

имеется… eem**yeh**-yetsa… there is…

иметь eem**yet** to have

имеются… eem**yeh**-yootsa… there are…

ими **ee**mee (by) them

имя **ee**mya name, first name

иначе ee**na**chyeh otherwise

инвалид eenva**leet** disabled

иногда ee**nagda** sometimes

иностранец eenastra**nyets**/ **иностранка** eenа**stranka** foreigner (*male/female*)

иностранный eena**stran**-ni foreign

институт иностранных

языков eensteet**oot** eenastran-níh yazi**kov** language school

инструктор eenstr**ook**tar instructor

инструмент eenstroom**yent** tool; instrument

интересный eentyer**yes**ni interesting

Интернет eentern**et** Internet

Интурист eentoor**eest** Intourist

информация eenfar**matsi**-ya information

Ирландия eerlan**dee**-ya Ireland

искать ees**kat** to look for

искренний **ees**kryen-nee sincere

искупаться eeskoo**pat**sa to go swimming

искусственный ees**koo**stvyen-ni artificial

искусство ees**koo**stva art

Испания eespan**ee**-ya Spain

исполнитель eespaln**ee**tyel executive; performer

использовать ees**pol**zavat to use

испорченный ees**por**chyen-ni faulty; rotten

исторический eestar**ee**chyeskee historical

история eestor**ee**-ya history

исчезать/исчезнуть eeschyez**at**/eeschy**ez**noot to disappear

Италия eetal**ee**-ya Italy

итог ee**tok** total; result

их eeн their; theirs; them; of them

июль ee-**yool** July

июнь ee-**yoon** June

К

к k to; towards

к. block

кабинет врача kabeenyet vracha doctor's surgery

каблук kablook heel

каждый kaJdi each; every

   каждый день kaJdi dyen every day

   каждый раз kaJdi ras every time

Казак kazak Cossack

Казахстан kazaнstan Kazakhstan

казачий kazachee Cossack

как kak like, as

   как? kak? how?

   как дела? kak dyela? how are you?, how are things?

календарь kalyendar calendar

камень kamyen stone

камера хранения kamyera нranyenee-ya left luggage office, baggage checkroom

Канада kanada Canada

канал kanal canal; channel

канат kanat rope

каникулы kaneekooli school holidays

канун Нового года kanoon novava goda New Year's Eve

канцтовары kantstavari stationery

капля kaplya drop

капот kapot bonnet, (US) hood

карандаш karandash pencil

карий karee brown (eyes)

карман karman pocket

карта karta map; playing card

картина karteena painting

картинная галерея karteen-na-ya galyeryeh-ya art gallery

картон karton cardboard

карточка (биснесмена) kartachka (beeznyesmyena) business card

Каспийское море kaspeeska-yeh moryeh Caspian Sea

касса kas-sa cash desk; booking office; box office

кассета kas-syeta cassette

кассетный магнитофон kas-syetni magneetafon cassette recorder

кастрюля kastryoolya saucepan

катастрофа katastrofa disaster

кататься на коньках katatsa na kankaн to skate

кататься на лыжах katatsa na liyJaн to ski

католик katoleek Catholic

кафе kafeh café

кафетерий kafyeteree cafeteria

качество kachyestva quality

кашель kashel cough

кашлять kashlyat to cough

каштановый kashtanavi brown, chestnut (hair)

каюта ka-yoota cabin

кв., квартира kvarteera flat, apartment

квартирная плата kvarteerna-ya plata, **квартплата** kvartplata rent

квитанция kveet**a**ntsi-ya receipt; ticket

кеды k**ye**di trainers

кем kem who; (by) whom

кемпинг k**e**mpeenk campsite

Киев k**ee**-yev Kiev

кило keel**o** kilo

километр keelam**ye**tr kilometre

кино(театр) keen**o**(-tyeh-**a**tr) cinema, movie theater

кинокамера keenak**a**myera camcorder

кинофильм keenaf**ee**lm film, movie

кислый k**ee**sli sour

кисть keest paintbrush

Китай keet**i** China

кладбище kl**a**dbeesh-chyeh cemetery

класс klas class

классика kl**a**seeka classical music or literature

классическая музыка klas**ee**chyeska-ya m**oo**zika classical music

классический klas-s**ee**chyeskee classical

класть/положить klast/ pala**j**eet to put; to lay

клей klyay glue

клейкая лента kl**yay**ka-ya l**ye**nta Sellotape, Scotch tape

клиент klee-**ye**nt client

климат kl**ee**mat climate

клиника kl**ee**neeka clinic

клуб kloop club

ключ kly**oo**ch key

книга kn**ee**ga book

книжечка kn**ee**Jechka book of 10 tickets

книжный магазин kn**ee**Jni magaz**ee**n bookshop, bookstore

ковёр kav**yo**r carpet; rug

когда? kagd**a**? when?

когда-нибудь kagd**a**-neeb**oo**t at some time; ever; one day

   вы когда-нибудь…? vi kagd**a**-neeb**oo**t…? have you ever…?

когда-то kagd**a**-ta one day; some time

кого kav**o** who; (of) whom

код kot code

кожа k**o**Ja skin; leather

кожаный k**o**Jani leather

койка k**oy**ka bunk bed

колготки kalg**o**tkee, **колготы** kalg**o**ti tights, pantyhose

колено kal**ye**na knee

колесо kalyes**o** wheel

количество kal**ee**chyestva quantity

коллекция kal-l**ye**ktsi-ya collection

колокол k**o**lakal bell

кольцо kalts**o** ring; circle

ком kom who; whom

команда kam**a**nda team

командировка kamand**ee**r**o**fka business trip

комар kam**a**r mosquito

комиссионный (магазин) kam**ee**s-see-**o**n-ni (magaz**ee**n) secondhand shop

Коммунистическая партия kam-mooneesteechyeska-ya partee-ya Communist Party

комната komnata room

компания kampanee-ya company

компостер kampostyer ticket punch

компьютер kampyootyer computer

кому kamoo who; (to) whom

конверт kanvyert envelope

кондитерская kandeetyerska-ya confectioner's

кондиционирование воздуха kandeetsi-aneeravanee-yeh vozdooна air-conditioning

конец kanyets end

конечно kanyeshna of course

конечный пункт kanyechni poonkt terminus

консервный нож kansyervni nosh tin-opener

консульство konsoolstva consulate

контактные линзы kantaktni-yeh leenzi contact lenses

контролёр kantralyor ticket inspector

конфета kanfyeta sweet, candy

концерт kantsert concert

концертный зал kantsertni zal concert hall

кончать/кончить kanchat/koncheet to finish

коньки kankee skates

кооператив ka-apyerateef co-operative

копейка kapyayka kopeck

у меня ни копейки денег oo myenya nee kapyaykee dyenyek I'm broke

корабль karabl ship

корзина karzeena basket

коридор kareedor corridor

коричневый kareechnyevi brown

коробка karopka box

коробка передач karopka pyeryedach gearbox

королева karalyeva queen

король karol king

короткий karotkee short

короткий путь karotkee poot shortcut

корп., корпус korpoos block

корь kor measles

косметика kasmyeteeka make-up; cosmetics

костыли kastilee crutches

кость kost bone

костюм kastyoom suit

который katori which

который час? katori chas? what time is it?

кофта kofta cardigan

кошелёк kashelyok purse, coin purse

кошка koshka cat

кошмар kashmar nightmare

к перронам k per-ronam to the platforms/tracks

к поездам k pa-yezdam to the trains

кража kraJa theft

край krı edge

крайний: по крайней мере pa krınyay myeryeh at least

кран kran tap, faucet

красивый kraseevi nice; beautiful; handsome

красить/покрасить kraseet/ pakraseet to paint

Красная Площадь krasna-ya plosh-chat Red Square

краснуха krasnooнa German measles

красный krasni red

красть/украсть krast/ookrast to steal

кредитная карточка kryedeetna-ya kartachka credit card

кредитный кризис kryedeetni kreezees credit crunch

крем kryem cream; butter cream

крем для бритья kryem dlya breetya shaving foam

крем для обуви kryem dlya oboovee shoe polish

крем для снятия косметики kryem dlya snyatee-ya kasmyeteekee cleansing cream

Кремль kryeml Kremlin

крепость kryepast fortress; strength

кресло-каталка kryesla-katalka wheelchair

критическое положение kreeteechyeska-yeh palaJenee-yeh emergency

кричать/закричать kreechat/ zakreechat to shout

кровать kravat bed

кровь krof blood

кроме kromyeh except

кроме воскресений kromyeh vaskryesyenee except Sundays

круглый kroogli round

круиз kroo-eez cruise

крутой krootoy steep

крыло krilo wing

Крым kriym Crimea

крыша kriysha roof

крышка kriyshka lid

к себе ksyebyeh pull

ксерокс ksyeraks photocopy; photocopier

кто? kto? who?

кто-нибудь kto-neeboot, **кто-то** kto-ta someone; anyone

кувшин koofsh**i**yn jug

кузен koozen, **кузина** koozeena cousin (male/female)

кукла kookla doll

кулинария kooleenaree-ya delicatessen

купальная шапочка koopalna-ya shapachka bathing cap

купальник koopalneek swimming costume

купаться/искупаться koopatsa/ eeskoopatsa to go swimming

купе koopeh compartment

купить koopeet to buy

купол koopal cupola, dome

курить/закурить kooreet/ zakooreet to smoke

курс (валюты) koors (valyooti)

exchange rate

куртка k**oo**rtka jacket; anorak

кусок k**oo**sok piece

кухня k**oo**hnya kitchen; cooking, cuisine

кухонная посуда k**oo**han-na-ya pas**oo**da cooking utensils

кухонное полотенце k**oo**han-na-yeh palat**ye**ntseh tea towel

Л

ладно l**a**dna all right, OK

лак для волос lak dlya val**o**s hair spray

лак для ногтей lak dlya nakt**yay** nail polish

лампа l**a**mpa lamp

лампочка l**a**mpachka light bulb

ластик l**a**steek rubber, eraser

Латвия l**a**tvee-ya Latvia

лгать/солгать lgat/salg**a**t to lie, to tell a lie

левша lyefsh**a** left-handed

левый l**ye**vi left

лёгкие ly**o**нkee-yeh lungs

лёгкий ly**o**нkee light (not heavy); easy

лёд lyot ice

леденец lyedyen**ye**ts lollipop

лезбиянка lyezbee-**ya**nka lesbian

лезвие бритвы l**ye**zvee-yeh br**ee**tvi razor blade

лейкопластырь lyaykapl**a**stir plaster, Bandaid

лекарство lyek**a**rstva medicine, drug

ленивый lyen**ee**vi lazy

лес lyes forest, wood

лестница l**ye**sneetsa stairs; ladder

летать/лететь lyet**a**t/lyet**ye**t to fly

лето l**ye**ta summer

летом l**ye**tam in summer

лечь lyech to lie down

ли lee question particle

ливень l**ee**vyen downpour

лист leest leaf

Литва leetv**a** Lithuania

литр leetr litre

лифт lift lift, elevator

лихорадка leeнar**a**tka fever

лицо leets**o** face

лишний l**ee**shnee spare

лишний вес багажа l**ee**shnee vyes bagaJ**a** excess baggage

А
Б
В
Г
Д
Е
Ё
Ж
З
И
Й
К
Л
М
Н
О
П
Р
С
Т
У
Ф
Х
Ц
Ч
Ш
Щ
Ъ
Ы
Ь
Э
Ю
Я

лоб lop forehead

ловить/поймать laveet/pImat to catch

лодка lotka boat

лодыжка ladIyshka ankle

ложиться/лечь laJeetsa/lyech to lie down

ложка loshka spoon

ложный loJni false

локоть lokat elbow

ломать/сломать lamat/slamat to break

ломтик lomteek slice

Лондон londan London

лосьон для загара lasyon dlya zagara suntan lotion

лосьон для снятия косметики lasyon dlya snyatee-ya kasmyeteekee make-up remover

лошадь loshat horse

луна loona moon

лучше looch-sheh better

лучший looch-shi better; best

самый лучший sami looch-shi the best

лыжи lIyJi skis

лыжные ботинки lIyJni-yeh bateenkee ski boots

лыжный спорт lIyJni sport skiing

любезный lyoobyezni kind, obliging

любимый lyoobeemi favourite

любить lyoobeet to love

любовь lyoobof love

люди lyoodee people

M

M gents' toilet, men's room; underground, metro, (US) subway

магазин magazeen shop

магазин беспошлинной торговли magazeen byesposhleen-ni targovlee duty-free shop

магнитофонная кассета magneetafon-na-ya kasyeta tape, cassette

мазь mas ointment

май mI May

маленький malyenkee small; little; short

мало mala not much; not many

мало времени mala vryemyenee not much time

мальчик malcheek boy

мама mama mum

марка marka stamp; make (of car etc)

марки markee stamps

март mart March

маршрут marshroot route, itinerary

маршрутное такси marshrootna-yeh taksee minibus

масло masla oil

масло для загара masla dlya zagara suntan oil

мастер mastyer foreman; expert; hair stylist

матрас matras mattress

матрёшка matryoshka Russian doll

мать mat mother

машина mashiyna car; vehicle

мебель myebyel furniture

медленно myedlyen-na slowly

медленный myedlyen-ni slow

медовый месяц myedovi myesyats honeymoon

медсестра myetsyestra nurse

между myeJdoo between

междугородный автобус myeJdoogarodni aftoboos coach, long-distance bus

междугородный звонок myeJdoo-garodni zvanok long-distance call

междугородный телефон myeJdoo-garodni tyelyefon long-distance phone

международные рейсы myeJdoonarodni-yeh ryaysi international flights

международный myeJdoonarodni international

международный звонок myeJdoonarodni zvanok international call

международный телефон myeJdoonarodni tyelyefon international telephone

мелочь myelach small change

менеджер menedjer manager

менее myenyeh-yeh less

меньше myensheh smaller; less

меня myenya me; of me

у меня oo myenya I have

менять/поменять myenyat/pamyenyat to change

мёртвый myortvi dead

мест нет myest nyet full

места myesta seats

местное время myesna-yeh vryemya local time

местность myesnast area

местный звонок myesni zvanok local call

место myesta place; seat

на месте na myestyeh on the spot

место для курения myesta dlya kooryenee-ya smoking area

месяц myesyats month

месячные myesyachni-yeh period

металл myetal metal

метр myetr metre

метро myetro underground, metro, (US) subway

мех myeH fur

меха myeHa fur shop

механик myeHaneek mechanic

меховая шапка myeHava-ya shapka fur hat

мешать myeshat to disturb; to stir; to mix; to prevent

милиционер meeleetsi-anyer policeman

милиция meeleetsi-ya police

миллион mee-lee-on million

Минск meensk Minsk

минута meenoota minute

мир meer world; peace

мне mnyeh me; to me

А
Б
В
Г
Д
Е
Ё
Ж
З
И
Й
К
Л
М
Н
О
П
Р
С
Т
У
Ф
Х
Ц
Ч
Ш
Щ
Ъ
Ы
Ь
Э
Ю
Я

многие mn**o**gee-yeh many; many people

много mn**o**ga a lot (of); many; much

мной mn**o**y (by) me

могу: я могу ya mag**oo** I can

мода m**o**da fashion

модный m**o**dni fashionable

моё ma**yo** my; mine

моего ma-yev**o** (of) my; (of) mine

моей ma-**yay** my; mine; of my; of mine; to my; to mine; by my; by mine

моём ma-**yo**m my; mine

моему ma-yem**oo** (to) my; (to) mine

может быть m**o**jet biyt maybe

можно m**o**jna one can, one may; it is possible

  можно…? m**o**jna…? can I…?

мои ma-**ee** my; mine; of my; of mine

моим ma-**ee**m (by) my; (by) mine; (to) my; (to) mine

моими mo-**ee**mee (by) my; (by) mine

моих ma-**ee**н, **мой** m**o**y my; mine

мокрый m**o**kri wet

Молдова mald**o**va Moldova

молния m**o**lnee-ya lightning; zip, zipper

молодой malad**o**y young

  молодые люди malad**iy**-eh ly**oo**dee young people

моложе mal**o**jeh younger

море m**o**ryeh sea

мороженое maro**J**ena-yeh ice cream

мороз mar**o**s frost

морозилка maraz**ee**lka freezer

Москва maskv**a** Moscow

мост mosst bridge

мотор mat**o**r engine

моторная лодка mat**o**rna-ya l**o**tka motorboat

мотоцикл matats**ee**kl motorbike

мочь/смочь moch/smoch can, to be able to

мою ma-**yoo** my; mine

моя ma-**ya** my; mine

муж moosh husband

мужская одежда moosshsk**a**-ya ad**ye**Jda menswear

мужской зал mooshsk**oy** zal men's hairdresser

мужской туалет mooshsk**oy** too-al**yet** gents' toilet, men's room

мужчина moosh-ch**ee**na man

музей mooz**yay** museum

Travel tip Opening hours for museums and galleries tend to be from 10am or 11am to 5pm or 6pm. They are closed at least one day a week, but there are no hard-and-fast rules as to which. In addition, one day in the month will be set aside as a *sanitarni dyen* or "cleaning day".

музыка m**oo**zika music

музыкальный mooz**ee**kalni musical

мусор **moo**sar rubbish, trash

мусорный ящик **moo**sarni **ya**sh-cheek dustbin, trashcan

муха **moo**нa fly (insect)

мы miy we

мыло **miy**la soap

мыть/помыть miyt/pam**iy**t to wash

мыть/помыть посуду miyt/pam**iy**t pas**oo**doo to do the washing-up

мышь miysh mouse

мягкие контактные линзы **mya**нkee-yeh kant**a**ktni-yeh **l**eenzi soft lenses

мягкий **mya**нkee soft

мясной магазин myasn**oy** magaz**een** butcher's

мясо **mya**sa meat

мяч myach ball

Н

на na on; at

наберите номер nabyer**ee**tyeh **no**myer dial the number

наб., набережная nabyerye**л**na-ya embankment

на вынос na v**iy**nas to take away, (US) to go

на себя na syeb**ya** pull

наверху navyerн**oo** at the top; upstairs

там наверху tam navyerн**oo** up there

над nat over; above

над головой nad galav**oy**

overhead

надеяться nad**yeh**-yatsa to hope

надо **na**da it is necessary; one must; need

мне надо… mnyeh **na**da… I need…

надоесть: мне надоело… mnyeh nada-**ye**la… I'm fed up with…

назад naz**at** back; backwards; ago

три дня назад tree dnya naz**at** three days ago

название naz**va**nee-yeh name; title

наиболее na-eeb**o**lyeh-yeh the most

найти n**ee**tee to find

накладная nakl**a**dna-ya invoice

наконец nakan**yets** at last

налево nal**ye**va to the left

наличные: платить наличными plat**ee**t nal**ee**chnimee to pay cash

налог nal**ok** tax

нам nam (to) us

нами n**a**mee (by) us

нападать/напасть napad**a**t/ nap**a**st to attack

напасть nap**a**st to attack

написать napees**a**t to write

напиток nap**ee**tak drink

наполнять/наполнить napaln**ya**t/nap**o**lneet to fill

направление napravl**ye**nee-yeh direction

направо napr**a**va to the right

А
Б
В
Г
Д
Е
Ё
Ж
З
И
Й
К
Л
М
Н
О
П
Р
С
Т
У
Ф
Х
Ц
Ч
Ш
Щ
Ъ
Ы
Ь
Э
Ю
Я

например napreemyer for
example

напрокат naprakat for hire, to
rent

напротив naproteef opposite

народ narot people; nation

народная музыка narodna-ya
moozika folk music

нарочно narochna deliberately

наружное narooJna-yeh for
external use only

наружный narooJni external;
outdoor

нас nas us; of us

у нас oo nas we have

насекомое nasyekoma-yeh insect

насморк nasmark cold

настольный теннис nastolni
ten-nees table tennis

настоящий nasta-yash-chee
genuine, real

настроение nastra-yenee-yeh

mood

натощак natash-chak on an
empty stomach

наука na-ooka science

научить na-oocheet to teach

нахальный naнalni cheeky,
impertinent

находить/найти naнadeet/nitee
to find

национальность natsi-analnast
nationality

начало nachala beginning

начальник nachalneek head,
chief, boss

начинать/начать nacheenat/
nachat to begin, to start

наш nash, наша nasha , наше
nasheh our; ours

нашего nasheva (of) our; (of)
ours

нашей nashay our; ours; of our;
of ours; to our; to ours; by our;

by ours

нашем nashem our; ours

нашему nashemoo (to) our; (to) ours

наши nashi our; ours

нашим nashim (by) our; (by) ours; (to) our; (to) ours

нашими nashiymee (by) our; (by) ours

наших nashih (of) our; (of) ours

нашу nashoo our; ours

не nyeh not

небо nyeba sky

неважно nyevaJna it doesn't matter

невероятный nyevyera-**ya**tni incredible

невеста nyev**ye**sta fiancée; bride

невозможно nyevazmoJna it's impossible

не высовываться из окон nyeh visovivatsa eez okan do not lean out of the windows

него nyevo his; its

у него oo nyevo he has; it has

недалеко (от) nyedalyeko (at) not far (from)

неделя nyedyelya week

в неделю vnyedyelyoo per week

на этой неделе na eti nyedyelyeh this week

две недели dvyeh nyedyelee fortnight, two weeks

недоразумение nyedarazoomyenee-yeh misunderstanding

неё nyeh-**yo** her; hers; it; its

у неё oo nyeh-**yo** she has; it has

независимый nyezav**ee**seemi independent

не за что nyeh za shta you're welcome, don't mention it

ней nyay her; it

некоторые nyekatari-yeh some; a few

не курить nyeh koor**ee**t no smoking

нелепый nyel**ye**pi ridiculous

нём nyom him; it

немедленно nyem**ye**dlyen-na immediately

немецкий nyem**ye**tskee German

немецкий язык nyem**ye**tskee yaz**i**yk German (language)

немного nyemn**o**ga a little bit

ненавидеть nyenav**ee**dyet to hate

не нырять nyeh nir**ya**t no diving

необходимо nyeh-apHad**ee**ema it's necessary

не останавливается в… nyeh astanavleeva-yetsa v… does not stop at…

неправильный nyepr**a**veelni wrong, incorrect

не прислоняться nyeh preeslan**ya**tsa do not lean against the door

неприятный nyepree-**ya**tni unpleasant

не работает nyeh rab**o**ta-yet out

А
Б
В
Г
Д
Е
Ё
Ж
З
И
Й
К
Л
М
Н
О
П
Р
С
Т
У
Ф
Х
Ц
Ч
Ш
Щ
Ъ
Ы
Ь
Э
Ю
Я

of order

не разрешается… nyeh razryesha-yetsa… do not…

нервный nyervni nervous

нёс nyos carried; was carrying; were carrying

несколько nyeskolka several; a few

несла nyesla carried; was carrying; were carrying

несли nyeslee carried; were carrying

несносный nyesnosni intolerable

нести nyestee to carry

нет nyet no

нет, спасибо nyet, spaseeba no, thank you

нет входа nyet fнoda no entry

нет выхода nyet viyнada no exit

не трогать nyeh trogat do not touch

неустойчивый nyeh-oostoycheevi changeable; unstable

ни… ни… nee… nee… neither… nor…

нигде neegdyeh nowhere

нижнее бельё neeлnyeh-yeh byelyo underwear

низкий neeskee low

никогда neekagda never

никто neekto nobody

ними: с ними sneemee with them

нитка neetka thread

них neeн their; theirs; them

у них оо neeн they have

ничего neechyevo, **ничто** neeshto nothing

но no but

Новая Зеландия nova-ya zyelandee-ya New Zealand

новогодняя ночь navagodnya-ya noch New Year's Eve

новости novastee news

новый novi new

новый год novi got New Year

с Новым годом! snovim godam! happy New Year!

нога naga leg; foot

ноготь nogat fingernail; toenail

нож nosh knife

ножницы noлneetsi scissors

ноль nol zero

номер nomyer number; hotel room

номер на двоих nomyer na dva-eeн double room

номер с двумя кроватями nomyer zdvoomya kravatyamee twin room

номерной знак namyernoy znak number plate

Норвегия narvyegee-ya Norway

нормально narmalna not bad, OK

нормальный narmalni normal

нос nos nose

носить/нести naseet/nyestee to carry

носки naskee socks

носовой платок nasavoy platok handkerchief

ноутбук no-ootbook laptop

ночная рубашка nachna-ya roobashka nightdress

ночь noch night

спокойной ночи spakoynı nochee good night

ноябрь na-yabr November

нравиться nraveetsa to like

мне нравится… mnyeh nraveetsa… I like…

нуль nool zero

нырять/нырнуть niryat/ nirnoot to dive

О

о a about

оба/обе oba/obyeh both

обед abyet lunch

обёрточная бумага abyortachna-ya boomaga wrapping paper

обещать abyesh-chat to promise

обижать/обидеть abeeJat/ abeedyet to offend

облако oblaka cloud

область oblast administrative region

облачный oblachni cloudy

обмен валюты abmyen valyooti currency exchange

обогреватель abagryevatyel heater

обратный адрес abratni adryes sender's address

обратный билет abratni beelyet return ticket, round-trip ticket

обручён/обручена abroochon/

abroochyena engaged (*male/ female*: to be married)

обслуживание apslooJivanee-yeh service

обслуживать/обслужить apslooJivat/apslooJit to serve

обувь oboof footwear

общежитие apsh-chyeJeetee-yeh hostel

общество opsh-chyestva society

объектив abyekteef lens

объяснение abyasnyenee-yeh explanation

объяснять/объяснить abyasnyat/abyasneet to explain

обыкновенный abiknavyen-ni usual

обычай abiychı custom

обычно abiychna usually

овощи ovash-chee vegetables

овощной магазин avash-chnoy magazeen greengrocer's

огонь agon fire

ограничение скорости agraneechyenee-yeh skorastee speed limit

одеваться/одеться adyevatsa/ adyetsa to get dressed

одежда adyeJda clothes

одеколон после бритья adyekalon poslyeh breetya aftershave

Одесса adyesa Odessa

одеться adyetsa to get dressed

одеяло adyeh-yala blanket

один adeen alone; one

одиннадцатый adeenatsati

eleventh

одиннадцать ad**ee**natsat eleven

одна adna alone; one

одно adno one

одноместный номер adna-
m**ye**sni n**o**myer single room

одолжить adal**J**eet to lend

ожерелье aJer**ye**lyeh necklace

ожог aJok burn

озеро o**ze**ra lake

окно akno window

около o**ka**la near; about

октябрь akty**a**br October

окулист akool**ee**st optician

он on he; it

она ana she; it

они anee they

онлайн anl**i**n online

оно ano it

опаздывать/опоздать (на)
ap**a**zdivat/apazd**a**t (na) to arrive/
be late; to miss

опасность ap**a**snast danger

опасный ap**a**sni dangerous

опера o**pye**ra opera

операция apyer**a**tsi-ya
operation

опоздать (на) apazd**a**t (na) to
arrive/be late; to miss

опрокинуть aprak**ee**noot to
knock over

оптика o**pt**eeka optician's

опухший ap**oo**Hshi swollen

оранжевый ar**a**nJevi orange
(colour)

организация argan**ee**z**a**tsi-ya
organization

организовать arga**nee**z**a**vat to
organize

оркестр ark**ye**str orchestra

оса asa wasp

осень o**s**yen autumn, (US) fall

   осенью o**s**yeny**oo** in the
   autumn, in the fall

осмотр asm**o**tr check-up

особенно as**o**byen-na especially

особняк asabn**ya**k detached
house

особый as**o**bi special

оставаться/остаться astav**a**tsa/
ast**a**tsa to stay; to remain

оставить ast**a**veet to leave
behind; to forget

остановиться astanav**ee**tsa
to stop

   остановитесь! astanav**ee**tyes!
   stop!

остановка astan**o**fka stop

остановка автобуса astan**o**fka
aft**o**boosa bus stop

остаток ast**a**tak rest

остаться ast**a**tsa to stay; to
remain

осторожно! astar**o**Jna! be
careful!; look out!

**осторожно, двери
закрываются!** astar**o**Jna,
dv**ye**ree zakriva-y**oo**tsa! caution,
the doors are closing!

осторожно, окрашено
astar**o**Jna, akr**a**shena wet paint

осторожный astar**o**Jni careful

остров o**st**raf island

острый o**st**ri hot, spicy; sharp

от ot from

ответ atv**yet** answer

ответить atv**yet**eet to answer

ответственный atv**yet**stvyen-ni responsible

отвечать/ответить atvyech**at**/ atv**yet**eet to answer

отвратительный atvrat**ee**tyelni disgusting

отдел ad-d**yel**, **отделение** ad-dyel**ye**nee-yeh department

отделение милиции ad-dyel**ye**nee-yeh meel**ee**tsi-ee police station

отдельно ad-d**yel**na separately

отдельный ad-d**yel**ni separate

отдельный номер ad-d**yel**ni **no**myer single room

отдохнуть ad-daHn**oot** to take a rest

отдых **o**d-diH holiday, vacation; rest

отдыхать/отдохнуть ad-diH**at**/ ad-daHn**oot** to take a rest

отец at**yets** father

открывалка atkriv**a**lka bottle-opener

открывать/открыть atkriv**at**/ atkr**it** to open

открытка atkr**it**ka card; postcard

открыто atkr**it**a open

открытый atkr**it**i open

открыть atkr**it** to open

отлично! atl**ee**chna! excellent!

отличный atl**ee**chni excellent

отменять/отменить

atmyen**yat**/atmyen**eet** to cancel

отоларинголог atalareeng**o**lak ear, nose and throat specialist

отопление ataply**e**nee-yeh heating

отправитель atprav**ee**tyel sender

отправить atprav**eet** to send

отправление atpravl**ye**nee-yeh departure

отправлять/отправить atpravl**yat**/atprav**eet** to send

от себя at syeb**ya** push

отъезд aty**est** departure

офис **o**fees waiter

официант afeetsi-**a**nt waiter

официантка afeetsi-**a**ntka waitress; barmaid

очаровательный acharav**a**tyelni lovely, charming

очевидец achyev**ee**dyets witness

очевидно achyev**ee**dna obviously

очень **o**chyen very; very much

очень приятно! ochyen pree-**ya**tna! pleased to meet you!

очередь ochyeryet queue, (US) line

    стоять в очереди sta-**ya**t vochyeryedee to queue, to line up

очки achk**ee** glasses, eyeglasses

очки от солнца achk**ee** at s**o**ntsa sunglasses

ошибиться ashib**ee**tsa to be mistaken

    я ошибся/ошиблась ya ash**iy**psa/ash**iy**blas I've made a mistake (**said by man/woman**)

ошибка ash**iy**pka mistake, error

П

падать/упасть p**a**dat/oop**a**st to fall

падать/упасть в обморок p**a**dat/oop**a**st v**o**bmarak to faint

пакет pak**ye**t packet; parcel; paper bag

палатка pal**a**tka tent

палец p**a**lyets finger

палец ноги p**a**lyets nag**ee** toe

палуба pal**oo**ba deck

пальто pal**to** coat

памятник p**a**myatneek monument

папа p**a**pa dad

папироса papeer**o**sa Russian non-filter cigarette

пара p**a**ra pair; couple

парикмахер pareekma**н**yer hairdresser

парикмахерская

pareekma**н**yerska-ya barber's, hairdresser's

парилка par**ee**lka steam room

парк park park

пароль par**o**l password

паром par**o**m ferry

пароход para**н**ot steamer

партер part**e**r stalls

партия p**a**rtee-ya party

парус p**a**roos sail

парусная лодка par**oo**sna-ya l**o**tka sailing boat

парусник par**oo**sneek sailing boat

парусный спорт par**oo**sni sport sailing

паспорт p**a**spart passport

паспортный контроль p**a**spartni kantr**o**l passport control

пассажир pasa**J**eer passenger

Пасха p**a**s**н**a Easter

паук pa-**oo**k spider

пахнуть pa**н**n**oo**t to smell

пачка p**a**chka packet; pack; bundle

педаль pyed**a**l pedal

пейзаж pyayz**a**sh landscape; scenery

пельменная pyelm**ye**n-na-ya café selling ravioli

пеницилин pyeneetsil**ee**n penicillin

пенсионер pyensee-an**ye**r

пенсионерка, pyensee-an**ye**rka old-age pensioner (**male/female**)

пепельница pyepyelneetsa
ashtray

пер. lane

первая помощь pyerva-ya
pomash-ch first aid

первый pyervi first

первый класс pyervi klas first
class

первый этаж pyervi etash
ground floor, (US) first floor

перевал pyeryeval pass (mountain)

переводить/перевести
pyeryevadeet/pyeryevyestee to
translate; to interpret

переводчик pyeryevotcheek
translator; interpreter

переговорный пункт
pyeryegavorni poonkt
communications centre

перед pyeryed in front of; just
before

передняя часть pyeryednya-ya
chast front

переезд pyeryeh-yest level
crossing, (US) grade crossing

перейти pyeryeh-eetee to cross

перекрёсток pyeryekryostak
cross-roads; junction,
intersection

перелом pyeryelom fracture

переодеться pyeryeh-adyetsa to
get changed

переполненный pyeryepolnyen-
ni crowded

перерыв pyeryeriyf break;
interval

перерыв на обед с… до…
pyeryeriyf na abyet s… do…

closed for lunch from… to…

пересадка pyeryesatka change;
transfer

пересесть pyeryesyest to change
(trains etc)

пересылать/переслать
pyeryesilat/pyeryeslat to forward

переулок pyeryeh-oolak lane

переход pyeryehot transfer;
passage; crossing; underpass,
subway

переходить/перейти
pyeryeHadeet/pyeryeh-eetee to
cross

переходник pyeryeHadneek
adaptor

перманент pyermanyent perm

перчатки pyerchatkee gloves

песня pyesnya song

> **Travel tip** Try to hear some
> Russian Orthodox church
> music, which is solely choral
> and wonderfully in keeping
> with the rituals of the faith.
> Russia's finest Orthodox
> choirs and bell-ringers per-
> form at annual festivals, and
> in monasteries and cathe-
> drals throughout Easter.

песок pyesok sand

петь pyet to sing

печатный материал pyechatni
matyeree-al printed matter

печень pyechyen liver

пешеход pyesheHot pedestrian

пешеходная зона pyesheHodna-
ya zona pedestrian precinct

А
Б
В
Г
Д
Е
Ё
Ж
З
И
Й
К
Л
М
Н
О
П
Р
С
Т
У
Ф
Х
Ц
Ч
Ш
Щ
Ъ
Ы
Ь
Э
Ю
Я

пешеходный переход
pyesheHodni pyeryeHot
pedestrian crossing

пешком pyeshkom on foot

пещера pyesh-chyera cave

пивной бар peevnoy bar,
пивнушка peevnooshka bar,
beer cellar, pub

пилка для ногтей peelka dlya
naktyay nailfile

писать/написать peesat/
napeesat to write

писчебумажный магазин
peesh-chyeboomaJni magazeen
stationer's

письмо peesmo letter

питательный peetatyelni
nutritious

пить/выпить peet/viypeet to
drink

питьевая вода peetyeva-ya vada
drinking water

пиццерия peetseree-ya pizzeria

пишущая машинка
peeshoosh-cha-ya mashiynka
typewriter

пищевое отравление peesh-
chyevo-yeh atravlyenee-yeh food
poisoning

пл. square

плавание plavanee-yeh
swimming

плавать запрещается
plavat zapryesh-cha-yetsa no
swimming

плавать/плыть plavat/pliyt to
swim

плавки plafkee swimming trunks

плакат plakat poster

плакать plakat to cry

пластинка plasteenka record

пластмассовый plasmas-savi
plastic

платите в кассу plateetyeh kas-
soo pay at the cash desk

платить/заплатить plateet/
zaplateet to pay

платный platni paid; to be paid
for

платок platok headscarf

платформа platforma platform,
(US) track

платье platyeh dress

плащ plash-ch raincoat

племянник plyemyan-neek
nephew

племянница plyemyan-neetsa
niece

плёнка plyonka film (for camera)

плечо plyecho shoulder

пломба plomba filling

плоский ploskee flat

плохо ploHa bad; badly

мне плохо mnyeh ploHa I feel
ill

плохой plaHoy bad

площадь plosh-chat square

плыть pliyt to swim

плэйер player personal stereo

пляж plyash beach

по po along; according to; on

по-английски pa-angleeskee
in English

поблагодарить pablagadareet
to thank

побриться pabreetsa to shave

повар povar cook

поверить pavyereet to believe

поворачивать/повернуть pavaracheevat/pavyernoot to turn

повредить pavryedeet to damage

повторять/повторить pavtaryat/paftareet to repeat

повязка pavyaska bandage

погладить pagladeet to iron; to stroke

погода pagoda weather

погулять pagoolyat to go for a walk

под pot below; under; underneath

под. entrance number

подавленный padavlyen-ni depressed

подарить padareet to give (present)

подарок padarak present, gift

подбородок padbarodak chin

подвал padval basement

подгузник padgoozneek nappy, diaper

поделиться padyeleetsa to share

подержанный padyerJan-ni secondhand

подмётка padmyotka sole

подниматься/подняться padneematsa/padnyatsa to go up

поднос padnos tray

подняться padnyatsa to go up

подобный padobni similar

подождать padaJdat to wait

подойти paditee to approach; to arrive; to come

подписать patpeesat to sign

подпись potpees signature

подросток padrostak teenager

подруга padrooga friend; girlfriend

подтвердить pat-vyerdeet to confirm

подумать padoomat to think

подушка padooshka pillow

подфарники patfarneekee sidelights

подходить/подойти padHadeet/paditee to approach; to arrive; to come

подъезд padyest entrance

подъёмник padyomneek ski-lift, chairlift

поезд po-yest train

посздка pa-yestka journey, trip

пожалуйста paJalsta please

пожар paJar fire, blaze

пожарная команда paJarna-ya kamanda fire brigade

пожарный выход paJarni viyHat fire exit

пожелание: с наилучшими пожеланиями sna-eeloochshimee paJelanee-yamee best wishes

поживаете: как вы поживаете? kak viy paJivayetyeh? how are you?

позаботиться о pazaboteetsa o to take care of

позавчера pazafchyera the day before yesterday

позвать pazvat to call

позвонить pazvan**eet** to ring; to phone

поздно p**o**zna late; it's late

поздравляю! pazdravl**ya**-yoo! congratulations!

позже p**o**J-Jeh later on

познакомить paznak**o**meet to introduce

познакомиться paznak**o**meetsa to get to know, to become acquainted with, to meet

поймать p**i**mat to catch

пока pak**a** while

пока! pak**a**! bye!

показывать/показать pak**a**zivat/pakaz**a**t to show

покидать/покинуть pakeed**a**t/pak**ee**noot to leave

по крайней мере pa kr**i**nyay m**ye**ryeh at least

покрасить pakr**a**seet to paint

покупатель pakoop**a**tyel customer; buyer

покупать/купить pakoop**a**t/koop**ee**t to buy

покупки pak**oo**pkee shopping

идти за покупками eet-t**ee** za pak**oo**pkamee to go shopping

пол pol floor; sex

полдень p**o**ldyen midday, noon

поле p**o**lyeh field

полезный pal**ye**zni useful

поликлиника paleekl**ee**neeka surgery; medical centre

политика pal**ee**teeka politics

политический paleet**ee**chyeskee political

поллитра pol-l**ee**tra half a litre

полночь p**o**lnach midnight

полный p**o**lni full

половина palav**ee**na half

половина второго palav**ee**na ftar**o**va half past one

положить pala**J**eet to put, to place

полотенце palat**ye**ntseh towel

получать/получить palooch**a**t/palooch**ee**t to receive

полчаса polchas**a** half an hour

поменять pamyen**ya**t to change

померить pamy**e**reet to try on

помнить/вспомнить p**o**mneet/fsp**o**mneet to remember, to recall

я помню ya p**o**mnyoo I remember

помогать/помочь pamag**a**t/pam**o**ch to help

помогите! pamag**ee**tyeh! help!

помощь p**o**mash-ch help, aid, assistance

помыть pam**i**yt to wash

помыть посуду pam**iy**t pas**oo**doo to do the washing-up

помыться pam**iy**tsa to wash (oneself)

понедельник panyed**ye**lneek Monday

понимать/понять paneem**a**t/ pan**ya**t to understand

я не понимаю ya nyeh paneem**a**-yoo I don't understand

понос pan**o**s diarrhoea

понять pan**ya**t to understand

поп-музыка pop-m**oo**zika pop music

попробовать papr**o**bavat to taste; to try

порт port harbour, port

портфель partf**ye**l briefcase

порция p**o**rtsi-ya portion

порядок par**ya**dak order

у меня всё в порядке oo myen**ya** fsyo fpar**ya**tkyeh fine, I'm OK, everything's OK

посадка pas**a**tka landing; boarding; arrival

посадочный талон pas**a**dachni tal**o**n boarding pass

посещать/посетить pasyesh-ch**a**t/pasyet**ee**t to visit

послание paslanee-yeh message

послать pasl**a**t to send

после p**o**slyeh after

последний pasl**ye**dnee last

послезавтра p**o**slyez**a**ftra the day after tomorrow

послушать pasl**oo**shat to listen (to)

посмотреть (на) pasmatr**ye**t (na) to look (at); to watch

посольство pas**o**lstva embassy

поставить past**a**veet to put

поставить машину pastaveet mashiynoo to park

постараться pastaratsa to try

постель pastyel bed

постельное бельё pastyelna-yeh byelyo bed linen

постирать pasteerat to do the washing

посторонним вход воспрещён pastaroneem fнot vaspryesh-chon private, staff only

посуда pasooda crockery

посылать/послать pasilat/ paslat to send

посылка pasiylka parcel

потерять patyeryat to lose

по техническим причинам pa tyeнneechyeskeem preecheenam for technical reasons

потолок patalok ceiling

потом patom then; afterwards

потому что patamoo shta because

потребитель patryebeetyel consumer

потрясающий patryasa-yoosh-chee tremendous

похмелье paнmyelyeh hangover

похожий paнoɹi like, similar to

поцеловать patselavat to kiss

поцелуй patseloo kiss

почему? pachyemoo? why?

починить pacheeneet to mend, to repair

почки pochkee kidneys

почта pochta post office; mail

почта до востребования pochta da-vastryebavanee-ya poste restante, general delivery

почтальон pachtalyon postman, mailman

почти pachtee almost

почтовая бумага pachtova-ya boomaga writing paper

почтовый индекс pachtovi eendeks postcode, zip code

почтовый ящик pachtovi yash-cheek letterbox, mailbox

пояс po-yas belt

потерять patyeryat to lose

пр. avenue

правильный praveelni right, correct

правительство praveetyelstva government

православная церковь pravaslavna-ya tserkaf Russian Orthodox Church

правый pravi right

праздник prazneek public holiday

празднование praznavanee-yeh celebration

практичный prakteechni practical

прачечная prachyechna-ya laundry

прачечная-самообслуживания prachyechna-ya-sama-apslooɹivanee-ya launderette

пребывание pryebivanee-yeh stay

предварительный заказ pryedvareetyelni zakas

reservation

**предварительный заказ
билетов** pryedvar**ee**tyelni z**a**kas
bee**lye**taf seat reservation

предлагать/предложить
pryedlag**a**t/pryedla**zh**eet to offer,
to suggest

предложение pryedla**zh**enee-yeh
offer, proposal

предложить pryedla**zh**eet to offer,
to suggest

предохранитель
pryeda**h**ran**ee**tyel fuse

предпочитать pryetpacheet**a**t
to prefer

председатель pryedsyed**a**tyel
chairman

представитель pryetstav**ee**tyel
representative; agent

презерватив pryezyervat**ee**f
condom

прекрасный pryekr**a**sni
beautiful; fine; excellent

прелестный pryel**ye**sni pretty

преподаватель pryepadav**a**tyel
teacher; lecturer

Прибалтика preeb**a**lteeka Baltic
States

прибыль pr**ee**bil profit

прибытие preeb**i**tee-yeh arrival

привет preev**ye**t hello, hi

прививка preev**ee**fka
vaccination

привлекательный
preevlyek**a**tyelni attractive

привычка preev**i**chka habit

привязной ремень
preevyazn**oy** ryem**ye**n seatbelt

приглашать/пригласить
preeglash**a**t/preeglas**ee**t to invite

приглашение preeglash**e**nee-yeh
invitation

пригород pr**ee**garat suburbs

пригородный поезд
pr**ee**garadni p**o**-yest local train,
suburban train

пригородная касса
pr**ee**garadna-ya k**a**s-sa ticket
office for suburban trains

приготовить preegat**o**veet to
cook; to prepare

приезд pree-**ye**st arrival

приезжать/приехать pree-
yez**zh**at/pree-**ye**hat to arrive (by
transport)

приём посылок pree-**yo**m
pas**i**lak parcels counter

приехать pree-**ye**hat to
arrive (by transport)

прийти preet**ee** to come, to
arrive (on foot)

**прикурить: у вас есть
прикурить?** oo vas yest
preekoor**ee**t? have you got a
light?

прилёт preel**yo**t arrival

пример preem**ye**r example

примерно preem**ye**rna
approximately

принадлежать preenadlye**zh**at
to belong

принимать/принять
preeneem**a**t/preen**ya**t to accept,
to take

принтер pr**ee**nter printer

приносить/принести

А
Б
В
Г
Д
Е
Ё
Ж
З
И
Й
К
Л
М
Н
О
П
Р
С
Т
У
Ф
Х
Ц
Ч
Ш
Щ
Ъ
Ы
Ь
Э
Ю
Я

preenaseet/preenyestee to bring

принять preenyat to accept, to take

природа preeroda nature

пристегните ремни preestyegneeteyh ryemnee fasten seat belts

приходить/прийти preeHadeet/preetee to come, to arrive (on foot)

причал preechal quay

причина preecheena cause; reason

приятного аппетита! preeyatnava apyeteeta! enjoy your meal!

приятный pree-yatni pleasant, nice

пробка propka plug; traffic jam

проблема prablyema problem

пробовать/попробовать probavat/paprobavat to taste; to try

проверять/проверить pravveryat/pravvereet to check

прогноз погоды pragnos pagodi weather forecast

программа program-ma programme

прогулка pragoolka walk

продавать/продать pradavat/pradat to sell

продаётся prada-yotsa for sale

продажа pradaJa sale; marketing

продажа билетов pradaJa beelyetaf tickets on sale

проданный pradan-ni sold

продать pradat to sell

продукция pradooktsi-ya product

проездной билет pra-yeznoy beelyet monthly season ticket

проживание с двухразовым питанием praJivanee-yeh zdvooH-razavim peetanee-yem half board

проживание с трёхразовым питанием praJivanee-yeh stryoH-razavim peetanee-yem full board

производство pra-eezvotstva production

произнести pra-eeznyestee to pronounce

произносить/произнести pra-eeznaseet/pra-eeznyestee to pronounce

прокат prakat rental, hire

прокат автомобилей prakat aftamabeelyay car rental

прокол prakol puncture

промышленность pramiyshlyen-nast industry

пропуск propoosk pass; hotel card

проснуться prasnootsa to wake up

проспект praspyekt brochure; avenue

простите prasteeteyh excuse me, sorry

простите? prasteeteyh? pardon?, pardon me?

простой prastoy simple

простыня prastinya sheet

просьба prosba request

просьба не... prosba nyeh...
please do not...

протестант pratyestant
Protestant

против proteef against

противозачаточное средство prateevazachatachna-yeh sryetstva contraceptive

прохладный praHladni cool

процент pratsent per cent

прочитать pracheetat to read

прошлый proshli last

в прошлом году fproshlam gadoo last year

на прошлой неделе na proshli nyedyelyeh last week

проявлять/проявить pra-yavlyat/pra-yaveet to develop

пруд proot pond

прыгать/прыгнуть priygat/priygnoot to jump

прыщик priysh-cheek spot, pimple

прямо pryama straight ahead

прямой pryamoy direct; straight

прямой номер pryamoy nomyer direct dialling

прямой рейс pryamoy ryays direct flight

птица pteetsa bird; poultry

публика poobleeka audience; public

пуговица poogaveetsa button

пункт poonkt point; station; place, spot; centre

пункт скорой помощи poonkt skori pomash-chee first-aid post

пустой poostoy empty

путеводитель pootyevadeetyel guidebook

путешествовать pootyeshestvavat to travel

путь poot path; way

пчела pchyela bee

пылесос pilyesos vacuum cleaner

пьеса pyesa play (theatre)

пьяный pyani drunk

пятка pyatka heel (of foot)

пятнадцатый pyatnatsati fifteenth

пятнадцать pyatnatsat fifteen

пятница pyatneetsa Friday

пятно pyatno stain

пятый pyati fifth

пять pyat five

пятьдесят pyadyesyat fifty

пятьсот pyatsot five hundred

Р

р. rouble

работа rabota job; work

работает с... до... rabota-yet s... do... open from... to...

работать rabotat to work

это не работает eta nyeh rabota-yet it's not working

рад rat glad

радио radee-o radio

раз ras time (occasion)

один раз adeen ras once

разбудить razboodeet to wake up

разве? razvyeh? really?

А
Б
В
Г
Д
Е
Ё
Ж
З
И
Й
К
Л
М
Н
О
П
Р
С
Т
У
Ф
Х
Ц
Ч
Ш
Щ
Ъ
Ы
Ь
Э
Ю
Я

разведён razvyedyon,
разведена razvyedyena
divorced (*male/female*)

развилка razveelka junction;
fork (**in road**)

разговаривать razgavareevat
to talk

**разговаривать с водителем
запрещается** razgavareevat
svadeetyelyem zapryesh-cha-
yetsa do not speak to the driver

разговор razgavor conversation

раздевалка razdyevalka
changing room

размен razmyen change

размер razmyer size

разный razni various, different

разочарованный razacharovan-
ni disappointed

разрешается razryesha-yetsa it
is allowed

разрешать/разрешить
razryeshat/razryeshiyt to let, to
allow

разрешение razryeshenee-yeh
permission; licence

разрешить razryeshiyt to let,
to allow

разумный razoomni sensible

район rion district

раковина rakaveena sink

ракушка rakooshka shell

рана rana injury

раненый ranyeni injured

рано rana early

раскладушка raskladooshka
campbed

распаковать (чемодан)
raspakavat (chyemadan) to unpack

расписание raspeesanee-yeh
timetable, (**US**) schedule

распродажа raspradaja sale

рассказ raskas story

рассказать raskazat to tell

расслабиться ras-slabeetsa to relax

расстояние ras-sta-**ya**nee-yeh distance

расстройство желудка rastroystva Jelootka indigestion

растение rastyenee-yeh plant

расчёска raschoska comb

ребёнок ryebyonak child; baby

ребро ryebro rib

ревматизм ryevmateezm rheumatism

ревнивый ryevneevi jealous

регистратура ryegeestratoora reception

регистрация ryegeestratsi-ya check-in; registration

регистрация багажа ryegeestratsi-ya bagaJa check-in

регулировщик ryegooleerovshcheek traffic warden

регулярный рейс ryegoolyarni ryays scheduled flight

редкий ryetkee rare

резать ryezat to cut

резина ryezeena rubber

резиночка ryezeenachka rubber band

рейс ryays flight

река ryeka river

реклама ryeklama advertisement; advertising

рекламировать ryeklameeravat to advertise

рекомендовать ryekamyendavat to recommend

религия ryeleegee-ya religion

ремень вентилятора ryemyen vyenteelyatara fan belt

ремесленные изделия ryemyeslyen-ni-yeh eezdyelee-ya crafts

ремонт ryemont repair

ремонт обуви ryemont oboovee shoe repairs

ремонт сумок ryemont soomak bag repairs

ресторан ryestaran restaurant

рецепт ryetsept prescription; recipe

решать/решить ryeshat/ryeshiyt to decide

решение ryeshyenee-yeh decision

Рига reega Riga

родина rodeena native country; home(land)

родители radeetyelee parents

родиться radeetsa to be born

родственники rotstvyen-neekee relatives

Рождество raJdyestvo Christmas

Travel tip Russians largely ignore the Western Christmas in the rush to prepare for New Year (*Novi Got*). This remains a family occasion until midnight, when a frenzied round of house-calling commences, getting steadily more drunken and continuing until dawn. Many Russians also celebrate the Orthodox New Year on the night of January 13–14.

с Рождеством!
sraJdyestv**o**m! merry Christmas!

роза r**o**za rose

розетка raz**ye**tka socket

розовый r**o**zavi pink

рок-музыка rok-m**oo**zika rock
music

роман ram**a**n novel

Россия ras-s**ee**-ya Russia

рот rot mouth

рубашка roob**a**shka shirt

рубль roobl rouble

руины roo-**ee**ni ruins

рука rook**a** arm; hand

руками не трогать rook**a**mee
nyeh tr**o**gat do not touch

руль rool steering wheel

русская r**oo**ska-ya Russian

русские r**oo**skee-yeh the Russians

русский r**oo**skee Russian

русский язык r**oo**skee yaz**i**yk
Russian (language)

Русь roos Russia (historical)

ручей rooch**yay** stream

ручка r**oo**chka handle; pen

ручная кладь roochn**a**-ya klat
hand luggage, hand baggage

ручной тормоз roochn**oy** t**o**rmas
handbrake

рыба r**i**yba fish

рыбная ловля r**i**ybna-ya l**o**vlya
fishing

рыбная ловля запрещена
r**i**ybna-ya l**o**vlya zapryesh-chyen**a**
no fishing

рыбный магазин r**i**ybni
magaz**ee**n fishmonger's

рыжий r**i**yЛi red-headed

рынок r**i**ynak market

Travel tip While local grocers
stock a range of Russian and
foreign products, the freshest
produce is found at markets
(*riynak*), where vendors tempt
buyers with nibbles of fruit,
cheese, sour cream, ham,
pickles and other home-made
delights.

рюкзак ryoogz**a**k rucksack

рюмка ry**oo**mka wine glass

ряд ryat row

рядом (с) ry**a**dam (s) next to

C

с s with

с нарочным sn**a**rachnim special
delivery

сад sat garden

садиться/сесть sad**ee**tsa/syest
to sit down; to get in

салфетка salf**ye**tka napkin

самовар samav**a**r samovar

Travel tip Traditionally,
Russian tea was brewed
and stewed for hours, and
topped up with boiling water
from an ornate tea urn, or
samovar, but nowadays even
the more run-of-the-mill cafés
use imported teabags. Most
Russians drink tea without
milk, and if you want it you
need to ask for it in cafés.

самолёт samal**yot** plane

самолётом samal**yo**tam by air

самообслуживание sama-aps**loo**Jivanee-yeh self-service

самый sami the most

санитарный день saneetarni dyen closed for cleaning

Санкт Петербург sankt pyetyer**boo**rk St Petersburg

сапог sapok boot

сауна sa-**oo**na sauna

свадьба svadba wedding

свежий svye**J** fresh

свёкор svyokar father-in-law **(husband's father)**

свекровь svyekrof mother-in-law **(husband's mother)**

свёрток svyortak package

свет svyet light

светло- svyetla- light **(colour)**

светофор svyetafor traffic lights

свеча svyecha candle

свеча зажигания svyecha zaJiganee-ya sparkplug

свинья sveenya pig

свитер svee**ter** sweater, jumper

свободно svabodna free; vacant; fluent

свободный svabodni free; vacant; fluent

свободных мест нет svabodniH myest nyet no vacancies

своё sva-**yo**, **свои** sva-**ee**, **свой** svoy, **своя** sva-**ya** my; your; his; its; her; our; their; mine; yours; hers; ours; theirs

свояченица sva-yachyeneetsa sister-in-law **(wife's sister)**

связываться/связаться (с) svyazivatsa/svyazatsa (s) to get in touch with

святой svyatoy holy; saint

священник svyash-chyen-neek priest

сгореть zgaryet to burn

сделать zdyelat to do; to make

сделать пересадку zdyelat pyeryesatkoo to change **(trains etc)**

себе syebyeh, **себя** syebya myself; yourself; himself; herself; itself; ourselves; yourselves; themselves

север syevyer north

к северу от k syevyeroo at north of

Северная Ирландия syevyerna-ya eerlandee-ya Northern Ireland

сегодня syevodnya today

сегодня вечером syevodnya vyechyeram this evening, tonight

сегодня днём syevodnya dnyom this afternoon

сегодня утром syevodnya **oo**tram this morning

седьмой syedmoy seventh

сейчас syaychas now, at the moment

секретарша syekryetarsha secretary

секретарь syekryetar secretary

секс seks sex

секунда syek**oo**nda second

семнадцатый syemnatsati seventeenth

семнадцать syemnatsat seventeen

семь syem seven

семьдесят syemdyesyat seventy

семьсот syemsot seven hundred

семья syemya family

сенная лихорадка syen-na-ya leeнaratka hayfever

сентябрь syentyabr September

сердечный приступ syerdyechni preestoop heart attack

сердитый syerdeeti angry

сердце syertseh heart

серебро syeryebro silver

середина syeryedeena middle

серый syeri grey

серьги syergee earrings

серьёзный syeryozni serious

сестра syestra sister

сесть syest to sit down; to get in

Сибирь seebeer Siberia

сигара seegara cigar

сигарета seegaryeta cigarette

сильный seelni strong

синий seenee blue

синяк seenyak bruise

скажите, пожалуйста… skaJeetyeh, paJalsta… can you tell me…?

сказать skazat to say; to speak

скала skala cliff; rock

скандальный skandalni shocking

скатерть skatyert tablecloth

сквозняк skvaznyak draught

скидка skeetka discount

складная детская коляска skladna-ya dyetska-ya kalyaska pushchair, (US) stroller

склон sklon slope

сковорода skavarada frying pan

скользкий skolskee slippery

сколько? skolka? how much?; how many?

сколько вам лет? skolka vam lyet? how old are you?

сколько это стоит? skolka eta sto-eet? how much is it?

скорая помощь skora-ya pomash-ch ambulance; first aid

скорее skaryeh-yeh rather

скорее! skaryeh-yeh! quickly!

скоро skora soon

скорость skorast speed; gear

скрывать/скрыть skrivat/skriyt to hide

скрыть skriyt to hide

скучный skooshni boring

слабительное slabeetyelna-yeh laxative

слабый slabi weak

сладкий slatkee sweet (to taste)

слайд slit slide (photographic)

слева slyeva on the left

следовать slyedavat to follow

следующая станция… slyedoo-yoosh-cha-ya stantsi-ya… next station…

следующий slyedoo-yoosh-chee next; following

в следующем году fslyedooyoosh-chyem gadoo next year

на следующей неделе na slyedoo-yoosh-chay nyedyelyeh next week

следующий день slyedoo-yoosh-chee dyen the next day

слепой slyepoy blind

слишком… sleeshkam… too…

слишком много sleeshkam mnoga too much

не слишком много nyeh sleeshkam mnoga not too much

словарь slavar dictionary

слово slova word

сложный sloJni complicated

сломанный sloman-ni broken

сломать slamat to break

сломаться slamatsa to break down

служащий slooJash-chee employee

служба slooJba service; employment; job; work;duty

служба размещения slooJba razmyesh-chyenee-ya reception desk

служебный вход slooJebni fHot staff entrance

случай sloochee chance

случайно sloochIna by chance

случаться/случиться sloochatsa/sloocheetsa to happen

слушать/послушать slooshat/paslooshat to listen (to)

слышать/услышать sliyshat/oosliyshat to hear

смерть smyert death

сметь smyet to dare

смешать smyeshat to mix

смеяться/засмеяться smyeh-yatsa/zasmyeh-yatsa to laugh

смотреть/посмотреть (на) smatryet/pasmatryet (na) to look (at); to watch

смочь smoch can, to be able to

вы сможете…? viy smoJetyeh…? will you be able to…?

он/она сможет on/ana smoJet he/she will be able to

смутно smootna vaguely

сначала snachala first; at first

снег snyek snow

снг es-en-geh CIS

снова snova again; once again

сноха snaHa daughter-in-law

собака sabaka dog

собачка sabachka little dog; at sign

соблюдайте тишину sablyoodItyeh teeshinoo please be quiet

собой saboy (by) myself; (by) yourself; (by) himself; (by) herself; (by) itself; (by) ourselves; (by) yourselves; (by) themselves

с собой s-saboy to take away, (US) to go

соболь sobal sable

собор sabor cathedral

собрание sabranee-yeh meeting

собственный sopstvyen-ni own; proper; personal

Советский Союз savyetskee sa-yoos Soviet Union

А
Б
В
Г
Д
Е
Ё
Ж
З
И
Й
К
Л
М
Н
О
П
Р
С
Т
У
Ф
Х
Ц
Ч
Ш
Щ
Ъ
Ы
Ь
Э
Ю
Я

современный savryem**yen**-ni
modern

**согласен: я согласен/
согласна** ya sagl**a**syen/sagl**a**sna
I agree (said by man/woman)

**согласованность
расписания** sagla**so**van-nast
raspees**a**nee-ya connection

**Соединённые Штаты
Америки** sayedeen**yon**-ni-yeh
sht**a**ti am**ye**reekee United States

сожаление: к сожалению k
saжal**ye**nee-yoo unfortunately

соки-воды s**o**kee-v**o**di fruit
juices and mineral water

солгать salg**a**t to lie, to tell a lie

солёный sal**yo**ni salty; savoury;
pickled

солнечный s**o**lnyechni sunny

солнечный ожог s**o**lnyechni
aж**o**k sunburn

солнечный свет s**o**lnyechni
svyet sunshine

солнечный удар s**o**lnyechni
oodar sunstroke

солнце s**o**ntseh sun

сон son dream; sleep

сопровождать saprava**j**dat to
accompany

сорок s**o**rak forty

сосед sas**yet**, **соседка** sas**ye**tka
neighbour (*male/female*)

сотовый телефон s**o**tavi
tyely**e**fon mobile phone, cell
phone

сохранять/сохранить
saнran**ya**t/saнran**ee**t to keep

социализм satsi-al**ee**zm socialism

Сочельник sach**ye**lneek
Christmas Eve

спальное место sp**a**lna-yeh
m**ye**sta couchette

спальный вагон sp**a**lni vag**o**n
sleeping car

спальный мешок sp**a**lni
mysh**o**k sleeping bag

спальня sp**a**lnya bedroom

спасатель spas**a**tel lifeguard

спасательный пояс spas**a**tyelni
p**o**-yas lifebelt

спасибо spas**ee**ba thank you

    спасибо большое spas**ee**ba
balsh**o**-yeh thank you very
much

спать spat to sleep

специальность spyetsi-**a**lnast
speciality

спешить spyesh**i**yt to hurry

СПИД speed Aids

спина speen**a** back (of body)

список sp**ee**sak list

спичка sp**ee**chka match

спокойной ночи spak**oy**nay
n**o**chee good night

спорт sport sport

спортивное оборудование
spart**ee**vna-yeh abar**oo**davanee-
yeh sports equipment

спортивный центр spart**ee**vni
tsentr sports centre

справа spr**a**va on the right

справедливый spravyedl**ee**evi
fair, just

справка spr**a**fka information

справочная spr**a**vachna-ya

enquiries; directory enquiries

справочное бюро spravachna-yeh byooro information office

справочный стол spravachni stol information desk

спрашивать/спросить sprashivat/spraseet to ask

спускаться/спуститься spooskatsa/spoosteetsa to go down

спущенная шина spoosh-chyen-na-ya shiyna flat tyre

среда sryeda Wednesday

среди sryedee among

среднего размера sryednyeva razmyera medium-sized

средство от насекомых sryetstva at nasyekomiн insect repellent

средство против загара sryetstva proteev zagara sunblock

срок srok period

срочно srochna urgent; urgently

срочный srochni urgent

СССР es-es-es-er USSR

ставить/поставить staveet/pastaveet to put

стадион stadee-on stadium

стакан stakan glass

становиться/стать stanaveetsa/stat to become

станция stantsi-ya station (underground, bus etc)

станция техобслуживания stantsi-ya tyeнap-slooжivanee-ya garage (for repairs), service station

стараться/постараться staratsa/pastaratsa to try

старше starsheh older

старый stari old

стать stat to become

стекло styeklo glass (material)

стена styena wall

стиральная машина steeralna-ya mashiyna washing machine

стиральный порошок steeralni parashok washing powder

стирать/постирать steerat/pasteerat to do the washing

сто sto hundred

стоимость sto-eemast charge, cost

стоимость международной отправки sto-eemast myeжdoonarodnay atprafkee overseas postage

стоить sto-eet to cost

стол stol table

столкновение stalknavyenee-yeh crash

столовая stalova-ya dining room; canteen

столовые приборы stalovi-yeh preebori cutlery

стоп-кран stop-kran emergency cord

сторона starana side

сто тысяч sto tiysyach hundred thousand

стоянка sta-yanka car park, parking lot

стоянка такси sta-yanka taksee taxi rank

стоять sta-yat to stand
страна strana country
страница straneetsa page
странный stran-ni strange
страх straH fear
страхование straHavanee-yeh insurance
стрижка streeshka haircut
стройный stroyni shapely
студент stoodyent, **студентка** stoodyentka student **(male/female)**
стул stool chair
стыдно: мне стыдно mnyeh stiydna I'm ashamed
стюард styoo-art steward
стюардесса styoo-ardesa stewardess
суббота soob-bota Saturday
сувенир soovyeneer souvenir
сумасшедший soomashetshi mad; madman
сумка soomka bag
сумочка soomachka handbag, **(US)** purse
сутки sootkee 24 hours, day and night
сухой sooHoy dry
сушить sooshiyt to dry
схема sHyema diagram; network map
сцепление stseplyenee-yeh clutch
счастливо оставаться! sh-chasleeva astavatsa! good night!; enjoy your stay!
счастливого пути! sh-chasleevava pootee! have a good trip!
счастливый sh-chasleevi happy
счастье sh-chastyeh happiness
   к счастью k sh-chastyoo

fortunately

счёт sh-chot bill, **(US)** check

США seh-sheh-**a** USA

сшить s-shit to sew

съесть s**y**est to eat

сыграть sigr**a**t to play

сын siyn son

сырой sir**oy** damp; raw

сюрприз syoorpr**ee**s surprise

Т

trolleybus or tram stop

та ta that; that one

табак tab**a**k tobacco

таблетка tabl**ye**tka pill, tablet

так tak so; this way; like this

   так! tak! well!

   так же красиво, как... tak Jeh kras**ee**va, kak... as beautiful as...

так как tak kak as; since

так себе tak syeb**ye**h so-so

также tagJeh also

такси taks**ee** taxi

таксофон taksaf**o**n public phone

талия t**a**lee-ya waist

талкучка talk**oo**chka flea market

Таллин t**a**l-leen Tallin

талон tal**o**n ticket

тальк talk talcum powder

там tam there

   там внизу tam vneez**oo** down there

таможенная декларация

тамоJen-na-ya dyeklaratsi-ya Customs declaration form

таможенный контроль tam**o**Jeni kantr**o**l Customs inspection

таможня tam**o**Jnya Customs

тампон tamp**o**n tampon

танцевать tantsev**a**t dance

тапочки tap**a**chkee slippers

таракан tarak**a**n cockroach

тарелка tar**ye**lka plate

тариф tar**ee**f charge, tariff

Ташкент tashk**ye**nt Tashkent

Тбилиси tbeel**ee**see Tbilisi

твёрдый tv**yo**rdi hard

твоего tva-y**e**vo (of) your; (of) yours

твоей tva-y**ay** your; yours; of your; of yours; to your; to yours; by your; by yours

твоему tva-y**e**moo (to) your; (to) yours

твоё tva-y**o** your; yours

твоём tva-y**o**m your; yours

твои tva-**ee** your; yours

твоим tva-**ee**m (by) your; (by) yours; (to) your; (to) yours

твоими tva-**ee**mee (by) your; (by) yours

твоих tva-**ee**H (of) your; (of) yours

твой tvoy your; yours

твою tva-y**oo** your; yours

твоя tva-y**a** your; yours

те tyeh those

театр tyeh-**a**tr theatre

театральная касса tyeh-atr**a**lna-

А
Б
В
Г
Д
Е
Ё
Ж
З
И
Й
К
Л
М
Н
О
П
Р
С
Т
У
Ф
Х
Ц
Ч
Ш
Щ
Ъ
Ы
Ь
Э
Ю
Я

ya **kas-sa** box office

тебе tyeb**yeh** you; to you

тебя tyeb**ya** you; of you

у тебя oo tyeb**ya** you have

телевизор tyelye**vee**zar television, TV set

телеграмма tyelyeg**ram**-ma telegram

тележка tyel**ye**shka trolley

телекс tye**lye**ks telex

телефон tyelye**fon** telephone

телефон-автомат tyelye**fon**-aftam**at** payphone

телефонная будка tyelye**fon**-na-ya b**oo**tka phone box

телефонный код tyelye**fon**-ni kot dialling code

телефонный справочник tyelye**fon**-ni spr**a**vachneek telephone directory

тело tye**la** body

тем tyem (by) that; (by) that one; (to) those

теми tye**mee** (by) those

тёмный tyomni dark

температура tyempyerat**oo**ra temperature

тени для век tye**nee** dlya vyek eye shadow

теннис tyen-nees tennis

тень tyen shadow; shade

в тени ftye**nee** in the shade

тепло tyep**lo** warm; it's warm

тёплый tyopli warm

термометр tyerm**o**myetr thermometer

термос termas Thermos flask

терпеть tyerp**yet** to bear, to stand

терять/потерять tyery**at**/patyery**at** to lose

тесный tyesni tight; cramped

тесть tyest father-in-law (**wife's father**)

тётя tyotya aunt

тех tyeн those; of those

течь tyech leak

течь tyech to flow; to stream; to leak

тёща tyosh-cha mother-in-law (**wife's mother**)

тихий tee**нee** quiet

тише tee**she** quieter

тише! tee**she**! quiet!

тишина teeshin**a** silence

ткань tkan material

то to that; that one

тобой tab**oy** (by) you

тогда tagd**a** then

того tav**o** (of) that; (of) that one

тоже to**ж**eh too; also

я тоже ya to**ж**eh me too

той toy that; that one; of that; of that one; to that; to that one

толкать/толкнуть talk**at**/talkn**oot** to push

толкнуть talkn**oot** to push

толпа talp**a** crowd

толстый tolsti fat (**adj**)

только tolka only; just

только по будним дням tolka pab**oo**dneem dnyam weekdays only

том tom that; that one

тому tamoo (to) that; (to) that one

тональный крем tanalni kryem
foundation cream

тонкий tonkee thin

тонуть/утонуть tanoot/
ootanoot to drown

торговый центр targovi tsentr
shopping centre

тормоза tarmaza brakes

тормозить/затормозить
tarmazeet/zatarmazeet to brake

тот tot that; that one

тот же самый tot Jeh sami the
same

тощий tosh-chee skinny

трава trava grass; herb; weed

традиционный tradeetsi-on-ni
traditional

традиция tradeetsi-ya tradition

транзитная посадка
tranzeetna-ya pasatka
intermediate stop

тратить trateet to spend

требовать tryebavat to demand

тревога tryevoga alarm

третий tryetee third

три tree three

тридцатый treetsati thirtieth

тридцать treetsat thirty

тринадцатый treenatsati
thirteenth

тринадцать treenatsat thirteen

триста treesta three hundred

трогать/тронуть trogat/
tronoot to touch

тройка troyka troika

тронуть tronoot to touch

тропинка trapeenka path

тротуар tratoo-ar pavement,
sidewalk

трубка troopka pipe (to smoke)

трубопровод troobapravot pipe;
pipeline

трудный troodni difficult

трусики trooseekee pants,
panties

трусы troosiy underpants

ту too that; that one

туалет too-alyet toilet, rest room

> Travel tip It's generally OK
> for non-customers to use
> the toilets in restaurants and
> hotels, since public toilets
> (too-alyet or WC) are few and
> far between – despite efforts
> to boost numbers by locating
> Portaloo-type cabins in parks
> and squares. There is a small
> charge, which includes a wad
> of toilet paper given out by
> the attendant.

туалетная бумага too-alyetna-
ya boomaga toilet paper

туалеты too-alyeti toilets, rest
rooms

туман tooman fog

туннель toon-nel tunnel

тургруппа toorgroop-pa tour
group

турист tooreest tourist

туристическая поездка
tooreesteechyeska-ya payeztka
package tour

Турция toortsi-ya Turkey

туфли tooflee shoes

А
Б
В
Г
Д
Е
Ё
Ж
З
И
Й
К
Л
М
Н
О
П
Р
С
Т
У
Ф
Х
Ц
Ч
Ш
Щ
Ъ
Ы
Ь
Э
Ю
Я

тушь для ресниц toosh dlya ryesn**ee**ts mascara

ты tiy you

тысяча t**iy**syacha thousand

тюрьма tyo**or**ma prison

тяжёлый tya**jo**li heavy

тянуть tyan**oo**t to pull

У

у oo at; by; near; with

у них oo nee**н** they have

у вас oo vas you have

у тебя oo tyeb**ya** you have

у неё oo nyeh-**yo** she has; it has

у нас oo nas we have

у него oo nyev**o** he has; it has

у меня oo myen**ya** I have

у вас есть…? oo vas yest…? have you got…?

у меня нет… oo myen**ya** nyet… I don't have…

убивать/убить oobeev**at**/oob**ee**t to kill

убирать/убрать oobeer**at**/oobr**at** to take away; to clean

убить oob**ee**t to kill

убрать oobr**at** to take away; to clean

уверенный oov**ye**ryen-ni sure

увидеть oov**ee**dyet to see

увлажняющий крем oovlaJn**ya**-yoosh-chee kryem moisturizer

увлекательный oovlyek**a**tyelni exciting

угол oogal corner

удар oodar blow; stroke

ударять/ударить oodar**ya**t/ood**a**reet to hit

удача ood**a**cha luck; success

> **Travel tip** Russians consider it bad luck to kiss or shake hands across a threshold, or return home to pick up something that's been forgotten. When buying flowers for your hostess, make certain that there's an odd number of blooms; even-numbered bouquets are for funerals. It's considered unlucky to whistle indoors, or put a handbag on the floor.

удивительный oodeev**ee**tyelni surprising

удлинитель oodleen**ee**tyel extension lead

удобный ood**o**bni comfortable

удостоверение oodasta-vyer**ye**nee-yeh certificate

уезжать/уехать ooyezJ**at**/oo**ye**Hat to leave

ужалить ooJ**a**leet to sting

ужас oo Jas, **ужасно** ooJ**a**sna it's awful, it's ghastly

ужасный ooJ**a**sni awful, terrible, ghastly

уже ooJ**eh** already

ужин oo Jin dinner; supper

ужинать oo Jinat to have dinner

узкий ooskee narrow

узнавать/узнать ooznav**at**/oozn**at** to recognize

уйти ooyt**ee** to go away

указатель поворота ookazatyel pavarota indicator

укладывать/уложить вещи ookladivat/oolaJeet vyesh-chee to pack

укол ookol injection

Украина ookra-eena Ukraine

украсть ookrast to steal

укус ookoos bite

ул., улица ooleetsa street

на улице na ooleetsyeh outside; in the street

уличное движение ooleechna-yeh dveeJenee-yeh traffic

Travel tip The signs on Moscow's metro are in Cyrillic. If you can't read them, listen to the tannoy announcements: if the voice is female you are heading out of the centre; if it is a man you are heading into the centre. All the lines are colour-coded and numbered.

уложить вещи oolaJeet vyesh-chee to pack

уложить волосы феном oolaJeet volasi fyenam to blow-dry

улучшить oolootshit to improve

улыбаться/улыбнуться oolibatsa/oolibnootsa to smile

улыбка ooliypka smile

улыбнуться ooliybnootsa to smile

умелый oomyeli skilful

умирать/умереть oomeerat/oomyeryet to die

умный oomni clever, intelligent

умывальник oomivalneek washbasin

универмаг ooneevyermak department store

универсам ooneevyersam supermarket

университет ooneevyerseetyet university

упасть oopast to fall

упасть в обморок oopast vobmarak to faint

управляющий oopravlya-yoosh-chee manager

уровень масла ooravyen masla oil level

уродливый oorodleevi ugly

урок oorok lesson

уронить ooraneet to drop

услышать oosliyshat to hear

успех oospyeн success

желаю успеха! Jelayoo oospyeнa! good luck!

успокойтесь ! oospakoytyes! calm down!

усталый oostali tired

устройство oostroystva device

усы oosiy moustache

утонуть ootanoot to drown

утро ootra morning

утра ootra in the morning; a.m.

в пять часов утра fpyat chasof ootra at 5 a.m.

утюг ootyook iron (for clothes)

ухо ooнa ear

уходить/уйти ooнadeet/ooytee to go away

А
Б
В
Г
Д
Е
Ё
Ж
З
И
Й
К
Л
М
Н
О
П
Р
С
Т
У
Ф
Х
Ц
Ч
Ш
Щ
Ъ
Ы
Ь
Э
Ю
Я

уходите! ooнadeetyeh! go away!

учёт oochot stocktaking

учитель oocheetyel,
учительница oocheetyelneetsa
teacher

учиться oocheetsa to learn; to
study

Уэльс oo-els Wales

уэльский oo-elskee Welsh

Ф

файл fil file

факс faks fax

факсимильный аппарат
fakseemeelni aparat fax machine

фамилия fameelee-ya surname

фары fari headlights

февраль fyevral February

фейерверк fyay-yervyerk
fireworks

фен fyen hairdryer

ферма fyerma farm

Финляндия feenlyandee-ya
Finland

фиолетовый fee-alyetavi purple

фирма feerma firm, company

флаг flak flag

флешка fleshka memory stick

фонарик fanareek torch

фонтан fantan fountain

формат farmat format

формат MP3 empetree MP3
format

фотоаппарат fata-aparat camera

фотограф fatograf photographer

фотографировать
fatagrafeeravat to take photos

фотография fatagrafee-ya
photograph

Франция frantsi-ya France

французский frantsooskee
French

французский язык frantsooskee
yazik French (language)

фрукты frookti fruit

фунт foont pound

фуражка foorashka cap

фургон foorgon van

футбол foodbol football

футболка foodbolka T-shirt

футбольное поле foodbolna-yeh
polyeh football pitch

Х

халат Halat dressing gown

химчистка Heemcheestka dry-
cleaner

хлеб Hlyep bread

хлопок Hlopak cotton

ходить Hadeet to go (on foot), to
walk; to suit

хозяин Hazya-een owner; host

хозяйственный магазин
Hazyistvyen-ni magazeen
hardware store

хоккей Hakyay hockey

Travel tip Ice hockey is one
of Russia's most popular
sports, and Moscow is a
major venue on the national
and international circuit.
Though the season runs
from September to April, the
highlights of the calendar for
many fans are the Spartak
Cup in August – a pre-season
tournament featuring the
Russian All-Stars – and the
World Championship in July.

холм Holm hill

холодильник Haladeelneek fridge

холодный Halodni cold

холостяк Halastyak bachelor

хороший Haroshi good

хорошо Harasho well

хорошо! Harasho! good!

мне хорошо mnyeh Harasho
I'm well

хотеть Hatyet to want

я хотел/хотела ya Hatyel/
Hatyela I wanted (said by man/
woman)

я хотел/хотела бы… ya
Hatyel/Hatyela bi… I would
like… (said by man/woman)

хотим Hateem we want

хотите Hateetyeh you want

хотя Hatya although

хотят Hatyat they want

хочет Hochyet he wants; she
wants; it wants

хочется: мне хочется… mnyeh
Hochyetsa… I feel like…

хочешь Hochyesh you want

А
Б
В
Г
Д
Е
Ё
Ж
З
И
Й
К
Л
М
Н
О
П
Р
С
Т
У
Ф
Х
Ц
Ч
Ш
Щ
Ъ
Ы
Ь
Э
Ю
Я

хочу Hachoo I want

храбрый Hrabri brave

храните в сухом/
прохладном/тёмном месте
Hraneetyeh fsooHom/praHladnam/
tyomnam myestyeh keep in a
cool/dark/dry place

хранить Hraneet to keep; to
preserve

хрустящий картофель
Hroostyash-chee kartofyel crisps,
(US) chips

художник HoodoJneek artist,
painter

худой Hoodoy thin

худший Hootshi worst

хуже HooJeh worse

Ц

царь tsar tsar

цвет tsvyet colour

цветная плёнка tsvyetna-ya
plyonka colour film

цветок tsvyetok flower

цветочный магазин
tsvyetochni magazeen florist's,
flower shop

цветы tsvyetiy flowers

целовать/поцеловать tselavat/
patselavat to kiss

целый tseli whole

цена tsena price

центр tsentr centre

центр города tsentr gorada city
centre

центральное отопление

tsentralna-yeh ataplyenee-yeh
central heating

цепочка tsepochka chain

церковь tserkav church

Ч

чаевые cha-yeviyeh tip

Travel tip In taxis, the fare
will usually be agreed in
advance so there's no need
to tip; in restaurants, no one
will object if you leave an
extra ten percent or so, but
in most places it's not com-
pulsory. Check, too, that it
hasn't already been included.

чайник chineek kettle;
teapot

чартерный рейс charterni ryays
charter flight

час chas hour; one o'clock

в… часа… chasa at… o'clock

в… часов… chasof at…
o'clock

часто chasta often

частый chasti often

часть chast part

часы chasiy watch;
clock; hours

часы приёма chasiy pree-yoma
visiting hours

часы работы chasiy raboti
opening hours, opening times

чашка chashka cup

чаще chash-chyeh more often

чего chyevo what; of what

чек chyek cheque, (US) check

чековая книжка
chyekava-ya kneeshka cheque/
check book

человек chyelavyek person

челюсть chyelyoost jaw

чем chyem than; what; by what

чём chyom what

чемодан chyemadan suitcase

чему chyemoo what; to what

через chyeryes through;
across; in

через три дня chyeryes tree
dnya in three days

чёрно-белый chorna-byeli black
and white

Чёрное море chorna-yeh moryeh
Black Sea

чёрный chorni black

честный chyesni honest

четверг chyetvyerk Thursday

четвёртый chetvyorti fourth

четверть chyetvyert quarter

четверть часа chyetvyert
chasa quarter of an hour

четверть второго chyetvyert
ftarova quarter past one

без четверти два byes
chyetvyertee dva quarter to two

четыре chetiyryeh four

четыреста chyetiyryesta four
hundred

четырнадцатый chetiyrnatsati
fourteenth

четырнадцать chetiyrnatsat
fourteen

Чешская республика
chyeshska-ya ryespoobleeka
Czech Republic

чинить/починить cheeneet/
pacheeneet to mend

число cheeslo date; number

чистить cheesteet to clean

чистый cheesti clean; pure

читать/прочитать cheetat/
pracheetat to read

что shto what; that

что-нибудь shto-neeboot
anything

что-то shto-ta something

чувство choostva feeling

чувствовать choostvavat to feel

чувствовать себя choostvavat
syebya to feel

чулки choolkee stockings

чуть choot hardly, scarcely; a little

чьё: чьё это? cho eta? whose
is this?

Ш

шампунь shampoon shampoo

шапка shapka hat (with flaps)

шариковая ручка shareekava-
ya roochka ballpoint pen

шарф sharf scarf (neck)

шашлычная shashliychna-ya
café selling kebabs

швейцар shvyaytsar porter;
doorman

Швейцария shvyaytsaree-ya
Switzerland

Швеция shvyetsi-ya Sweden

шевелиться/шевельнуться shevyeleetsa/shevyelnootsa to move; to stir

шезлонг shezlonk deckchair

шёл shol went; was going

шёлковый sholkavi silk

шерсть sherst wool

шестнадцатый shesnatsati sixteenth

шестнадцать shesnatsat sixteen

шестой shestoy sixth

шесть shest six

шестьдесят shesdyesyat sixty

шестьсот shes-sot six hundred

шея sheh-ya neck

шина shiyna tyre

широкий shirokee wide

шить/сшить shit/s-shit to sew

шкаф shkaf cupboard; wardrobe, closet

школа shkola school

шла shla went; was going

шли shlee went; were going

шло shlo went; was going

шляпа shlyapa hat

шнурки shnoorkee shoelaces

шоколад shakalat chocolate

шорты shorti shorts

шоссе shas-seh highway

Шотландия shatlandee-ya Scotland

шотландский shatlandskee Scottish

штепсельная вилка shtepsyelna-ya veelka plug (electric)

штопор shtopar corkscrew

штраф shtraf fine

шум shoom noise

шумный shoomni noisy

шурин shooreen brother-in-law (wife's brother)

шутка shootka joke

Щ

щётка sh-chotka brush

Э

экипаж ekeepash crew

эластичный elasteechni elastic

электрический elyektreechyeskee electric

электричество elyektreechyestva electricity

электричка elyektreechka suburban train

электронная почта elyektron-na-ya pochta electronic mail

Эстония estonee-ya Estonia

эт. floor

эта eta it (is); that; this; this one

этаж etash floor; storey

первый этаж pyervi etash ground floor, **(US)** first floor

эти etee these; those

этим eteem (by) this; (by) this one; (to) these

этими eteemee (by) these

этих eteeн these; of these

это eta it (is); that; this (one)

этого etava (of) this; (of) this one

этой eti this; this one; of this; of this one; to this; to this one; by this; by this one

этом etam this; this one

этому etamoo (to) this; (to) this one

этот etat it (is); that; this; this one

эту etoo this; this one

Ю

юбка yoopka skirt

ювелирные изделия yoovyeleerni-yeh eezdyelee-ya jewellery

ювелирный магазин yoovyeleerni magazeen jeweller's shop

юг yook south

к **югу от** k yoogoo at south of

Южная Африка yooлna-ya afreeka South Africa

южный yooлni southern

юмор yoomar humour

Я

я ya I

явиться на регистрацию yaveetsa na ryegeestratsi-yoo to check in

яд yat poison

язык yaziyk tongue; language

Ялта yalta Yalta

январь yanvar January

ярлык yarliyk label

ярмарка yarmarka fair; market

ярус yaroos circle; tier

ясный yasni clear; obvious

А
Б
В
Г
Д
Е
Ё
Ж
З
И
Й
К
Л
М
Н
О
П
Р
С
Т
У
Ф
Х
Ц
Ч
Ш
Щ
Ъ
Ы
Ь
Э
Ю
Я

MENU READER

Food

Essential terms

bread хлеб Hlyep

butter масло masla

cup чашка chashka

dessert десерт dyesyert

fish рыба riyba

fork вилка veelka

glass стакан stakan

knife нож nosh

main course основное блюдо
asnavno-yeh blyooda

meat мясо myasa

menu меню myenyoo

pepper перец pyerets

plate тарелка taryelka

salad салат salat

salt соль sol

set menu комплексный обед
komplyeksni abyet

soup суп soop

spoon ложка loshka

starter закуска zakooska

table стол stol

another..., please ещё
одно..., пожалуйста yesh-
cho... peeva, paJalsta

excuse me! простите!
prasteetyeh!

could I have the bill, please?
счёт, пожалуйста sh-chot,
paJalsta

I'd like... (said by man/woman) я
бы хотел/хотела... ya biy
HatYel/HatYela...

А–Я

абрикос abreek**o**s apricot

азу az**oo** small pieces of meat in a savoury sauce

ананас ananas pineapple

антрекот antryek**o**t entrecote steak

апельсин apyels**ee**n orange

апельсиновое варенье apyels**ee**nava-yeh var**ye**nyeh marmalade

арахис araнees peanuts

арбуз arb**oo**s water melon

ассорти мясное asart**ee** myasn**o**-yeh assorted meats

ассорти рыбное asart**ee** r**iy**bna-yeh assorted fish

баклажан bakla**J**an aubergine

банан banan banana

баранина baraneena mutton, lamb

баранина на вертеле baraneena na v**ye**rtelyeh mutton grilled on a skewer

баранки barankee ring-shaped rolls

бараньи котлеты baranee katl**ye**ti lamb chops

батон bat**o**n baguette

бекон byek**o**n bacon

белый хлеб b**ye**liy нl**ye**p white bread

беф строганов byef-str**o**ganaf beef Stroganoff

битки beetk**ee** rissoles; hamburgers

битки из баранины beetk**ee** eez bar**a**nini lamb meatballs

бифштекс beefsht**e**ks steak

бифштекс натуральный beefsht**e**ks natoor**a**lni fried or grilled steak

блинчики bl**ee**ncheekee pancakes

> **Travel tip** Russian culinary traditions remain strong, especially with regard to *blini* (pancakes), one of the best-loved of Russian *zak-ooskee* – small dishes or *hors d'oeuvres*, which are often a meal in themselves. Zakuski traditionally form the basis of the famous "Russian table": a feast of awesome proportions accompanied by tea.

блинчики с вареньем bl**ee**ncheekee svar**ye**nyem pancakes with jam

блины bleen**iy** buckwheat pancakes, blini

блины с икрой bleen**iy** sikr**o**y blini with caviar

блины со сметаной bleen**iy** sa smyetan**i** blini with sour cream

блюда из птицы bl**yoo**da ees pt**ee**tsi poultry dishes

блюдо bl**yoo**da dish, course

бородинский хлеб barad**ee**nskee нl**ye**p dark rye bread

борщ borsh-ch beef, beetroot and cabbage soup

брынза br**i**ynza sheep's cheese, feta

брюссельская капуста bryoos-s**ye**lska-ya kap**oo**sta Brussels sprouts

бублик b**oo**bleek type of bagel

буженина с гарниром booJen**ee**na zgarn**ee**ram cold boiled pork with vegetables

булки b**oo**lkee rolls

булочка b**oo**lachka roll

бульон bool**yon** clear meat soup, bouillon

бульон с пирожками bool**yon** speerashkamee clear meat soup served with small meat pies

бульон с фрикадельками bool**yon** sfreekadelkamee clear soup with meatballs

бутерброд booterbr**ot** sandwich

бутерброд с мясом booterbr**ot** sm**ya**sam meat sandwich

бутерброд с сыром booterbr**ot** s-s**i**yram cheese sandwich

буханка boo**H**anka loaf

ванильный van**ee**lni vanilla

вареники var**ye**neekee curd or fruit dumplings

варёный var**yo**ni boiled

варенье var**ye**nyeh jam, preserve

ватрушка vatr**oo**shka cheesecake

вермишель vyermeesh**e**l vermicelli

вегетарианский vyegyetaree-**a**nskee vegetarian

ветчина vyetch**ee**na ham

взбитые сливки vzb**ee**ti-yeh sl**ee**fkee whipped cream

винегрет veenyegr**ye**t Russian vegetable salad: beetroot, potatoes, onions, peas, carrots and pickled cucumbers in mayonnaise or oil

виноград veenagr**a**t grapes

вишня v**ee**shnya sour cherries

галушка gal**oo**shka Ukrainian dumpling

гамбургер g**a**mboorgyer hamburger

гарнир garn**ee**r vegetables

говядина gav**ya**deena beef

говядина отварная с хреном gav**ya**deena atvarna-ya s**H**r**ye**nam boiled beef with horseradish

говядина тушёная gav**ya**deena toosh**o**na-ya stewed beef

голубцы galoopts**i**y cabbage leaves stuffed with meat and rice

горох gar**o**H peas

горошек gar**o**shek peas

горчица garch**ee**tsa mustard

горячие закуски gar**ya**chee-yeh zak**oo**skee hot starters, hot appetizers

горячий gar**ya**chee hot

грейпфрут gr**a**ypfroot grapefruit

гренки gr**ye**nkee croutons

гренок gr**ye**nak toast

грецкие орехи gr**ye**tskee-yeh ar**ye**нee walnut

гречка gryechka buckwheat

гречневая каша gryechnyeva-ya kasha buckwheat porridge

грибы greebiy mushrooms

грибы в сметане greebiy fsmyetanyeh mushrooms in sour cream

грибы маринованные greebiy mareenovani-yeh marinated mushrooms

груша groosha pear

гуляш из говядины goolyash eez gavyadeeni beef goulash

гусь goos goose

десерт dyesyert dessert

джем djem jam

дичь deech game

домашний damashnee home-made

домашняя птица damashnya-ya pteetsa poultry

дыня diynya melon

еда yeda food; meal

ежевика yeJeveeka blackberries

жареная рыба Jaryena-ya riyba fried fish

жареный Jaryeni grilled; fried; roast

жареный картофель Jaryeni kartofyel fried potatoes

жареный на вертеле Jaryeni na vyertyel-yeh grilled on a skewer

желе Jelyeh jelly

жир Jiyr lard

жульен Joolyen mushrooms or meat cooked with onions and sour cream

завтрак zaftrak breakfast

закуска zakooska snack; starter, appetizer

закуски zakooskee starters, appetizers

заливная рыба zaleevna-ya riyba fish in aspic

заливной zaleevnoy in aspic

замороженные продукты zamaroJen-ni-yeh pradookti frozen food

запеканка zapyekanka baked pudding; shepherd's pie

запечённый zapyechonni baked

зелёный горошек zyelyoni garoshek green peas

зелёный лук zyelyoni look spring onions

зелёный салат zyelyoni salat green salad

земляника zyemlyaneeka wild strawberries

зразы zrazi meat cutlets stuffed with rice, buckwheat or mashed potatoes

изделия из теста eezdyelee-ya ees tyesta pastry dishes

изюм eezyoom sultanas; raisins

икра eekra caviar

икра баклажанная eekra baklaJanna-ya mashed fried aubergines with onions and tomatoes икра зернистая eekra zyerneesta-ya fresh caviar

икра кетовая eekra kyetova-ya red caviar

индейка eendyayka turkey

инжир eenJiyr figs

кабачки kabachkee courgettes

камбала kambala plaice

капуста kapoosta cabbage

карп karp carp

карп с грибами karp zgreebamee carp with mushrooms

картофель kartofyel potatoes

картофельное пюре kartofyelna-yeh pyooreh mashed potatoes

картофель с ветчиной и шпиком kartofyel zvyetcheenoy ee shpeekam potatoes with ham and bacon fat

картофель фри kartofyel free chips, French fries

каша kasha porridge

каштан kashtan chestnut

кебаб kebap kebab

кекс kyeks fruit cake

кета kyeta Siberian salmon

кетчуп kyetchoop ketchup

кильки keelkee sprats

кисель keesyel thin fruit jelly

кисель из клубники keesyel ees kloobneekee strawberry jelly

кисель из чёрной смородины keesyel ees chornı smarodeenı blackcurrant jelly

кислая капуста keesla-ya kapoosta sauerkraut

кислые щи keesli-yeh sh-chee sauerkraut soup

клубника kloobneeka strawberries

клюква klyookva cranberries

колбаса kalbasa salami sausage

комплексный обед komplyeksnı abyet set menu

компот kampot stewed fruit in a light syrup; compote

компот из груш kampot eez groosh stewed pears

компот из сухофруктов kampot ees sooxa-frooktaf stewed dried fruit

консервы kansyervi tinned foods

конфета kanfyeta sweet, candy

копчёная колбаса kapchona-ya kalbasa smoked sausage

копчёная сёмга kapchona-ya syomga smoked salmon

копчёные свиные рёбрышки kapchoni-yeh sveeniy-yeh ryobrishkee smoked pork ribs

копчёный kapchonı smoked

коржики korJikee shortbread

корица kareetsa cinnamon

котлета katlyeta cutlet; burger; rissole

котлеты по-киевски katlyeti pa-kee-yefskee chicken Kiev

котлеты с грибами katlyeti zgreebamee steak with mushrooms

кофейный kaf**ya**yni coffee-
flavoured; coffee

краб krap crab

крабовые палочки k**ra**bavi-yeh
p**a**lachkee crab sticks

красная икра k**ra**sna-ya **ee**kr**a**
red caviar

красная смородина k**ra**sna-ya
sm**a**r**o**deena redcurrants

креветки krye**vye**tkee prawns

крем kryem butter cream

кровь: с кровью s k**ro**vyoo rare

кролик kr**o**leek rabbit

кукуруза kookoor**oo**za sweet
corn

кулебяка koolye**bya**ka pie with
meat, fish or vegetables

курица k**oo**reetsa chicken

лапша lapsha noodles

лесные орехи lyesn**i**y-yeh
ar**ye**нee hazelnuts

лимон leem**o**n lemon

ломтик l**o**mteek slice

лососина lasas**ee**na smoked
salmon

лосось las**o**s salmon

лук look onions

майонез mi-an**e**s mayonnaise

макаронные изделия
makar**o**n-ni-yeh eezd**ye**lee-ya
pasta

макароны makar**o**ni macaroni

малина mal**ee**na raspberries

мандарин mandar**ee**n mandarin;
tangerine

манная каша man-na-ya kasha
semolina

маргарин margar**ee**n margarine

маслины masl**ee**ni olives

масло m**a**sla butter; oil

мёд myot honey

медовый myed**o**vi honey

меню myen**yoo** menu

мидии m**ee**dee-ee mussels

миндаль meend**a**l almonds

моллюски mal-l**yoo**skee shellfish

молоко malak**o** milk

молочный mal**o**chni milk; dairy

молочный кисель mal**o**chni
kees**ye**l milk jelly

морковь mark**o**f carrots

мороженое mar**o**Jena-yeh ice
cream

мороженое малиновое
mar**o**Jena-yeh mal**ee**nava-yeh
raspberry ice cream

мороженое 'пломбир'
mar**o**Jena-yeh plamb**ee**r
originally ice cream with
candied fruit, but nowadays
often just plain vanilla ice cream

мороженое клубничное
mar**o**Jena-yeh kloobn**ee**chna-
yeh strawberry ice cream

мороженое молочное
mar**o**Jena-yeh mal**o**chna-yeh
dairy ice cream

**мороженое молочное с
ванилином** mar**o**Jena-yeh
mal**o**chna-yeh svaneel**ee**nam
vanilla dairy ice cream

мороженое шоколадное
mar**o**Jena-yeh shakal**a**dna-yeh

chocolate ice cream

морская капуста marska-ya
kapoosta sea kale

морские продукты marskee-
yeh pradookti seafood

мука mooka flour

мясной myasnoy meat

мясной бульон myasnoy
boolyon clear meat soup

мясо myasa meat

на вертеле na vyertyelyeh on a
skewer

на вынос na viynas to take away,
to go

**национальные русские
блюда** natsi-analni-yeh rooskee-
yeh blyooda Russian national
dishes

начинка nacheenka filling

обед abyet lunch

овощи ovash-chee vegetables

овощной avash-chnoy vegetable

овощной суп avash-chnoy soop
vegetable soup

огурец agooryets cucumber

огурцы со сметаной agoortsiy
sa smyetani cucumber with sour
cream

окорок okarak gammon

окрошка akroshka cold soup
made with kvas (see **квас**
p.249), vegetables and meat

оладьи aladee thick pancakes

оливки aleefkee olives

омар amar lobster

омлет amlyet omelette

омлет натуральный amlyet
natooralni plain omelette

омлет с ветчиной amlyet
svyetcheenoy ham omelette

орехи aryeHee nuts

осётр запечённый в сметане
asyotr zapyechoni fsmyetanyeh
sturgeon baked in sour cream

осетрина заливная asyetreena
zaleevna-ya sturgeon in aspic

осетрина под белым соусом
asyetreena pat byelim so-oosam
sturgeon in white sauce

осетрина с гарниром
asyetreena zgarneeram sturgeon
with vegetables

**осетрина с пикантным
соусом** asyetreena speekantnim
so-oosam sturgeon in piquant
sauce

основное блюдо asnavno-yeh
blyooda main course

отбивная котлета atbeevna-ya
katlyeta chop

отварная рыба atvarna-ya riyba
poached fish

отварной atvarnoy boiled;
poached

отварной цыплёнок atvarnoy
tsiplyonak boiled chicken

палтус paltoos halibut

панированный paneerovanni in
breadcrumbs

панированный цыплёнок
paneerovanni tsiplyonak chicken
in breadcrumbs

паштет pash**tyet** pâté; pie

пельмени pyel**myenee** type of ravioli

первое блюдо **pyer**va-yeh bl**yoo**da first course

перец **pyer**yets pepper

персик **pyer**seek peach

петрушка pyet**roo**shka parsley

печёнка pye**chon**ka liver

печёный pye**cho**ni baked

печенье pye**chye**nyeh biscuit, cookie; pastry

печень трески в масле **pye**chyen t**rye**skee v**ma**sl-yeh cod liver in oil

пирог pee**rok** pie; tart; cake

пирог с повидлом pee**rok** spa**vee**dlam jam tart

пирог с мясом pee**rok** sm**ya**sam meat pie

пирог с яблоками pee**rok** s**ya**blakamee apple pie

пирожки peera**shkee** pies

пирожки с капустой peera**shkee** ska**poo**sti cabbage pies

пирожки с мясом peera**shkee** sm**ya**sam meat pies

пирожки с творогом peera**shkee** st**vo**ragam cottage cheese pies

пирожное pee**ro**Jna-yeh pastries; cake, pastry

пицца **pee**tsa pizza

плавленый сыр **plav**lyeni siyr processed cheese

плов plof pilaf

повидло pa**vee**dla jam

под белым соусом pat b**ye**lim so-**oo**sam in white sauce

поджаренный padJ**a**ryen-ni grilled; fried

поджаренный хлеб padJ**a**ryen-ni Hl**yep** toast

под майонезом pad mI-an**e**zam in mayonnaise

подсолнечное масло pat**so**lnyechna-yeh **ma**sla sunflower oil

пожарские котлеты paJ**a**rskee-yeh kat**lye**ti minced chicken patties

помидор pamee**dor** tomato

пончики **pon**cheekee doughnuts

порция **por**tsi-ya portion

почки **po**chkee kidneys

приправа к салату pree**pra**va k sa**la**too salad dressing

простокваша prastak**va**sha natural set yoghurt

пряник p**rya**neek gingerbread

пряность p**rya**nast spice

птица p**tee**tsa poultry

рагу из баранины ra**goo** eez ba**ra**neeni lamb ragout

рагу из говядины ra**goo** eez gav**ya**deeni beef ragout

рак rak crayfish

рассол ras-**sol** pickle

рассольник ras-**sol**neek meat or fish soup with pickled cucumbers

ржаной хлеб rJa**noy** Hl**yep** rye

bread

рис rees rice

ромштекс с луком romshteks sl**oo**kam rump steak with onions

ростбиф с гарниром r**o**stbeef zgarn**ee**ram roast beef with vegetables

рубленое мясо r**oo**blyena-yeh m**ya**sa minced meat

рубленые котлеты r**oo**blyeni-yeh katl**ye**ti rissoles

рулет rool**ye**t meat and potato roll; swiss roll

рулет из рубленой телятины rool**ye**t eez r**oo**blyeni tyel**ya**teeni minced veal roll

русская кухня r**oo**ska-ya k**oo**Hnya Russian cuisine

рыба r**iy**ba fish

рыбные блюда r**iy**bni-yeh bl**yoo**da fish dishes

рыбный r**iy**bni fish

ряженка rya**J**enka fermented baked milk, similar to thick yoghurt

салат sal**a**t lettuce; salad

салат зелёный sal**a**t zyel**yo**ni green salad

салат из картофеля sal**a**t ees kart**o**fyelya potato salad

салат из лука sal**a**t eez l**oo**ka spring onion salad

салат из огурцов sal**a**t eez agoorts**of** cucumber salad

салат из помидоров sal**a**t ees pameed**o**raf tomato

salad

салат из помидоров с брынзой sal**a**t ees pameed**o**raf zbr**iy**nzi tomato salad with sheep's cheese

салат из редиски sal**a**t eez ryed**ee**skee radish salad

салат из яблок sal**a**t eez **ya**blak apple salad

салат мясной sal**a**t myasn**oy** meat salad

салат с крабами sal**a**t skr**a**bamee crab salad

салат столичный sal**a**t stal**ee**chni potato salad with meat, carrots, peas and mayonnaise

сало s**a**la salted pork fat, sliced and eaten with rye bread (Ukrainian)

самообслуживание sama-apsl**oo**Jivanee-yeh self-service

сандвич s**a**ndveech sandwich

сардельки sard**e**lkee thick frankfurters

сардины sard**ee**ni sardines

сардины в масле sard**ee**ni vm**a**slyeh sardines in oil

сахар s**a**Har sugar

свежий sv**ye**Ji fresh

свёкла sv**yo**kla beetroot

свинина sveen**ee**na pork

свинина жареная с гарниром sveen**ee**na **J**aryena-ya zgarn**ee**ram fried pork with vegetables

свинина с квашеной капустой sveen**ee**na skv**a**sheni

kap**oo**stl pork with sauerkraut

свиной sveen**oy** pork

свиные отбивные sveen**iy**-yeh atbeevn**iy**-yeh pork chops

с гарниром zgarn**ee**ram with vegetables

селёдка малосольная syel**yo**tka malas**o**lna-ya slightly salted herring

сельдь syeld herring

сёмга s**yo**mga salmon

скумбрия горячего копчения sk**oo**mbree-ya gar**ya**chyeva kapch**ye**nee-ya smoked mackerel

скумбрия запечённая sk**oo**mbree-ya zapyech**o**na-ya baked mackerel

сладкий sl**a**tkee sweet

сладкое sl**a**tka-yeh dessert, sweet course

слива sl**ee**va plum

сливки sl**ee**fkee cream

сливочное масло sl**ee**vachna-yeh m**a**sla butter

с майонезом smi-an**e**zam with mayonnaise

сметана smyet**a**na sour cream

солёное печенье sal**yo**na-yeh pyech**ye**nyeh savoury biscuits

солёные огурцы sal**yo**ni-yeh agoorts**iy** pickled cucumbers

солёные помидоры sal**yo**ni-yeh pameed**o**ri pickled tomatoes

солёный sal**yo**ni salty; savoury; salted; pickled

соль sol salt

солянка sal**ya**nka spicy soup made from fish or meat and vegetables; stewed meat and

cabbage with spices

сосиски sas**ee**skee frankfurters

соус s**o**-oos sauce

спаржа spar**Ja** asparagus

с рисом s r**ee**sam with rice

стерлядь st**ye**rlyat small
sturgeon

студень st**oo**dyen meat jelly;
galantine; aspic

судак s**oo**dak pike-perch

судак в белом вине s**oo**dak
vb**ye**lam veen-**yeh** pike-perch in
white wine

судак жареный в тесте s**oo**dak
Jaryeni ft**ye**styeh pike-perch fried
in batter

суп s**oo**p soup

суп из свежих грибов s**oo**p
ees sv**ye**Jih gree**bof** fresh
mushroom soup

суп картофельный s**oo**p
kart**o**fyelni potato soup

суп-лапша с курицей s**oo**p
lapsha sk**oo**reetsay chicken
noodle soup

суп мясной s**oo**p myasn**oy** meat
soup

суп с грибами s**oo**p zgreeb**a**mee
mushroom soup

суп томатный s**oo**p tam**a**tni
tomato soup

с хреном sHr**ye**nam with
horseradish sauce

сыр siyr cheese

сырник s**iy**rneek small
cheesecake; cottage cheese
pancake or fritter

сырой sir**oy** raw

творог tvar**o**k cottage cheese

телятина tyel**ya**teena veal

телячьи отбивные tyel**ya**chee
atbeevn**iy**-yeh veal chops

тесто t**ye**sta pastry; dough

тефтели с рисом tyeft**ye**lee
sr**ee**sam meatballs with rice

тмин tmeen thyme

томатный соус tam**a**tni s**o**-oos
tomato sauce

торт tort cake, gateau

> **Travel tip** Russians are very
> fond of cakes (*tort*). In the cit-
> ies, chains of patisseries sell
> all kinds of freshly made fruit
> or chocolate gateaux, while
> supermarkets stock various
> cakes whose main ingre-
> dients are sponge dough,
> honey and a distinctive spice
> like cinnamon or ginger – or
> lots of cream and jam.

травы tr**a**vi herbs

треска tryesk**a** cod

тунец toon**ye**ts tuna fish

тушёный toosh**o**ni stewed

укроп ookr**o**p dill

уксус **oo**ksoos vinegar

устрицы **oo**streetsi oysters

утка **oo**tka duck

уха oo**Ha** fish soup

фаршированная рыба
farshir**o**van-na-ya r**iy**ba stuffed

fish

фаршированные помидоры farshirovan-ni-yeh pameedori stuffed tomatoes

фаршированный farshirovan-ni stuffed

фасоль fasol French beans; haricot beans

филе filyeh fillet

фирменные блюда feermyen-ni-yeh blooda speciality dishes

фисташки feestashkee pistachio nuts

форель faryel trout

фрикадельки freekadyelkee meatballs

фрикадельки из телятины в соусе freekadyelkee ees tyelyateeni vso-oosyeh veal meatballs in gravy

фруктовое мороженое frooktova-yeh maroJena-yeh fruit ice cream

фрукты frookti fruit

харчо Harcho Georgian thick, spicy mutton soup

хлеб Hlyep bread

холодной Halodni cold

холодные закуски Halodni-yeh zakooskee cold starters, cold appetizers

хорошо прожаренный Harasho praJaryen-ni well-done

хрен Hryen horseradish

хрустящий картофель Hroostyash-chee kartofyel crisps,

(US) chips

цветная капуста tsvyetna-ya kapoosta cauliflower

цыплёнок tsiplyonak chicken

цыплёнок в тесте tsiplyonak ftyestyeh chicken in pastry

цыплёнок по-охотничьи tsiplyonak pa-aHotneechee chicken chasseur

цыплёнок 'табака' tsiplyonak tabaka Georgian chicken with garlic, grilled or fried

цыплёнок фрикасе tsiplyonak freekaseh chicken fricassee

чахохбили chaHoHbeelee Georgian-style chicken casserole

черешня cheryeshnya sweet cherries

чёрная смородина chorna-ya smarodeena blackcurrants

чёрника chyerneeka bilberries

чёрный перец chorni pyeryets black pepper

чёрный хлеб chorni Hlyep black bread, rye bread

чеснок chyesnok garlic

чечевица chyechyeveetsa lentils

шашлык shashliyk kebab

шашлык из баранины shashliyk eez baraneeni lamb kebab

шашлык из свинины с рисом shashliyk ees sveeneeni sreesam pork kebab with rice

шницель shneetsel schnitzel

шницель с яичницей глазуньей shneetsel sya-eeshneetsay glazoonyay schnitzel with fried egg

шоколад shakalat chocolate

шпинат shpeenat spinach

шпроты shproti sprats

щи sh-chee cabbage soup

щука sh-chooka pike

эскалоп eskalop escalope

эскимо eskeemo choc-ice

яблоко yablaka apple

яблочный пирог yablachni peerok apple pie

язык yaziyk tongue

яичница ya-eeshneetsa fried egg; omelette

яичница болтунья ya-eeshneetsa baltoonya scrambled eggs

яичница глазунья ya-eeshneetsa glazoonya fried eggs

яйцо yitso egg

яйцо вкрутую yitso fkrootoo-yoo hard-boiled egg

яйцо всмятку yitso fsmyatkoo soft-boiled egg

яйцо под майонезом yitso pad mi-anezam egg mayonnaise

Drink

Essential terms

beer пиво peeva

bottle бутылка bootiylka

brandy коньяк kanyak

coffee кофе kofyeh

cup чашка chashka

fruit juice фруктовый сок frooktovi sok

gin джин djin

gin and tonic джин с тоником djin stoneekam

glass стакан stakan (wine glass) бокал bakal

milk молоко malako

mineral water минеральная вода meenyeralna-ya vada

red wine красное вино krasna-yeh veeno

soda (water) газированная вода gazeerovan-na-ya vada

soft drink безалкогольный напиток byezalkagolni napeetak

sugar сахар saнar

tea чай chi

tonic (water) тоник toneek

vodka водка votka

water вода vada

whisky виски veeskee

white wine белое вино byela-yeh veeno

wine вино veeno

wine list карта вин karta veen

another beer, please
ещё одно пиво,
пожалуйста yesh-cho adno
peeva, paлalsta

a cup of tea, please чашку
чая, пожалуйста chashkoo
cha-ya, paлalsta

a glass of... стакан... stakan

А–Я

абрикосовый сок abrekosavi
sok apricot juice

Акашени akashenee Georgian
red wine

апельсиновый сок apyelseenavi
sok orange juice

аперитив apyereeteef aperitif

Арарат ararat brandy from
Armenia

армянский коньяк armyanskee
kanyak Armenian brandy

бальзам balzam alcoholic herbal
drink flavoured with honey
and fruit

безалкогольный напиток
byezalkagolni napeetak soft drink

безо льда byezalda without ice

без сахара byes saнara without
sugar

белое вино byela-yeh veeno
white wine

Белый Аист byeli a-eest brand
of cognac

Боржоми barлomee brand of
mineral water

брют bryoott dry, brut

вермут vyermoot vermouth

вино veeno wine

виноградный сок veenagradni
sok grape juice

виски veeskee whisky

вишнёвый сок veeshnyovi sok
cherry juice

вода vada water

водка votka vodka

водка Зубровка votka zoobrofka
bison grass vodka

водка Лимонная votka leemon-
na-ya lemon vodka

водка Московская votka
maskofska-ya brand of vodka

водка Охотничья votka
aнotneechya hunter's vodka
flavoured with juniper berries,
ginger and cloves

водка Перцовка votka
pyertsovka pepper vodka

водка Старка votka starka apple
and pear-leaf vodka

водка Столичная votka
staleechna-ya votka brand of
vodka

газированная вода
gazeerovan-na-ya vada fizzy
water

газированный gazeerovan-ni
fizzy

горилка gareelka Ukrainian
vodka

Гурджани goordJanee Georgian
dry white wine

грузинское вино groozeenska-
yeh veeno Georgian wine

джин djin gin

джин с тоником djin stoneekom
gin and tonic

заварка zavarka strong leaf tea
brew to which boiling water
is added

игристое вино eegreesta-yeh
veeno sparkling wine

какао kaka-o cocoa

карта вин karta veen wine list

квас kvas kvas – non-alcoholic
drink made from fermented
bread and water

кефир kyefeer sour yoghurt
drink

Киндзмараули kindzmara-oolee
Georgian red wine

кисель keesyel thickened fruit
juice drink

клюквенный морс klyookvyen-
ni mors cranberry drink

Кока-Кола koka-kola Coca-Cola

коктейль kaktayl cocktail

компот kampot fruit syrup drink
with pieces of fresh or dried
fruit

коньяк kanyak brandy

кофе kofyeh coffee

кофе по-турецки kofyeh
pa-tooryetskee Turkish coffee

кофе с молоком kofyeh
smalakom coffee with milk

красное вино krasna-yeh veeno
red wine

креплёное вино kryeplyona-yeh
veeno fortified wine

кумыс koomiys fermented drink
made from mare's milk

лёд lyot ice; ice cubes

ликёр leekyor liqueur

лимон leemon lemon

лимонад leemanat lemonade

Массандра mas-sandra Crimean
fortified wine

минеральная вода
meenyeralna-ya vada mineral
water

молоко malako milk

Московское maskofska-yeh
brand of bottled light ale

Мукузани mookoozanee
Georgian red wine

напитки napeetkee drinks

напиток napeetak drink

Нарзан narzan brand of mineral
water

настойка nastoyka liqueur made
from berries or other fruit

пиво peeva beer

пиво Балтика peeva balteeka brand of bottled beer

пиво Жигулёвское peeva jigoolyofska-yeh brand of bottled beer

пиво Очаковское peeva achakofska-yeh brand of bottled beer

пиво Тверское peeva tvyersko-yeh dark beer

полусладкий palooslatkee medium-sweet

полусладкое вино palooslatka-yeh veeno medium-sweet wine

полусухое вино poloosoono-yeh veeno medium-dry wine

полусухой poloosoonoy medium-dry

Пепси pepsee Pepsi

портвейн portvyayn port-style drink

растворимый кофе rastvareemi kofyeh instant coffee

ром rom rum

Саперави sapyeravi Georgian red wine

сахар saHar sugar

светлое пиво svyetla-yeh peeva lager

сладкий slatkee sweet

сладкое вино slatka-yeh veeno dessert wine

сливки sleefkee cream

с молоком smalakom with milk

сок sok juice

со льдом saldom with ice

с сахаром s-saHaram with sugar

столовое вино stalova-yeh veeno table wine

сухой sooHoy dry

томатный сок tamatni sok tomato juice

травяной чай travyanoy chi herbal tea

Фанта Fanta

Цинандали tsinandalee Georgian dry white wine

чай chi tea

чай с лимоном chi sleemonam lemon tea

чёрный кофе chorni kofyeh black coffee

шампанское shampanska-yeh champagne

яблочный сок yablachni sok apple juice

Picture credits

All photographs by Jonathan Smith, © Rough Guides.

Front cover: © Graham Lawrence/Alamy.
Back cover: Jonathan Smith, © Rough Guides.

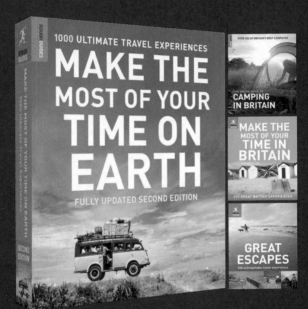